Language Teacher Noticing in Tasks

PSYCHOLOGY OF LANGUAGE LEARNING AND TEACHING

Series Editors: Sarah Mercer, *Universität Graz, Austria* and Stephen Ryan, *Waseda University, Japan*

This international, interdisciplinary book series explores the exciting, emerging field of Psychology of Language Learning and Teaching. It is a series that aims to bring together works that address a diverse range of psychological constructs from a multitude of empirical and theoretical perspectives, but always with a clear focus on their applications within the domain of language learning and teaching. The field is one that integrates various areas of research that have been traditionally discussed as distinct entities, such as motivation, identity, beliefs, strategies and self-regulation, and it also explores other less familiar concepts for a language education audience, such as emotions, the self and positive psychology approaches. In theoretical terms, the new field represents a dynamic interface between psychology and foreign language education and books in the series draw on work from diverse branches of psychology, while remaining determinedly focused on their pedagogic value. In methodological terms, sociocultural and complexity perspectives have drawn attention to the relationships between individuals and their social worlds, leading to a field now marked by methodological pluralism. In view of this, books encompassing quantitative, qualitative and mixed methods studies are all welcomed.

All books in this series are externally peer-reviewed.

Full details of all the books in this series and of all our other publications can be found on http://www.multilingual-matters.com, or by writing to Multilingual Matters, St Nicholas House, 31–34 High Street, Bristol BS1 2AW, UK.

PSYCHOLOGY OF LANGUAGE LEARNING AND TEACHING: 14

Language Teacher Noticing in Tasks

Daniel O. Jackson

MULTILINGUAL MATTERS
Bristol • Blue Ridge Summit

DOI https://doi.org/10.21832/JACKSO1234

Library of Congress Cataloging in Publication Data
A catalog record for this book is available from the Library of Congress.
Names: Jackson, Daniel O., author.
Title: Language Teacher Noticing in Tasks/Daniel O. Jackson.
Description: Bristol; Blue Ridge Summit: Multilingual Matters, [2021] |
   Series: Psychology of Language Learning and Teaching: 14 | Includes bibliographical references and index. | Summary: "This book provides an accessible account of teacher noticing, the process of attending to, interpreting and acting on events which occur during engagement with learners, in contexts of language teacher education. It presents an innovative study of task-based interaction and emphasizes the role of reflective practice in professional development"— Provided by publisher. Identifiers: LCCN 2020053017 | ISBN 9781800411234 (hardback) | ISBN 9781800411227 (paperback) | ISBN 9781800411241 (pdf) | ISBN 9781800411258 (epub) | ISBN 9781800411265 (kindle edition)
Subjects: LCSH: English language—Study and teaching—Foreign speakers—Case studies. | English language—Study and teaching—Psychological aspects—Case studies. | English language—Study and teaching—Japan—Case studies. | Teachers—Training of—Japan—Case studies. | Situational awareness. | Language awareness. | Second language acquisition. | Teacher-student relationships. | Reflective teaching. | Teaching—Methodology.
Classification: LCC PE1128.A2 J33 2021 | DDC 428.0071—dc23
LC record available at https://lccn.loc.gov/2020053017

British Library Cataloguing in Publication Data
A catalogue entry for this book is available from the British Library.

ISBN-13: 978-1-80041-123-4 (hbk)
ISBN-13: 978-1-80041-122-7 (pbk)

Multilingual Matters
UK: St Nicholas House, 31–34 High Street, Bristol BS1 2AW, UK.
USA: NBN, Blue Ridge Summit, PA, USA.

Website: www.multilingual-matters.com
Twitter: Multi_Ling_Mat
Facebook: https://www.facebook.com/multilingualmatters
Blog: www.channelviewpublications.wordpress.com

Copyright © 2021 Daniel O. Jackson

All rights reserved. No part of this work may be reproduced in any form or by any means without permission in writing from the publisher.

The policy of Multilingual Matters/Channel View Publications is to use papers that are natural, renewable and recyclable products, made from wood grown in sustainable forests. In the manufacturing process of our books, and to further support our policy, preference is given to printers that have FSC and PEFC Chain of Custody certification. The FSC and/or PEFC logos will appear on those books where full certification has been granted to the printer concerned.

Typeset by Nova Techset Private Limited, Bengaluru and Chennai, India.

Contents

Tables and Figures	ix
Acknowledgments	xi
Abbreviations Used in the Book	xiii

Part 1: Situating Noticing among Teachers

1	Introduction and Overview	3
	Introduction	3
	The Path to this Book	6
	Overview of the Book	10
2	Noticing: An Integrative Perspective	11
	Noticing as a Confluence	11
	Noticing in SLA Research	13
	Interaction in SLA Research	17
	A Holistic View of Teacher–Learner Noticing	21
	An Analytic View of Teacher–Learner Noticing	24
	Summary	26
3	Language Teacher Noticing	28
	What Does Teacher Noticing Have to Offer?	28
	Teacher Cognition	29
	Reflective Teaching	31
	Defining Teacher Noticing	35
	Language Teacher Noticing	40
	Summary	44

Part 2: A Study of Pre-Service Teachers

4	Contextualizing the Study	49
	The Psychology of Language Teaching	49
	The Context of Noticing: From Meso to Micro Levels	50
	The School and Community	52
	The Teacher Education Program	54
	The Tasks	55
	Noticing Based on Video	59
	Summary	62

5	Researching Teacher Noticing	64
	Challenges in Researching Noticing	64
	Methodological Options	66
	Research Design and Questions	67
	Participants	69
	Data Collection and Procedure	70
	Validity and Reliability	72
	Summary	76
6	Influences on Teacher Noticing	78
	Issues and Hypotheses	78
	Data Coding	81
	Descriptive Statistics	82
	Quantitative Analyses of Noticing	84
	Taking Teacher Noticing to Task	87
	Putting Teacher Noticing in Perspective	89
	Summary	91
7	Noticing of Embodied Resources	93
	The Role of Embodied Resources	93
	Facial Expressions	97
	Gaze	100
	Movement	103
	Tasks and Embodiment	105
	Summary	106
8	Noticing of Verbal Resources	108
	Meaning and Usage-Based Learning in Tasks	108
	Constructional Meaning	113
	Landmark Descriptions	119
	Route Directions	121
	Tasks and Language	123
	Summary	124
9	Noticing and Pre-Service Teachers	126
	Overview of the Main Findings	126
	Integrating the Findings	129
	Study Limitations	134
	Implications for Pre-Service Teachers	135
	Summary	137

Part 3: Conclusion

10	Future Directions	141
	A Role for Teacher Noticing	141
	Language Teacher Education	142
	Language Teacher Development	144

Language Teaching Research	148
Reflecting on Noticing as Teacher Psychology	149
Appendices	151
Appendix A: Map Gap Task Materials (Teacher Versions)	151
Appendix B: Coding Guidelines (Excerpt)	153
Appendix C: Transcription Conventions	155
References	156
Index	172

Tables and Figures

Tables

Table 2.1	Characterizations of L2 learning in terms of the cognitive processes invoked	14
Table 3.1	Distinctions between teacher noticing and related concepts	34
Table 4.1	Samuda and Bygate's (2008) features applied to the tasks used in the study	58
Table 5.1	Participant characteristics ($N = 32$)	69
Table 5.2	Data sources in the study	70
Table 5.3	Scoring rubric for direction-giving map tasks	73
Table 5.4	Task completion scores for each map task	73
Table 5.5	Task completion scores: Mean differences across simple versus complex tasks	74
Table 5.6	Time on task: Mean differences across simple versus complex tasks	75
Table 6.1	Stimulated recall results: Means for participants	83
Table 6.2	Recall comments by task and perspective	84
Table 6.3	Noticing instances by task and perspective	84
Table 8.1	Usage-based L2 learning opportunities within meaning-focused tasks	111
Table 9.1	Links between the quantitative and qualitative dimensions of the study	130
Table 9.2	Qualitative aspects of teacher noticing and their implications	137
Table 10.1	Practical suggestions for using language teacher noticing	144

Figures

Figure 3.1	Continua for observing teacher noticing in practice	40
Figure 3.2	Individual and joint attention in noticing	41
Figure 4.1	Multi-level framework depicting the embedded context of teacher noticing	51
Figure 5.1	MMR design with the research questions and data sources	68

Figure 5.2 Bar plot of time on task 75
Figure 6.1 Plot of teacher noticing instances by complexity and
          perspective 85
Figure 7.1 Detail of the Shops task map (student version) 102
Figure 8.1 Detail of the Campus task map (student version) 117
Figure 8.2 Detail of the Museum task map (student version) 122

Acknowledgments

This being a book for teachers, I am particularly grateful to all of mine for their inspiration and guidance. Over the years, I have been fortunate to learn from many fantastic teachers – I hope to thank you all personally! My most influential mentors were Tere Pica and Dick Schmidt, the legacy of whose teaching this book is intended to honor. I trace my views on second language learning to them. They should be credited for my scholarly development, although I am solely to blame for this book's shortcomings.

The study reported in this volume was supported by institutional grants provided by the Research Institute of Language Studies and Language Education at Kanda University of International Studies (KUIS). I am deeply grateful to Yasuko Ito, Noriko Fujimoto, Kevin Garvey, Tomoya Shirakawa, Masaru Yamamoto, Yuri Nagai and all of the participants for their contributions. My colleagues in the English Department and MATESOL Program at KUIS, including Masaki Kobayashi, Tim Murphey, Siwon Park and Yasushi Sekiya, have offered moral support and valuable insights, too.

I also wish to acknowledge those who organized a number of conferences at which aspects of this research were presented and discussed. These include the Psychology of Language Learning Conference (2018, Tokyo), the International Conference on Thinking, Doing, Learning: Usage-based Perspectives on Second Language Learning (2019, Jyväskylä) and the International Conference on Task-Based Language Teaching (2019, Ottawa). In Finland, Niina Lilja and Leila Kääntä's pre-conference workshop helped me to craft the qualitative chapters in this book. I am thankful to KUIS for funding my participation in these events.

Several others, in particular Alfred Rue Burch, Minyoung Cho and Matthew T. Prior, have fostered my growth and understanding in ways that enhanced this book. I am also grateful to Laura Longworth at Multilingual Matters for her advice throughout the writing process and to the series editors, Sarah Mercer and Stephen Ryan, for their excellent feedback. My greatest thanks I owe to my family for their love and encouragement, and to Misa and Noe-chan, especially.

Daniel Jackson

Abbreviations Used in the Book

AIDE	Attention, Interpretation and Decision-making during Engagement
BAK	Beliefs, Assumptions and Knowledge
CA	Conversation Analysis
CA-for-SLA	Conversation Analysis-for-Second Language Acquisition
CDST	Complex Dynamic Systems Theory
CLIL	Content and Language Integrated Learning
EFL	English as a Foreign Language
ESL	English as a Second Language
L2	Second Language
MMR	Mixed-Methods Research
NNEST	Non-Native English Speaking Teacher
PLLT	Psychology of Language Learning and Teaching
PST	Pre-Service Teacher
QUANT	Quantitative
QUAL	Qualitative
SCT	Sociocultural Theory
SLA	Second Language Acquisition
SLTE	Second Language Teacher Education
TBLT	Task-Based Language Teaching
TESOL	Teaching English to Speakers of Other Languages
ZPD	Zone of Proximal Development

Part 1
Situating Noticing among Teachers

1 Introduction and Overview

Introduction

This book seeks to describe what pre-service English teachers notice as they guide a partner through a series of communicative tasks varying in complexity. Books like this one are commonly introduced with language such as 'this topic is gaining popularity worldwide'. In the present case, such a statement would be partly true. Teacher noticing in mathematics education does indeed seem to be growing in popularity. Many research articles in journals such as the *Journal of Teacher Education* and *Teaching and Teacher Education* have addressed it, as have edited volumes (Schack *et al.*, 2017; Sherin *et al.*, 2011; Simpson *et al.*, 2020). It is not the case that teacher noticing applies solely to math teaching; the construct has been used to explore the thinking of teachers of biology (Russ & Luna, 2013) and jazz (Ankney, 2016) as well. Yet, for some reason, teacher noticing has not appeared often in the literature on second language (L2) teaching. This book is intended to change that situation by providing an accessible, evidence-based account of how teacher noticing can be examined in contexts of language teacher education.

Based on a review of the literature in mathematics education and language teacher cognition, I define language teacher noticing as 'a form of reflection entailing processes of attending to events, interpreting them, and deciding how to act on them, which occurs during engagement with learners'. Therefore, it can be classified under the larger umbrella of language teacher psychology and it more specifically focuses on teachers' interactive thinking (Borg, 2019). Later, I expand on this definition using models of joint attention, and suggest the mnemonic AIDE for the key components of <u>a</u>ttention, <u>i</u>nterpretation, <u>d</u>ecision-making and <u>e</u>ngagement. I also situate pre-service teacher (PST) noticing within an ecological perspective that acknowledges the potential influences of institution, program and task. One of the main findings of the study reported in this book is that PSTs encounter particular challenges and solutions while implementing tasks. Their raw insights can be useful to language teachers and teacher educators, perhaps as much as theoretical constructs.

What these insights reflect is the nature of language teacher noticing in actual practice, or 'dynamic interactions among cognition, context and experience' (Borg, 2015: 324). The primary source of data here was stimulated recall interviews conducted with PSTs enrolled in an undergraduate teacher training course at the university where I teach. Assigned to teacher and student roles, they interacted in pairs to complete a series of four map gap tasks, and those in the teacher role reflected aloud while watching a video of their teaching immediately after completing each task.

Based on these interview data, the study drew upon 64 transcripts containing PSTs' thoughts about what they noticed. These transcripts were translated, then coded for noticing instances by two experienced teachers. The study then tested relevant hypotheses regarding the effects of task complexity and perspectival memory on teacher noticing. However, these teachers' comments are even more informative when seen as offering an emic perspective on the dynamic act of thinking-for-teaching. Thus, conversation analysis was also used to explore the particular interactions that gave rise to teacher noticing, with reference to the resources used by the teacher and student participants.

To be clear, this book makes the case that teacher noticing is distinct from broader notions already used to describe language teachers' innermost thoughts, such as reflective teaching or teacher cognition. This case partly rests on the use of research methods designed to elicit PSTs' relevant thoughts *during* engagement with learners in the act of teaching. This study adopted task-based language teaching (TBLT) as a framework representing particular challenges and options for engaging with learners that PSTs may potentially encounter in their future careers in the Japanese educational context (Butler, 2011; Fukuta *et al.*, 2017). Within and beyond Japan, the use of tasks in a wide range of language classrooms is growing in popularity (Jackson & Burch, 2017; Samuda *et al.*, 2018; Shintani, 2016). Readers of this book, I hope, will come to appreciate how novice educators might implement tasks and, more importantly, better understand the struggles they face in doing so.

How might studying language teacher noticing make a difference? More than in the past, we are witnessing an expansion of the language teaching field in terms of types of instruction, types of learners and types of outcomes sought and, along with all of these changes, increasing professionalism. This post-methods era of language education emphasizes context sensitivity, practitioner theories and learner identities (Kumaravadivelu, 2006). Teachers, using tasks, are seen as active agents who spontaneously shape the classroom environment in response to diverse student needs (Samuda, 2015; Van den Branden, 2016). The importance of reflective practice for professional development (Crookes, 2003; Farrell, 2015; Mann & Walsh, 2017) has also been emphasized. In general, the pendulum has gravitated toward humanistic, critical accounts of the teacher *with* the learners (Freire, 2007). Increasingly, we find more and more attention paid to learner and teacher psychology (Mercer & Kostoulas, 2018a; Williams *et al.*, 2016).

Mercer and Kostoulas (2018b) recently made the rationale for studying language teacher psychology explicit:

> Teachers are absolutely defining in terms of a person's educational experience as well as often in terms of their life trajectories after school. Surely these people, who have the privilege and considerable responsibility of crafting learning experiences, are so important that understanding their characteristics, personalities, needs, motivations and well-being should be a priority. And yet, in second language acquisition (SLA) to date, this has not been the case. (Mercer & Kostoulas, 2018b: 1)

This book attempts to integrate related lines of scholarship by focusing on what language teachers see, think and do, the study of which is neither new (Fanselow, 1988) nor specific to language teaching professionals (Goodwin, 1994). Nonetheless, teacher noticing and the resulting conversations about what they see in their work remain underspecified, despite their enormous significance.

Later in the book, I propose that the value of teacher noticing for language education resides in how it is used to:

(1) Develop rapport. Teachers who notice their students will have more opportunities to establish rapport. This in turn creates a positive dynamic in the classroom and better experiences, with deeper engagement, throughout the period of instruction (Dörnyei & Murphey, 2003). There is consequently more student engagement for the teacher to notice, so that a virtuous cycle is created.
(2) Support acquisition. Teachers must notice and act upon learners' use of language to be able to support their linguistic development. A major tenet of contemporary language teaching is that instructors should, during communication, notice learners' production and guide them toward more effective usage, through focus on form (Long & Robinson, 1998).

Yet, acquisition is not the only thing that matters; as Ortega (2011) reminded us, participation is another powerful metaphor for learning.

(3) Enhance participation. Participation, if understood as engagement during lessons, drives learners' educational experiences. Teachers who notice various dimensions of student engagement, including cognitive, affective, behavioral and social engagement (Philp & Duchesne, 2016), can better assist students in terms of fostering active participation in learner-centered classrooms.

I also suggest that teacher noticing can be applied to professional development to:

(4) Foster reflection. Pre-service and novice teachers need meaningful opportunities to use an array of tools to reflect with others, and these should be data led, as argued by Mann and Walsh (2017). These

authors also claimed that confusing terminology relating to reflective practice is one reason for the lack of data-based accounts. This book seeks to offer terminological clarity and to illustrate the operationalization of language teacher noticing, also elaborating on the use of stimulated recall interviews, which Mann and Walsh regard as a valuable means of reflection.
(5) Guide observation. Post-observation feedback to support development or evaluation (Copland & Donaghue, 2019) is a central feature of language teachers' career advancement. One possibility for focusing such observations, described later, is for observers to pay attention to how the teacher 'does noticing' during classroom interaction, which can be regarded as one part of their embodied and jointly accomplished management of classroom practices (Hall & Looney, 2019). Language teachers display their attention to learners in myriad ways, including pointing to nominate speakers, scowling at disruptions and using recasts to correct pronunciation. These displays are all social acts of doing noticing, which are obviously less appropriate outside the classroom context!

The Path to this Book

At this point, a few words about how I became interested in the topic of teacher noticing may be in order. The turn of this century marked the start of my teaching career, as that is when I received my MS in TESOL/Education from the Graduate School of Education at the University of Pennsylvania. At Penn, I became familiar with the cognitive-interactionist approach (Pica, 1994; for book-length accounts, see Long, 2015; Mackey, 2012). Over a number of years circulating around classrooms to listen, ask questions and offer language support – and reflecting on my practice – I felt that my teaching was gradually accompanied by a heightened sense of awareness, including a better idea of when and how to pay attention, a finer understanding of my students' thinking and an intuitive grasp of what knowledge might be needed in a given context. At best, I would have described these moments as 'acts of cognition' (Freire, 2007), liberating me from teaching only syllabus or textbook content, because they initiated communication to resolve students' concerns at the point of need. Yet I felt I lacked precise terms to describe this subjective impression, even though I had read up on language teacher cognition (Borg, 2015). So, it was a pleasant epiphany when I first encountered Miriam Sherin and Elizabeth van Es' work on teacher noticing (Sherin & van Es, 2003, is a highly accessible introduction).

I then joined the Second Language Studies Department at the University of Hawai'i at Mānoa, where I completed a dissertation on artificial language learning under the supervision of the late Richard Schmidt, whose noticing hypothesis I came to understand better through my studies. Fully aware of its importance and deeply appreciative of the insights it brings though I am, at some point it struck me as slightly incongruous that SLA deals much more with learner noticing than with teacher noticing. One could easily counter that learner noticing applies to all adult language learning, whether inside or outside the classroom, and teacher noticing only to instructed language learning, so an imbalance is understandable. However, there was still no research seeking to connect teacher noticing and language teaching after I completed my dissertation in 2014. Nor do language teacher trainers mention it in their numerous how-to books, which might surprise no one. In hindsight, I was no longer satisfied with waiting for someone else to do a study of language teachers' noticing, more familiar with the caveats such a study would involve and somehow undeterred by the fact that the only available literature was in math and science education. Besides, my own teaching experience had convinced me that it was a worthy topic, and Dick also showed enthusiasm for the project. So, I teamed up with then PhD candidate Minyoung Cho to conduct a classroom study in her course for the BA program in Second Language Studies, later published in *Language Teaching Research* as Jackson and Cho (2018).

In our study, we employed a combination of stimulated recall methodology (Gass & Mackey, 2017) and analyses of classroom discourse to probe noticing by eight language teachers-in-training. The results were intriguing to me and when writing up the paper I could easily anticipate future studies, as well as pitfalls to avoid and enhancements to the design and methodology. Besides, the idea seemed to go over well at academic conferences, and we received positive responses from audiences in the United States, Belgium and Japan. Along the way to my degree, I had also done some research on task complexity (Jackson & Suethanapornkul, 2013) and had become acquainted with conversation analytic perspectives on TBLT (Jackson & Burch, 2017). Those viewpoints and my subsequent experiences, including my deepening involvement with language teacher education, are reflected in this book.

Regarding this involvement, I am currently an Associate Professor in the English Department and a member of the steering committee and teaching staff for the MA TESOL program at Kanda University of International Studies in Japan. In these roles, I engage with pre-service and in-service teachers, especially in my courses on applied linguistics, SLA and TBLT. The project reported in this book evolved from discussions with colleagues interested in supporting the development of undergraduate students on their way to becoming English language teachers (by now, many of these individuals have entered the profession – congratulations to them!). Based on these conversations, the project was eventually awarded institutional support, which provided funding for two student assistants as well as compensation for the study participants. As a teacher–researcher, I feel glad that this research has led to mutually beneficial relationships with many students, as we share the goal of promoting English education in Japan. One aim of this book is to share these PSTs' insights more broadly. It is indeed fortunate that the present book series has created a venue for such work.

At the time of writing, social inequality and health crises have had a profound impact on language educators around the globe. Their long-term effects on mental and physical well-being are a cause for deep concern. Regarding the COVID-19 pandemic, early in 2020 many of us shifted to emergency remote teaching (Hodges *et al.*, 2020). The abrupt change from classroom-based to fully online instruction has influenced English teaching and teacher reflection in a multitude of ways (for a timely collection of papers, see Morris *et al.*, 2020). Based on my own experiences during this time, it is now even clearer: teaching is essentially embodied and emotional labor. Our dynamic work environment has implications for our ability to notice students' thinking. This is a valid concern which needs to be addressed. Although this book hardly addresses such major issues, it is some consolation that the PLLT series, and Multilingual Matters, offer wide space for such discussions.

It is also encouraging that several recent publications in English language education have cited work on teacher noticing (Borg, 2019; Hüttner, 2019; Jackson & Cho, 2018; Jackson & Shirakawa, 2020; Lengeling *et al.*, 2020; Mann *et al.*, 2020; Yuan *et al.*, 2020). This suggests to me that it has its place in the broader context of language teaching and learning, whether it be face to face or fully online.

The transdisciplinary spirit of this project might help to explain why I prefer, whenever possible, to integrate various theories and methods in order to consider their complementarity. Although my primary graduate training has focused on cognitive-interactionist perspectives on SLA, and I specialize in TBLT and individual differences, my coursework and reading have been in education, linguistics and psychology, and I have attended workshops on conversation analysis and multimodal approaches in L2 research. My position is that language teacher noticing can, and should, be studied from a wide range of theoretical perspectives (epistemologies) and that a variety of tools (methodologies) are suitable. Primarily owing to my experience, I consider language teacher noticing to be a subjective phenomenon. It is also true that different audiences are convinced by different approaches and sources of evidence, and whether others value the treatment of teacher noticing in this book may depend on their experience, training and preferences. Given that tolerance and respect for different values is of the utmost importance, the guiding epistemology for this book is pragmatism (Patton, 1997). In designing this project, I tried to consider a range of applications of teacher noticing in language education, and these led to different research questions. These distinct research questions called for different methods. The main questions addressed in this book are glossed here:

- Does task complexity affect recall of teacher noticing?
- Does perspectival memory affect recall of teacher noticing?
- What do teachers notice about students' use of embodied resources?
- What do teachers notice about students' use of verbal resources?

As a consequence of this range of questions, this monograph bears hallmarks of mixed-methods research (e.g. Brown, 2014), including triangulation of data from various sources, use of quantitative and qualitative analyses, and integration of results at the level of interpretation. Regarding this last point, a final question addressed at the end of the book is:

- How can the qualitative and quantitative results be integrated to form a pluralistic, evidence-based understanding of language teacher noticing?

One must admit, however, that mixing methods convincingly is not a simple or easy thing to do. Any shortcomings inherent in this particular attempt at satisfying a wide audience, I hope, will inspire future practitioner accounts and specialist research on language teacher noticing.

To summarize, this book is based on the view that the field of second language teacher cognition (Borg, 2015) has provided fertile ground for the deepening of our understanding of language teacher psychology (Mercer & Kostoulas, 2018a) and that, as in the past, it is natural to look beyond our immediate experience to other educational domains for insight. Drawing on mathematics education, the construct of teacher noticing has been applied to novice language teacher cognition among those preparing to teach languages in Hawaii (Jackson & Cho, 2018). This construct can inform contemporary language teaching frameworks, such as TBLT, where more research is needed to understand how instructors learn to recalibrate their actions *in situ* to enhance student learning and participation once a task is in progress (Samuda, 2015). Furthermore, task design and methodological factors may affect recall of teacher noticing, although little is known about these influences. The study reported in this book therefore occupies gaps in research on TBLT and also illustrates, through close analyses of task interaction coupled with recall data, the ways in which PSTs notice their student partners' use of embodied and linguistic resources. This focus, on what teachers attend to, how they interpret it and their subsequent decisions, has multiple implications for language learning and teacher development. These have yet to be fully explored. This book therefore also serves as a call for future work in a diverse range of contexts that adopts varying epistemologies and methodologies to understand language teacher noticing.

Overview of the Book

This book has three aims, which correspond to its three parts. In Part 1, 'Situating Noticing among Teachers', it seeks to provide an introduction to language teacher noticing. The present Chapter 1 serves as an introduction. Chapter 2 revisits the noticing construct in SLA before introducing perspectives on teacher–learner noticing. Chapter 3 then defines and discusses teacher noticing to extend it to the specific context of language education.

Part 2, 'A Study of Pre-Service Teachers', aims to report on research into this topic that is integrative in its conceptual background and innovative in its methodological approach. Chapter 4 uses an ecological framework (Douglas Fir Group, 2016; Mercer, 2018; Williams *et al.*, 2016) to contextualize the study, which was conducted within a teacher preparation program at a Japanese university. Chapter 5 then considers options in researching teacher noticing and gives methodological details relevant to understanding the study design. Chapter 6 addresses the influence of task and perspective on the number of noticing instances reported by participants. Chapters 7 and 8 complement this quantitative perspective by reporting qualitative results from the study. Chapter 7 deals with the PSTs' noticing of embodied resources and Chapter 8 turns to their noticing of verbal resources. Then, Chapter 9 summarizes and synthesizes the findings of the quantitative and qualitative strands of the investigation, describing the practical and theoretical implications of teacher noticing.

Lastly, in Part 3, 'Conclusion', the book expands on how studying what teachers notice can provide fresh insight. Three areas in which broader implications may be found include L2 teacher education, professional development and language teaching research. I conclude with reflections on how noticing, as an instance of teacher psychology, may lead to a better understanding of the challenges facing those who are new to language teaching.

2 Noticing: An Integrative Perspective

Noticing as a Confluence

One could think of this book as depicting the confluence of two intellectual streams that form a deep river. One of those streams is learner noticing. Noticing, in the field of second language teaching and learning, has been discussed and debated for many years, in particular since the publication of Richard Schmidt's (1990) seminal article describing this construct. It concerns an individual's subjective awareness of the language she or he is learning. This brief definition has led scholars to revisit fundamental questions about SLA and reimagine how to answer them. This in turn fuels discussion and debate in programs intended to educate language teachers and researchers. Because this book is intended primarily for second language (L2) teachers, this chapter first escorts the reader to a place which is often vividly recalled from one's coursework, but in which perhaps not enough time has been spent to fully grasp the nuances and complexities of noticing. Many language teachers have read or heard about noticing, yet the construct is a deceptively simple one that deserves fuller treatment than is sometimes offered. Moreover, all psychological constructs, noticing included, evolve over time. A great deal of work has informed – and will continue to inform – the development of the noticing construct, and revisiting it now reveals new perspectives based on the fundamental ideas in Schmidt's landmark proposal. The influence of noticing on second language acquisition (SLA) can be seen in a wide array of research agendas and scholarly publications. To name but a recent few, these include diverse works by Bergsleigthner *et al.* (2013), Gass *et al.* (2017), Leow (2015), Rebuschat (2015) and Roehr-Brackin (2018).

Interestingly, outside the literature on SLA, there has also been recent attention to the rather different idea of teacher noticing. This is the second stream, which is the main focus of this book. Building on a framework proposed by van Es and Sherin (2002), researchers in math and science education have applied this construct in teacher training, resulting in a growing body of work that explores the ways in which teachers, rather than learners, rely on professional knowledge to notice classroom processes, link them to pedagogic rationales and purposely act on them during instruction (for book-length treatments, see Schack *et al.*, 2017; Sherin *et al.*, 2011a). Thus, another goal of this chapter is to acquaint readers with this strand of research. In keeping with this book's overall purpose, justifications for, research on and implications of teacher noticing in L2 contexts will be elaborated on in later chapters.

At times, it is important to consider these two streams – noticing by learners and noticing by teachers – separately because each is distinct in terms of its history, development and scope. Also, although these two varieties of noticing are both central to classroom L2 acquisition, they suggest distinct empirical questions, methodological implications and research outcomes. However, one can also observe many occasions when teachers and learners seem to notice a particular aspect of language at the same time and are aware of sharing this focus. In fact, this is the basis for focus on form, which involves momentary shifts in attention to linguistic features by the teacher during otherwise communicative lessons (Long, 1991, 2015; Long & Robinson, 1998; see also Williams, 2001, on learner-generated focus on form; Kasper & Burch, 2016, on focus on form outside classroom settings). Thus, at the confluence of learner and teacher noticing there is a notion – focus on form – that has attained the status of a principle underpinning contemporary L2 teaching (Long, 2015; see, for discussion, R. Ellis, 2018). Surprisingly, though, focus on form has not often been investigated in terms of teacher cognition. It also is noteworthy that the intertwining of teacher and learner attention has many potential outcomes, of which focus on form is but one. L2 learning and teaching is complex and includes, of course, cognitive and linguistic dimensions, but its critical and social dimensions (Ortega, 2005) must not be neglected either. Therefore, teacher noticing encompasses a wide range of aspects of classroom interaction. In these ways, noticing by teachers and learners is like a river that stretches out to touch many diverse realities of L2 classroom life.

As indicated by its title, this chapter seeks to begin to integrate teacher and learner noticing at a conceptual level. In line with recent discussions of transdisciplinarity in SLA, the goal is to engage with the constructs of teacher and learning noticing based on research in the disciplines of teacher education and L2 learning, respectively, so that their complementarity becomes clearer (Douglas Fir Group, 2016: 23). This of course does not mean that integrating these views will be easy and at times it is necessary to distinguish their separate contributions. Part of the challenge (which I personally find intriguing) is that, currently, little cross-referencing seems to have occurred in these areas: those writing about teacher noticing have not cited the SLA literature, nor have scholars in SLA begun to cite work on teacher noticing. An exception to this is the literature review in Jackson and Cho (2018). In this book, I hope to lay the groundwork for future cross-pollination and integrated research to explore noticing from these dual perspectives. As a complement to this goal of offering an integrative theoretical perspective, the design of the research reported on in this book drew on mixed methods (Brown, 2014; Riazi, 2017) in order to situate the construct of L2 teacher noticing within qualitative and quantitative paradigms.

To trace these two threads – learner and teacher noticing – and to attempt to describe how they contribute to classroom L2 learning, this chapter first reviews core tenets of the noticing hypothesis and how it has influenced views on language education. Subsequently, views within SLA on interaction, which often surrounds noticing, will be described. Examples of L2 discourse are then presented and discussed in terms of teacher and learner noticing. Afterwards, similarities and differences in these constructs are described. The viewpoint offered is a notable reversal of how L2 education has long been seen. Traditionally, it is teachers who lead learners to notice, but what I, in line with many others, strongly feel is needed in L2 education is for learner psychology to become the basis for teacher noticing, reasoning and action. This chapter closes with a discussion of the implications of studying teacher noticing in L2 classroom settings.

Noticing in SLA Research

Labels abound for conscious experience, that great blooming, buzzing confusion described by James (1890). Thus, a century later, one impetus for Schmidt's (1990) article on the role of consciousness in L2 learning or acquisition was to begin to untangle the various senses of consciousness, focusing particularly on consciousness as awareness. Noticing refers to a level of awareness at which stimuli are subjectively experienced. Schmidt used the psychological construct of noticing to examine theoretical views on the relationship between awareness and SLA, which centered on the key roles of the available input and the learners' intake, whether this process of incorporating input was deliberate or not. Largely based on an earlier diary study conducted with Sylvia Frota of his own learning of Brazilian Portuguese (Schmidt & Frota, 1986), it was concluded that 'noticing is the necessary and sufficient condition for converting input to intake' in adult SLA (Schmidt, 1990: 129).

To foster comprehension of the noticing construct, a number of closely related concepts are briefly introduced here. These are based on Schmidt's views (1990, 1993, 2001). Firstly, noticing involves the co-occurrence of attention and awareness. Attention is used here primarily in the sense of stimulus detection, which can be voluntary (in the case of paying attention) or involuntary (where no intention is present). Awareness can be broken down into perception, focal awareness (i.e. noticing) and understanding. Noticing and understanding are distinct in that the former deals with registering surface instances whereas the latter entails deeper abstraction of rules or patterns. Noticing occurs in working memory, which involves temporary processing and storage of information. This permits rehearsal and maintenance (Robinson, 2003). Learning processes can be described as explicit or implicit, depending on whether or not they involve awareness. These processes are described in the next section, where all of the terms are consolidated further.

Process versus product

It should be noted that Schmidt maintained a clear distinction between learning as a process and learning as a product. In his own words, 'implicit and explicit learning and implicit and explicit knowledge are related but distinct concepts that need to be separated. The first set refers to the processes of learning, the second to the end-products of learning (or sometimes to knowledge that is innate and not learned at all)' (Schmidt, 1994: 20). This is important because the noticing hypothesis concerns learning processes that occur at the time of encoding. As noted already, these processes include attention and awareness as well as, sometimes, intention. One can think of noticing as a proposal related to explicit learning, which covers intentional or incidental learning and stands apart from implicit learning. Table 2.1 lists these types of L2 learning, also differentiating them according to the cognitive processes they are said to invoke. The binary classification used for the sake of convenience here is not to deny that these processes are in fact continuous in nature. Typically, learners experience fluctuating levels of attention, awareness or intention (which may be related to motivational states) in accordance with the ebb and flow of daily life. Based on Table 2.1, noticing encompasses both intentional and incidental learning and it excludes implicit learning. Importantly, the labels *explicit* and *implicit* mean something very different when used to refer to teaching (see DeKeyser, 2003).

An example

Naturally, questions arise from the aforementioned definition of noticing, and these often concern precisely when and how learners subjectively experience input. Schmidt clarified that 'what is noticed ... is not the raw

Table 2.1 Characterizations of L2 learning in terms of the cognitive processes invoked

	Attention	Awareness	Intention
Explicit learning			
Intentional learning	+	+	+
Incidental learning	+	+	−
Implicit learning	+	−	−

data of the input ... to which attention is directed, but input as interpreted by existing schemata' (Schmidt, 2001: 31). Such schemata can include previously acquired phonological or orthographic systems which, by filtering input, may prompt learners to notice certain surface features.

As an example of noticing, consider the diary entry in Box 2.1, which I wrote one summer. At the time of this entry, I had lived in Honolulu for around three years and I had enrolled in a Hawaiian language class for beginners at a community school. My interest in learning Hawaiian grew out of my belief that learning the basics of another L2 (or, more precisely, L4, after German and Japanese) would be a good use of the summer break and would enhance my appreciation for Hawaiian culture. At the time, though, I had had very little exposure to the language, apart from the reference materials that a couple of friends had lent me and the weekly class meetings I attended. Also, prior language learning experience led me to focus more heavily on written Hawaiian than on its rich oral traditions, much to my detriment. This entry was made after the second meeting of the class.

Box 2.1 Diary entry on noticing Hawaiian in Waikiki

6-24-2012
Had my eyes peeled in Waikiki for Hawaiian today. Saw little of it, but what I did see led me back to another puzzle I'd wanted to solve. I knew that *nā* is another form of the article. For example, today we passed the jewelry shop, *nā hōkū*, and sat across from a surfer sporting a hat with the words *nā keiki*... on the bus home. I imagined that this *nā* might be the indefinite article; however, upon checking *NPHD* [*New Hawaiian Pocket Dictionary*, Pukui & Elbert, 1992] I now see that it's the plural definite article. This makes sense. The phrases mean 'the stars' and 'the children', respectively. Apparently, *he* is the indefinite article, although I've yet to come across that outside of dictionary examples (e.g. *he pepa kēia* – this is a paper).

Taking Robinson's (2003) model of noticing as a guide, I had allocated selective focal attention to the feature *nā* and detected it in two separate contexts on this day. I possessed some awareness of *nā* as an article, likely reinforced by its occurrence before nouns, which prompted me to formulate the incorrect hypothesis that it is the indefinite article. This was evidently not my first encounter with *nā*, but it is also certain that, at this point, although I knew the word class to which it belonged, I did not grasp its meaning. As Schmidt (1993: 213) wrote, noticing concerns item learning, whereas understanding concerns system learning. Here, the item *nā* was just beginning to make sense to me. I was still quite far from a proper understanding of the article system.

The influence of my L1 (English) in filtering input can also be seen in this example. Firstly, this knowledge would facilitate reading in Hawaiian, as its alphabet was adapted from English. Secondly, I had not anticipated that Hawaiian would mark plurality in this way because in English –*s* on the end of a noun typically marks plurals. It is at least possible then that implicit L1 knowledge shaped my noticing. N.C. Ellis (2005) has elaborated that implicit and explicit knowledge commingle during conscious L2 processing. Although no mental process can be described as entirely explicit, this episode was a conscious process involving rehearsal in working memory and encoding in long-term memory, shown by the fact that I was able to recall this experience in my diary. This example furthermore depicts noticing as a subjective experience that is not based solely on the raw input. Later in this chapter, additional examples of noticing embedded in social interaction within classroom contexts are described.

Issues in noticing

The noticing hypothesis has garnered much attention, along with, inevitably, criticisms, to which Schmidt (2012) replied in detail. Frequently, the issues are methodological, as some have objected that: (1) diary studies are not appropriately fine-grained to allow inspection of attention (Tomlin & Villa, 1994) and (2) constructs within the hypothesis (e.g. levels of awareness) are not easily nor uniformly defined (Leow, 2015: 73). Others have challenged the view of language learning implied, stating that (3) certain linguistic features (words, sounds, orthography) may require noticing, while others (phonological, morphological and syntactic rules) may not (Schachter, 1998), or that (4) models relying on environmental input as the sole source of adult L2 acquisition are insufficient (Carroll, 1999; see Gass, 1997, for a similar view that universal grammar influences intake). Furthermore, the contribution of awareness to learning is to some degree debatable. Consequently, some take the position that (5) only attention is necessary. According to these researchers, SLA may proceed in the absence of awareness (Carr & Curran, 1994; Tomlin & Villa, 1994; Williams, 2005; see Rebuschat, 2015). Lastly, another argument is not so much a criticism of the noticing hypothesis itself, but an observation that it constitutes a cognitivist perspective on SLA, which is accompanied by the assertion that (6) alternative theoretical viewpoints are also necessary to understand the complexity and multidimensionality of SLA (Atkinson, 2011).

Regarding these concerns, in line with Schmidt (2012), I would suggest that Issues 1 and 2 apply to all psychological constructs, not simply noticing. Researchers have pursued the measurement of noticing for quite some time now, resulting in gradual improvements to conceptual and methodological clarity (Godfroid *et al.*, 2010). Issue 3 raises interesting points, some of which might be fruitfully addressed through research on statistical learning (Rebuschat & Williams, 2012). Issue 4 seems to have been dealt with insofar as Schmidt (2001) allowed a role for schemata (see above). The raw input is certainly not the only factor involved in what gets noticed. The debate over Issue 5, regarding whether implicit learning plays a role, has a long tenure in SLA, spanning its disciplinary history from Krashen's (1982) monitor hypothesis to the volume edited by Rebuschat (2015). Despite this longstanding theoretical interest, and substantial attempts at empirical research into the issue, the possible role of implicit learning in instructed SLA remains relatively obscure, regardless of occasional assertions that it is the default learning mechanism (Doughty, 2003; Long, 2015). Finally, Issue 6, which is not necessarily a drawback because work on cognitive-interactionist SLA has shed much light on language education, targets a perceived neglect of the social aspects of learning in some early studies that has begun to resolve itself in work based on sociocultural theory and other complementary approaches to SLA. In fact, Schmidt's noticing has been integrated into sociocultural (Alanen, 2013; Swain, 2000) and sociocognitive (Jacknick & Thornbury, 2013) perspectives, and thus it need not be considered a purely cognitivist construct.

Summary

Despite or perhaps because of these controversies, Schmidt's noticing hypothesis, which stated that input cannot be converted to intake unless it is noticed, continues to fuel a diverse array of empirical agendas. Studies of noticing have theoretical implications for understanding the role of L2 learner-internal processes, but also are important for classroom practice, where the crucial importance of input, output and feedback have long been recognized as conditions for SLA (Pica, 1994). Approaches to language pedagogy in which materials designers attempt to manipulate input (e.g. input enhancement, see Lee & Huang, 2008) may claim the noticing hypothesis as a theoretical rationale. Likewise, pedagogic practices that encourage spoken or written output are regarded as serving the function of helping learners notice (Swain, 1995). Lastly, the interactional feedback afforded by negotiation of meaning with teachers or peers during classroom tasks is important to L2 development. The next section builds on this background to illustrate how noticing is often shaped by interaction, which is central to accounts of SLA.

Interaction in SLA Research

No one disagrees that interaction is necessary for language learning. The debate is mainly over whether it is sufficient for child language development. Some argue that 'the child knows vastly more than experience has provided' (Chomsky, 2000: 6). Others contend that mechanisms of usage-based learning, such as intention reading and pattern finding, provide all that is needed (Tomasello, 2003). Since its early days, SLA researchers have focused on the role of experience and interaction in learning. Yet there is a contrast between views on how the experience of interacting facilitates L2 development. The interactional context of noticing is considered in terms of three views summarized here: the cognitive-interactionist approach, sociocultural theory (SCT) and conversation analysis-for-SLA (CA-for-SLA).

These words from the late Charlene J. Sato succinctly summarize the cognitive-interactionist approach: 'conversational interaction selectively facilitates the acquisition of linguistic devices that code various semantic and functional domains' (Sato, 1986: 24). Worth noting, especially, are her cautious use of 'selectively' and the restriction to meaning-laden L2 features. This approach has been applied within classroom-oriented SLA research since the 1980s, at which time researchers began to scrutinize Krashen's (1982) theoretical claim that SLA requires comprehensible input and to seek out mechanisms that would account for the popular notion in language pedagogy of 'talking to learn', to borrow the title of the seminal collection edited by Day (1986).

Early work in this vein by Long considered the roles of linguistic and conversational modifications in establishing comprehension, suggesting that such adjustments might serve a crucial function. Namely, if adjustments facilitate comprehension, and comprehension facilitates acquisition (as Krashen claimed), then it can be deduced that such adjustments facilitate acquisition (Long, 1983a). In addition, Long (1983b) emphasized that input comprehensibility often appeared to be enhanced by conversational adjustments, describing a number of interactional devices used to achieve this end. To illustrate briefly, consider the exchange in Example 2.1, in which the student uses a conversational modification to clarify the teacher's message.

Example 2.1

Teacher: Have you ever seen the mural at the campus center?
Student: What's a mural?
Teacher: It's a large painting on a wall.

Thereafter, interaction rose to the forefront of the agenda in language teaching research, especially that concerning task-based language teaching (TBLT) (e.g. Gass, 1997; Long, 1991; Pica, 1994; Pica *et al.*, 1993; Sato, 1986; Varonis & Gass, 1985). According to the interaction hypothesis, modified interaction 'connects input, internal learner capacities, in particular selective attention, and output in productive ways' (Long, 1996: 452). Interaction, or conversation in face-to-face or computer-mediated environments, may be modified through the use of confirmation checks (*did you say on the left?*), clarification requests (*pardon?*) or comprehension checks (*do you understand?*). Development depends upon the creation of meaningful opportunities to interact in the L2, which then facilitates acquisition of L2 lexis and morphosyntax (Mackey & Goo, 2007).

The principal classroom implication here is that language instructors should attempt to maximize student talk in order to provide a context for experimenting with language (Philp *et al.*, 2014). This not only affords learners more opportunity for interaction and noticing, but also presents the teacher with more opportunity to notice. Teachers themselves can partake of the interaction by dropping in on conversations as students conduct pair and group work. Based on their observations, they can negotiate meaning, offer recasts or provide brief metalinguistic explanations of challenging linguistic aspects of a task, either immediately or at a later stage in the lesson. As such, studies following the interactionist approach have also addressed teacher roles (Polio & Gass, 2017; Polio *et al.*, 2006) and characteristics (Gurzynski-Weiss, 2017).

Turning to the sociocultural view, this perspective first attracted interest around the turn of the century when Lantolf and others (Lantolf, 2000; Lantolf & Appel, 1994) began to elaborate on its consequences for understanding SLA. Its historical provenance is much older and its application more general, however, as it draws on the work of the Russian psychologist Lev Vygotsky, whose selected works on child development were published posthumously in English as *Mind in Society* in 1978. At the core of Vygotsky's view of the mind was the notion of mediation, or how thinking is constructed through physical or symbolic tools (Lantolf, 2000). As a means of articulating thought, verbalization functions as a tool to mediate development, which can include L2 development – this process has been called languaging (Swain, 2006a). Development is assumed to occur in a zone of proximal development (ZPD), which describes the difference between a child's actual developmental level in independent problem solving and her potential developmental level during collaboration with more developed peers (Vygotsky, 1978). In SLA, collaborative activity between peers at different proficiency levels, or a teacher and a learner, can exemplify this space. Also, largely in contrast to cognitive-interactionist approaches, interaction in SCT is not only between individuals but encompasses an individual's interaction with artifacts, such as written texts (Lantolf & Thorne, 2007).

Under this view, interaction may prompt language use, as either self-directed or collaborative talk. Self-directed talk serves functions in connection with interaction that include eavesdropping on conversations and focusing learners on features of the target language they wish to learn (Lantolf, 2011). Shadowing, too, can involve repeating an interlocutor's speech silently during an interaction. In these ways, self-directed talk is considered beneficial to learning. Collaborative talk, or collaborative dialogue, is directly focused on interaction. It refers specifically to interaction in which 'speakers are engaged in problem solving and knowledge building' (Swain, 2000: 102). Thus, the purpose of interaction here is not strictly viewed as facilitating the comprehension of input (Storch, 2017). Swain's (2000) discussion of collaborative talk notes that one of its roles is to promote noticing, in two ways: learners may notice a gap (Schmidt & Frota, 1986) when they become aware of the difference between their use of the L2 and that of others; or they may notice a hole, when during production they notice their inability to express a certain meaning in the L2.

It should be recalled that SCT views interaction as more than dyadic. Anytime a learner interacts with the world, mediation can occur. Thus, Alanen has pointed out an even deeper link between noticing and SCT. To her, 'noticing as the conscious registration of linguistic elements can be viewed as an instantiation or reflex of mediation' (Alanen, 2013: 338). That is, mediation may give rise to the subjective awareness of language as an object and this noticed object may in turn mediate further thought or activity. In this way, noticing can be associated with learning mechanisms in SCT.

Sociocultural theory and concepts are crucial to understanding interaction within an environment to learn an L2. The ZPD, for instance, draws attention to the fact that teacher–learner and learner–learner mediation involve distinct interactional processes (Guk & Kellogg, 2007). The broadening of the notion of talk to include self-directed and collaborative forms suggests that interacting involves more than what is publicly displayed during a conversation. Also, the associated notion of interacting with the world in terms of symbols, objects or human relations, based on activity theory, has implications for L2 learning in tasks (Coughlan & Duff, 1994).

Yet another view on interaction comes from conversation analysis (CA), or 'the systematic analysis of the talk produced in everyday situations of human interaction' (Hutchby & Wooffitt, 2008: 11). Like the sociocultural view, it developed outside SLA and is not exclusively concerned with language development. Instead, it originated in ethnomethodology, a branch of sociology developed by Harold Garfinkel which aims to describe how people organize and understand social interaction. Conversation analysts adopt an emic perspective in seeking to understand the methods participants use to carry out ordinary social actions during talk. Some methods, or procedures, referred to in this endeavor include those involving turn-taking, conversational sequences, repair of miscommunication, and the display of preferences, or norms, regarding actions (Pekarek Doehler & Pochon-Berger, 2015; Schegloff, 2007). This view encompasses both verbal and nonverbal actions; there is an increasing recognition of the role of embodied resources, such as gesture, posture and gaze (Hall & Looney, 2019; Mondada, 2016). Regarding language, the relationship between social interaction and grammar, or morphosyntax, can be construed in three ways: grammar is a resource for interaction, an outcome of it (as in acquisition) and an inherent part of it (Schegloff et al., 1996).

Owing to their emic nature, studies on CA-for-SLA contrast with theory-driven approaches. Two general strands have emerged from the literature. The first focuses on gathering detail regarding situated, interactional processes that may support L2 learning. Such studies have been conducted in various settings, from formal classroom instruction (Lee & Burch, 2017) to educational spaces such as book clubs (Ro, 2018) to informal conversations (Kasper & Burch, 2016). The second, based on longitudinal data, uses learner behavior tracking to observe the trajectory of development of specific language features over time in talk-in-interaction (Markee, 2008; see Hauser, 2017; Kunitz & Skogmyr Marian, 2017). For reasons that should already be clear, CA-for-SLA studies are unconcerned with observing cognitive processes. Nonetheless, they have illustrated how teachers construct opportunities for students to notice and hold their students accountable for doing so through social actions (Markee, 2008).

Many implications can be drawn from the focus on interaction that CA-for-SLA provides. Regarding TBLT, because CA focuses on social organization and goals, it is highly suitable for inspecting task processes (Seedhouse, 2005), including how learners open (Hellerman, 2007) and close (Hellerman & Cole, 2008) discussions. Learners' *in situ* group planning processes leading toward task completion have also been explored (Lee & Burch, 2017). Other studies foster understanding of embodied construction learning (Eskildsen & Wagner, 2015) and L2 interactional competence (Pekarek Doehler & Pochon-Berger, 2015), thereby offering fresh perspectives on what it means to learn and use an L2, respectively. On top of this, CA has had an impact on understanding the contributions of teachers in terms of their classroom interactional competence (Walsh, 2011), as well as students in terms of interactional noticing (Kääntä, 2014). Later in this book, I will return to the concept of interactional noticing.

In sum, although child language learners know more than, or at least as much as, interaction provides, adults, whose learning is based to a considerable extent on what they notice, typically seem to know less, owing partly to individual differences and L1 influence, but also to the quantity and quality of interaction they engage in. Interaction plays a major role in SLA and different views on interaction have provided distinct perspectives on noticing.

A Holistic View of Teacher–Learner Noticing

So far, this chapter has given an account of noticing by learners and viewed the interactional processes surrounding noticing from three distinct theoretical perspectives. This section presents examples of focus on form embedded in social interaction within communicative classroom contexts in order to describe features of such interaction that teachers and learners may notice together. These examples build on the premise that understanding classroom discourse can help teachers develop professionally (Walsh, 2011). Here, I will focus on what teachers need to notice in order to manage discourse in ways that are conducive to learner noticing and, potentially, L2 development. These anecdotal examples are based on my own experiences teaching English in Japanese university classrooms. Some assumptions from the previous section, as well as some new ones, resonate throughout the discussion of these examples.

The first two examples demonstrate how the teacher can initiate a language focus. In Example 2.2, two students have paired up to complete a task in which they discuss which items to bring on vacation. They are discussing items to add to their list, while the teacher is listening in on the conversation.

Example 2.2

Student 1: I also need to bring *hoshitsu* [moisturizing] cream
Teacher: How do you say *hoshitsu* in English?
Student 2: Moisturizing cream

Here, the teacher notices Student 1's use of the L1 and interrupts to initiate a focus on the equivalent English term. The teacher uses a display question to elicit this term. Having Student 2 produce this expression serves as an opportunity for Student 1 to notice a hole while also returning control of the conversation to the students. In fact, Student 1's language use could be said to fall on a continuum of translanguaging that extends from using the L1 as a resource to become bilingual to using two languages as a bilingual normally would (Cenoz & Gorter, 2015: 6). Teachers should be sensitive to this continuum and try to notice whether instances of L1 use are better categorized as L2 learning opportunities or bilingual language use.

Example 2.3 provides another example of how the teacher may intervene in student discourse. In this example, students had prepared a role-play to demonstrate how to make a business telephone call. One student began as follows.

Example 2.3

Student: It is Naoko Takahashi. May I speak to Ms Jones, please?
Teacher: Normally, we say, 'Hello. This is so and so' to start a phone call

The teacher's response here involves noticing the opener, comparing it with pragmatic norms in the L2 and determining an effective method of repairing the utterance. Such repair options include clarification requests (*I'm sorry?*) and recasts (*This is Naoko Takahashi*) but, in the present case, these may lack clarity compared to the metalinguistic explanation provided. By explaining the typical opening, the teacher provides the student with the opportunity to notice a gap. Clearly, there are a number of decisions to be made by the teacher in such cases, not least of which is whether to correct an utterance or not. If, as in this case, the student is thought to be at a stage where such advice may be beneficial, the actions above are warranted.

The next two examples show how, conversely, students can initiate a focus on language by appealing to the teacher. In Example 2.4, which occurred during a writing lesson, the teacher was explaining a grammar point (i.e. use of collocations to make writing sound more natural) to the entire class.

Example 2.4

Teacher: Just remember there are different types of collocations, like verb-noun, adjective-noun, noun-noun
Student: Noun-noun?
Teacher: Sure, climate change for example

The student's question here provides a clear opportunity to elaborate on the explanation. This student's brief turn, which consisted of segmenting and repeating the teacher's utterance with rising intonation, elicited an example that might otherwise not have been presented during the lesson. Students need, of course, to notice specific exemplars and not merely abstract categories in order to develop functional communicative ability. This example also shows how teacher noticing is closely tied in with the concept of teacher language awareness (Andrews, 2007). Responding promptly to student questions requires attention to the nature of those questions as well as the explicit knowledge of the L2 system to answer them. Of course, not all such questions are as easily handled as the one in this example.

In Example 2.5 the focus is on a different skill, pronunciation. This example occurred during a reading lesson. The students were reviewing words from a passage they read in groups, when one student asked for help with the word *eloquence*.

Example 2.5

Student: Where is [the] accent? [pointing to the word *eloquence*]
Teacher: /ˈeləkwəns/ listen /ˈeləkwəns/ It's at the beginning
Student: Okay

This example reveals another way of dealing with student questions about language. Again, the student effectively elicits additional, specific information about the L2, to which the teacher responded first by saying the word aloud twice with a focus on the stress. Doing so offers a direct route to the student's noticing of the word stress. Interestingly, it also enabled the teacher to reflect on the question in order to give an accurate answer: the stress is at the beginning. Teacher noticing, therefore, might sometimes involve the teacher using the target language for the purpose of accessing explicit knowledge about it. This information also benefits students.

An important general point here is that while student-initiated questions are largely unpredictable, the teacher must be socially attuned to noticing the kinds of brief interventions students may benefit from, which may depend not solely on the context and the learner's psycholinguistic and communicative capacities in the L2 (see Harley, 1993) but also upon aptitude, personality, motivation and, as experienced teachers realize, mood, which changes according to the time of day (e.g. morning versus afternoon classes). At the same time, being free of expectations leaves room for learners to grow and change along any of these dimensions. Sometimes, unexpected student questions are pleasant surprises.

These four examples were intended to help readers see the practical side of noticing in language classrooms and consider ways in which they might act on it in their own teaching. Thus, these teacher responses may be improved upon. It should be noted, of course, that most learner noticing is not externally guided. However, by taking a holistic perspective, a case can be made that, at certain times, noticing involves mutual engagement and shared attention by the teacher and learner. Teacher noticing can guide learner noticing, or it can be the other way around. As these examples show, there is a good deal of thinking going on when teachers determine a course of pedagogic action in flight. Whether attention to form is teacher or learner generated, the features of the classroom setting, the language focus, the task objective(s) and the individual learner are important because they suggest contextual constraints as well as pedagogic principles to be considered during teacher noticing, which informs the management of classroom interaction.

An Analytic View of Teacher–Learner Noticing

In contrast to the preceding section, this one takes an analytic perspective on teacher–learner noticing. There are substantial differences in the ways in which learner and teacher noticing have been dealt with in their respective literatures. These are to be expected owing to the distinct nature of, and the scholarly traditions behind, professional learning, on the one hand, and language learning, on the other. However, there are also similarities – they are both learning, after all. For instance, the default stance in both accounts is that awareness based on selective attention leads to improved performance and development. To tease apart these separate constructs, I review their similarities and differences here. In the following chapter, I present a more detailed model describing their integration.

Similarities

The main similarities across teacher and learner noticing are that, in either case, noticing involves: (1) subjective experience, (2) attention and

(3) awareness. However, a closer look at these commonalities reveals subtle differences in the treatment of teacher versus learner noticing.

To begin with, noticing, as a teacher or a learner, arises from one's personal experience of what is perceived. Thus, Schmidt called noticing a 'private experience' (Schmidt, 1990: 132) that is the 'subjective correlate' (Schmidt, 2001: 5) of attention. This raises intriguing philosophical queries about the reducibility of noticing to neuroscientific processes (not to mention thorny issues of measurement) which are beyond the scope of this book. It is worth noting here that the perceptions that feed into subjective psychological states need not be fully conscious (or accurate), as when, for example, a teacher entering the classroom senses that a student is absent before looking around to confirm whether this is impression is factual.

Consequently, noticing by teachers and learners results from attending to events in the environment, whether during teaching or learning. It follows that these forms of noticing are contingent upon events experienced by the teacher or language learner in real time. Several models of attention have been cited in support of noticing and these vary in emphasis depending on whether the goal is to describe teacher (van Es, 2011) or learner (Robinson *et al.*, 2012) noticing. For instance, the notion of attention-dependent knowledge encompasses skills that experienced teachers recruit when paying attention to cognitive and affective dimensions of classroom interaction (van Es, 2011: 135). On the other hand, the study of attention in SLA has expanded to include the neurobiological level and the information processing level, each of which attempts to explain its role in different contexts, and leads to controversies over the most useful explanatory models (Robinson *et al.*, 2012).

Lastly, noticing is equated with focal awareness in Schmidt's (1990) account. This is considered to be a lower level of conscious awareness than understanding. Teacher noticing also involves awareness. However, more specifically, teacher noticing is considered to be a form of situation awareness. Following Endsley (2000), situation awareness in teaching entails perceiving meaningful events, comprehending their significance and projecting their future status (Miller, 2011: 53). To the best of my knowledge, the notion of situation awareness has not entered the discussion of noticing in SLA. At the same time, awareness is a hotly debated topic in SLA research and, while this area has been the focus of novel experiments and replication studies, it is difficult to argue that any clear consensus exists on its role in adult learning. In attempting to define explicit versus implicit learning (which is not the same as knowledge), one major point of controversy regards the stage of learning at which awareness is claimed to operate (or not), which has led researchers to urge that 'on-line learner awareness in the process of learning be assessed before claims of implicit learning are advanced' (Schmidt, 1994: 20; see also Leow & Hama, 2013; Leow *et al.*, 2011, 2014).

Differences

As for the major differences, their professional status obviously accounts for large gaps in how teachers and learners think about classroom events. It should already be clear that teacher noticing is viewed as being shaped by professional acumen. There are numerous labels attached to the varied abilities that contribute to making teachers good noticers, including professional vision (Sherin & van Es, 2009) and sense making (Sherin & Russ, 2015), which are described in the next chapter. These are closely associated with teaching expertise. On the other hand, in his commentary on two decades of research into noticing, Schmidt (2012) acknowledged that while an individual's language learning history is an important factor, the idea of someone being a good noticer in SLA remains under-explored. Unfortunately, little is known about the role of expertise in learner noticing.

Another obvious difference concerns the object of noticing. Teacher noticing concerns significant or meaningful classroom events. Furthermore, it is sometimes presumed to allow teachers to 'see' student thinking. This seems to pose a conundrum because, as stated already, subjective experiences are private and not accessible to others. However, in theory, if one assumes that L2 use, which teachers do have access to, reflects learner cognition to some extent, then research should address this assumption within language teaching. Conversely, what learners notice, as already described, are features of target language input as filtered through existing knowledge.

Summary

In this chapter the concept of noticing in SLA has been presented in order to argue for an expanded view. Traditionally, noticing refers to the subjective correlate of attention and 'the objects of attention and noticing are elements of the surface structure of utterances in the input' (Schmidt, 2001: 5). Following in this tradition, one may argue that, at times, learners and teachers experience such utterances in a process of joint attention. The main site in which teacher–learner noticing is relevant is during classroom interaction. Three perspectives on interaction, including cognitive-interactionist, sociocultural theory and conversation-analytic approaches, were considered. Each of these diverse views allows for the possibility of language development situated in encounters where a teacher and student notice jointly. Furthermore, teacher–learner noticing was introduced as a construct that can be viewed holistically or analytically. The examples offered in this chapter were intended to show how skilled language teachers manage classroom interaction in order to encourage a focus on form. However, these are not the only way in which teacher noticing is used (see Chapter 3). There are similarities between teacher and learner noticing insofar as they both involve subjectively experiencing phenomena, which is linked to attention and some level of awareness. The psychological models recruited in discussions of each of these areas differ somewhat, however. There are also other major differences between teacher and student noticing, which include the role of knowledge or expertise and the object of noticing. Some of these points raise issues that cannot be easily resolved in this book, which will focus mostly on teacher noticing. Nonetheless, if classroom psychology is to be understood more fully, it makes sense to consider the merger of learner and teacher noticing. This chapter attempted to shed initial light on the concept of noticing as a confluence. In Chapter 3, teacher noticing is further defined and situated within other processes in language teacher cognition.

3 Language Teacher Noticing

What Does Teacher Noticing Have to Offer?

The previous chapter provided the background for an understanding of language teacher noticing that is deep because it can at times be considered facilitative of learner noticing and also broad because it draws on educational literature in various domains. As noted earlier, the approach taken in this book is integrative and transdisciplinary. One formulation of this approach is that it aims to integrate teacher and learner noticing and to look across disciplinary boundaries for insight into language teaching. The purpose of this approach is to introduce the construct of language teacher noticing in a way that will allow it to complement empirical research and professional development. Admittedly, these are long-term goals. However, there is good reason to believe that language teacher noticing can bridge gaps in research and practice.

Namely, it is clear that the teacher's role in language instruction has expanded. In the case of task-based language teaching (TBLT), for instance, teachers are called upon to make decisions and carry out actions at the pre-task, task and language focus phases of a lesson (see Willis, 1996). However, their role is more than the sum of these practices because teachers are also regarded as change agents who think critically about task implementation and raise questions that inform future classroom practice (Van den Branden, 2016). To achieve these goals effectively, teachers must notice dimensions of learning at multiple stages of their lessons and reflect upon them. It could be argued that self-observation in the form of teacher noticing is one of the simplest tools available for improving classroom instruction and enhancing professional growth. This is true of both pre-service and in-service teachers, although the resources to support a better understanding of teacher noticing vary across these contexts. In either case, it would help to start with a careful definition.

Definition

The goal of this chapter is to provide and unpack a definition of language teacher noticing that can be useful for research and practice. To that end, I propose the following definition, which draws on various sources described throughout this chapter:

> Language teacher noticing is a form of reflection entailing processes of attending to events, interpreting them, and deciding how to act on them, which occurs during engagement with learners.

The remainder of the chapter will provide accounts of related constructs, specify the niche that language teacher noticing occupies, and position this idea within the broader perspective of the psychology of language learning and teaching, referring to TBLT as an example at times.

Teacher Cognition

The general view of the role of the teacher in language teaching has transitioned fairly recently from being a vehicle for the implementation of a particular method (e.g. the audiolingual method) to being a facilitator of communication responsive to student needs. Commenting on this transition, one of the earliest proponents of using tasks in language teaching, N.S. Prabhu, proclaimed that there is no best language teaching method for all contexts and argued that attempts to understand the 'pedagogic perceptions' of teachers and researchers (Prabhu, 1990: 176) might offer a suitable alternative to the hunt for the best method. This idea of perception fits well with noticing, although teacher cognition research has expanded in somewhat broader directions to account for the various demands placed on language teachers in the post-methods era.

Within a climate of concern for context sensitivity, practitioner theories and learner identities (Kumaravadivelu, 2006), TBLT, as an approach that has grown out of communicative language teaching, puts a premium on learner needs and language use and thereby redefines the teacher's role. Yet it has also been argued that TBLT, too, is presented at times as having a procedural emphasis; that is, if done right, task design may appear to supersede considerations of the essential role of skilled teaching (see Atkinson, 2017; for contrasting viewpoints, see among others Norris, 2011; Samuda, 2015; Van den Branden, 2016). The problem, perhaps, is that language teachers do so much that the specific thought processes they engage in during tasks risk under-specification in the literature.

The understandable tendency for teachers to wish to adopt innovative practices, whether based on tasks, genre, content or something else, further reinforces the notion that teachers' pedagogic perceptions need to be accounted for overtly. Teacher noticing may encourage such accounting. Historically, it can be seen as the continuation of a trend in language teaching research of adapting concepts from general education in order to offer new perspectives on teachers' mental work, which Freeman (2016) has called, 'the same things done differently'. That is, what is seen as important in general education is no less important in language teaching, albeit reframed by the particular challenges of classroom second language (L2) learning.

Borg's conceptualization of teacher cognition

Another example of how researchers have imported ideas from general education into language teaching comes from Borg (2015). This approach synthesized various points of view that had accumulated since the 1970s regarding what teachers think, know and believe, referring to them collectively as teacher cognition. Teacher cognitions (in plural) arise from four sub-constructs, the first two of which can be grouped under teacher learning, in the form of (1) schooling in a general sense and (2) professional coursework. These are distinct from (3) contextual factors, within which (4) classroom practice is nested. These four sub-constructs feed into language teacher cognition. Borg's conceptualization therefore highlights the broad range of influences on teacher thinking that accrue over the lifespan and stem from the immediate context. This schematic view includes statements on how the four major elements 'define', 'limit' and 'influence' each other, as well as various other perceptions and cognitions. For instance, Borg concludes that the relationship between cognition and practice is not linear or unidirectional, but rather that language teaching consists of 'dynamic interactions among cognition, context and experience' (Borg, 2015: 324).

This view has spawned a number of empirical studies that focus on language teacher cognition (Borg, 2019, is a recent review). For example, it is not uncommon for researchers working within the educational framework of TBLT to refer to Borg's work (e.g. Van den Branden, 2016). Several studies have attempted to link in-service teachers' beliefs about TBLT to practice, in a wide range of settings. Some of these studies have used classroom observations combined with interviews (e.g. Andon & Eckerth, 2009; Carless, 2004; Zheng & Borg, 2014) to illustrate how teachers experimenting with TBLT often flexibly adopt its principles upon consideration of issues such as established curriculum guidelines or classroom management issues, as well as their prior teaching beliefs or additional contextual factors. Thus, the way teachers think about and use tasks needs to be integrated into their own broader perception of themselves and their work.

Borg's influential work provides a sophisticated and comprehensive description of the potential influences on teachers' pedagogic perceptions during classroom practice. It emphasizes a rich variety of aspects of cognition, including 'beliefs, knowledge, theories, attitudes, assumptions, conceptions, principles, thinking, decision-making' (Borg, 2015: 333). This is helpful because any of these concepts may come into play when teachers are conducting lessons, they may assist teachers in understanding their own development and they may guide further research. However, this list can be seen as both a challenge and an opportunity. It is a challenge to delineate these concepts and to know their relative significance in terms of teaching and learning outcomes. In this regard, it is worth pointing out that Borg does not refer to his conceptualization as a model. Its goal seems to be to describe teacher cognition in general rather than to make explicit predictions regarding which elements interact and how. Borg thus regards it as one tool within an overall framework for language teacher cognition research. The utility of this framework, he argues, is to relate connected studies, enhance awareness of key elements in teacher cognition and highlight gaps in order to prompt attention to them. This is where researchers and teachers can look for opportunities. The four major factors that Borg identified (schooling, coursework, context and practice) can act as separate inroads into teacher cognition concerning either generic processes (e.g. planning) or domain-specific ones (e.g. writing), as he pointed out. As a generic process, teacher noticing represents a gap in language teaching research.

Noticing as a cognition

Within Borg's account, the obvious starting point for studying teacher noticing is classroom practice (including practice teaching) because this deals with actual teaching and contextual factors. In line with his usage, noticing can be considered as a specific instance of a cognition that involves other cognitions (namely, selective attention, use of interpretive frames and decision-making). Teacher noticing, thus defined, is not overtly mentioned by Borg, although it may be assumed to be important. The main advantage of considering teacher noticing in light of teacher cognition is that it allows for a broad range of potential influences to be considered, while also situating it firmly in practice. In turn, teacher noticing research may reveal specific factors that interface with teacher cognition.

Furthermore, when teachers focus and sustain their noticing, they can use it to foster exploratory practice. This involves 'attending more intensively to what is going on' (Allwright, 2003: 124), which can lead to action for understanding and working with those understandings. Such work nurtures classroom learning as well as teacher development.

Reflective Teaching

Reflective teaching, in contrast to teacher cognition, has also been used to describe teachers' thoughts about classroom teaching. In general, the English teaching profession has used the term *reflection* to mean 'conscious, experientially informed thought' (Anderson, 2020: 4). Crookes (2003) reviews narrow and broad definitions of reflective teaching and specifies that the latter entails two relationships: one between an individual teacher's thinking and acting and another between the teacher and the society to which he or she belongs. Acknowledging the individualistic nature of reflective teaching, Crookes emphasizes the value of distancing oneself from one's teaching experiences during reflection and asserts that the responsibility for reflection should not rest solely upon the teacher (Crookes, 2003: 183). The terms *reflective teaching* and *teacher reflection* therefore both suggest that teachers independently problematize or question their teaching. It is argued that this process is more efficient when collegial support is available to help teachers view their teaching less subjectively.

Reflective practice

Reflective practice is a similar label for the process of taking an evaluative stance on one's teaching with the assistance of others. As defined by Farrell (2015: 123), it is a 'process accompanied by a set of attitudes in which teachers systematically collect data about their practice, and while engaging in dialogue with others use the data to make informed decisions about their practice inside and outside the classroom'. In addition, Farrell recognizes a distinction based on Schön (1983; see Farrell, 2015; see also Bailey, 2012; Freeman, 2016) that contrasts reflection-in-action and reflection-on-action. These two types happen during and after teaching, respectively, while Farrell also considers reflection-for-action to be a third type that is proactive (Farrell, 2015: 82). This tripartite division means that the timing of reflection can be classified as before, during or after a lesson. For a comprehensive review of related research, see Farrell (2016).

Reflection-in-action is arguably a highly neglected area of research in language teaching. However, this lack of attention may be at least partly attributable to the description of it as 'tacit' (Farrell, 2015: 81), 'inaccessible' (Freeman, 2016: 212) or inexpressible (Burton, 2009: 300). This characterization, however, seems inconsistent with both the definitions of reflection found in the language teaching literature and the general understanding of reflection as a conscious process. The possibility of classroom events unconsciously influencing teacher cognitions (Borg, 2015) notwithstanding, the usage of reflection strongly implies awareness. Moreover, skilled language teachers certainly base many decisions on in-the-moment conscious reflection – the notion of focus on form would not exist if they could not (Long & Robinson, 1998; see also Long, 1977, cited in Allwright & Bailey, 1991). Instead, the main obstacle to studying reflection-in-action, if one accepts a simple definition of it as spontaneous reflection during teaching, appears to be its intractability. It is easier to capture culminated reflections exhibited by, for instance, lesson plans and classroom materials, which do not necessarily refer to any specific in-the-moment cognitions.

This gap in research on reflection-in-action is directly related to concerns raised by Walsh and Mann (2015). These authors presented a case for more evidence-based approaches to reflective practice, which they view as often unsupported by data, overly focused on individuals (rather than collaborative) and predominately carried out in writing. They commented on the need to clarify how teachers do reflective practice and to expand the range of data elicitation tools used, in particular those based on recordings of classroom interaction. Making a strong argument for improving reflective practice through data collection and peer dialogue, Walsh and Mann provide helpful examples of the use of self-observation and stimulated recall in reflective practice. Particularly in the case of stimulated recall, this may bring us closer to the possibility of investigating reflection-in-action, although it must be kept in mind that recall may at times be used in ways that favor explanation or justification (i.e. reflection-on-action) instead of in-the-moment reflection. For an earlier critique, see Mann and Walsh (2013).

A recent study by Anderson (2019) sought to capture reflection-in-action using video-based stimulated recall methodology. Four English as a foreign language (EFL) teachers (with a minimum of four years' experience) were shown video-recordings of their lessons immediately after teaching and prompted to recall what they noticed. These reflections were coded to develop a typology of interactive thought containing eight categories. Of particular interest is the category of perception, which was described as 'seeing, hearing, noticing, or perceiving something' (Anderson, 2019: 7). It included two subcategories: perception of learner actions, contributions or moods and perception of other factors (including materials, time and board work). The first of these subcategories was the most frequent across all four teachers. This important study shows that there is much work to be done in the area of language teachers' reflection-in-action, which includes, prominently in this study, their noticing of student contributions (see also Jackson & Cho, 2018).

Lastly, beyond defining and engaging with it, another challenge is the question of how such reflection might facilitate learning by teachers. Burton (2009: 300) helpfully described how reflective sequences can lead to experiential learning on the part of a teacher. Among these were included:

(1) Noticing a concern
(2) Clarifying the concern
(3) Responding to the concern
(4) Processing it as a whole
(5) Acting on insights gained.

This series of steps, beginning with noticing, might then also be used to describe how teacher noticing, as a form of reflection, potentially feeds into the teacher's long-term thinking and development. Similarly, a recent study by Lengeling *et al.* (2020) linked noticing and reflection, based on qualitative research with 22 students in a classroom observation course offered through a BA TESOL program in Mexico. The study found that noticing was useful for professional development as it led to participants' understanding of when to attend to classroom events, reflection on why they occurred and examination of how to improve their teaching practices.

Noticing as a form of reflection

Reflective practice as a concept within language teacher education appears to be maturing as different authors situate it within and establish its importance to professional development. As with all constructs, it can be partitioned into sub-constructs, and the distinction between reflection *in* versus *on* action has been imported from outside the language teaching field to explain physical and temporal constraints on how teachers think. It is important to note that Schön's (1983) description of reflection-in-action as a process based on tacit knowing-in-action, which leads expert practitioners to generate novel theories independent of established ideas, is different in kind from teacher noticing. Teacher noticing need not rely solely upon internalized knowledge about practice.

As described by Schön (1983), the timescale of reflection-in-action is also more flexible, because noticing is limited to engagement with learners, whereas the length of reflection-in-action varies according to the type of practice. This early formulation by Schön has been treated in different ways by different authors in the TESOL field (e.g. Anderson, 2019; Farrell, 2015). Suffice it to say that teacher noticing may lead to further reflection and this process may influence subsequent thought and action (Burton, 2009; Criswell & Krall, 2017; Mason, 2002).

To summarize and delineate further, Table 3.1 offers a comparison between teacher noticing and the concepts closest to it.

Table 3.1 Distinctions between teacher noticing and related concepts

Concept	Main components	Context
Teacher cognition	Schooling, professional coursework, contextual factors, classroom practice	Interacting 'personal, physical, sociocultural, and historical milieus' (Borg, 2019: 6)
Interactive thought	Planned intention, knowledge/memory access, perception, decision, affordance awareness, uncertainty awareness, value judgement, reflexivity (Anderson, 2019)	During a lesson
Teacher noticing	Attention, interpretation, decision making	During engagement with learners

Defining Teacher Noticing

This section focuses on the definition of teacher noticing, as a specific case of noticing by developing professionals, in order to then clarify what is unique about language teacher noticing. Essentially, teaching involves noticing. This is true whether teaching is defined in broad terms, including forms such as social tolerance, opportunity provisioning, input enhancement, corrective feedback and direct instruction (Atkinson, 2017), or as 'discussion about the nature and demands of the task, talk about strategies, interim performance analysis, general and specific feedback, provision of information and relevant supplementary skill practice' (Bygate, 2016: 10). Learning to notice how to productively shape environments or how to promote discussion and performance is a fundamental aspect of language teacher development.

The discipline of noticing

In 2002, John Mason, a professor of mathematics education at the Open University, offered a prescient, book-length account of noticing as a tool for researching one's practice. Taking teaching to be any profession involving caring for or supporting others, Mason introduced the concept of noticing by emphasizing the importance of professionals being awake to the possibility of making appropriate changes. As an instance of the aforementioned reflection-in-action, he described how a teacher who is angered by a student's childish behavior may say that they are angry not with the individual responsible for the behavior, but with the behavior itself. In doing so, the teacher relies on an 'inner witness' (Mason, 2002: 19), who functions as an emotionally distant observer facilitating the resolution of classroom conflicts. This example shows how the distinct mental experiences (i.e. emotional versus rational) of a single teacher can be partitioned and reflected upon spontaneously in order to enhance instruction. Unavoidably, there are times when language teachers experience negative emotions, such as anxiety (Benesch, 2017; Horwitz, 1996). On a positive note, trait emotional intelligence has been linked to a range of teaching skills, including classroom management and pedagogical skills (Dewaele *et al.*, 2018). Thus, cultivating the ability to notice and regulate one's emotions can be a powerful teaching tool (King & Ng, 2018).

Mason used noticing to refer to 'a collection of practices both for living in, and hence learning from, experience, and for informing future practice' (Mason, 2002: 29). He posited three levels of noticing. The first is perceiving, in which physical, emotional or cognitive changes are detected. This, he argues, allows for memory traces to be established, although this level may not involve much awareness. The second level, marking, entails perceiving but with the additional possibility of being able to independently recall and describe, or re-mark on the event. The third level is recording. This can take a multitude of forms, including written or mental notes. One example of recording carried out in language classrooms would be when the teacher circles words in a passage that individual students have looked up while they were reading, as a reminder to check comprehension with the whole class. Importantly, each level demands intention and commitment for it to foster the next level. Teachers perceive many things that they do not mark, and also mark things that are soon forgotten. So, in order to develop, it is necessary to look for opportunities to extend noticing within classroom environments. Based on the centrality of noticing to a wide range of professional contexts, Mason included practical suggestions to enhance one's sensitivity to these levels. For instance, he suggested trying to recall episodes related to noticing, marking and recording at the end of each day.

The Discipline of Noticing, as Mason refers to it, involves sensitizing oneself to practice, in order to become better at noticing. Of course, noticing can and does happen by chance, but this is not the same as intentional noticing. To help foster noticing, Mason describes how professionals can keep accounts, develop sensitivity, recognize choices, prepare to notice, label events and validate with others. Labels are interesting because they sometimes reflect coinages developed within groups of professionals to succinctly describe certain complex phenomena they encounter in their work. For example, *re-tasking* versus *de-tasking* refers to the ways teachers may enhance or reduce the potential of a task-based lesson plan during a lesson (Samuda, 2015). Mason considers such brief-but-vivid accounts of practice highly useful in professional communication because they label not just a single experience but a general category of experience shared by others (Mason, 2002: 81). In these ways, noticing is not confined to the classroom, but enters into teachers' preparation and reflection outside of it.

Mason's work has often been discussed in the literature on mathematics teacher education. However, given its scope, it certainly deserves fuller attention by members of other teaching fields, including L2 teaching. The approach he developed has been cited widely by others and built upon in more recent contributions, including Mason (2011, 2017). The next section focuses on how teacher noticing has grown through empirical work with teachers of a range of academic subjects and student levels.

Teacher noticing and professional vision

Beginning in the same year that Mason's book appeared, Miriam Sherin and Elizabeth van Es published a series of articles that investigated teacher noticing and showed this construct to be valuable in mathematics teacher education (Sherin & van Es, 2009; van Es & Sherin, 2002, 2006, 2008). In the process, their collaboration has redefined and expanded the construct of teacher noticing. Their initial stance was that math and science education reforms in the United States called for a new understanding of teachers' roles, emphasizing flexibility and the capacity to 'see' students' thinking. They characterized this ability as noticing, specifying that it involved three parts: (1) identifying important aspects of teaching situations; (2) connecting specific details of classroom interaction with teaching and learning principles; and (3) reasoning about these interactions using contextual knowledge (van Es & Sherin, 2002: 573). They also noted that skilled teachers possess these qualities, and aimed to explore whether they could be developed through teacher training. To do so, they conducted a pre–post experimental study with 12 pre-service math and science teachers. The dependent variable was teachers' written reflections on their teaching, scored for levels of development in noticing. The intervention involved having six experimental participants use a video analysis support tool to reflect on their teaching, while six control participants did not use this tool. At posttest, only the scores of the experimental group increased. Therefore, some methods of helping teachers develop their noticing appear more effective than others. Recent studies in this vein have gone on to explore in detail how video tools can act as a scaffold to teacher noticing (Superfine et al., 2017).

Written reflections are but one potential source of data on teacher noticing. In another study, van Es and Sherin (2006) addressed noticing in the context of video clubs. The premise here is that, like professional development in general, the development of teacher noticing may best be fostered in groups. Video clubs bring teachers together in a meeting to view and discuss videotaped segments of teaching. Such meetings may include novice and expert teachers and, optionally, researchers who participate as a facilitators or observers. In this study, teachers were interviewed before and after participating in a series of video club meetings. Following a qualitative approach, aspects of both what teachers noticed (the agent and topic) and how (their stance and focus) were analyzed, based on data from 13 participants in two different video clubs. The results indicated that the perspectives of participants in both clubs changed, becoming either narrower or broader (this classification concerns whether teachers primarily focused on one or multiple aspects, respectively). The authors argued that both of these changes can be valuable in different ways, and that the design of video clubs, including the artifacts used, participant roles and format (i.e. organization and length) seemed to matter.

The video club setting was explored in further detail in a follow-up with seven participants from one club, whose noticing over time revealed three distinct trajectories (van Es & Sherin, 2008). Here, interview comments were again shown to differ in terms of specificity. The analysis uncovered three distinct paths followed by the teachers: direct (broad → narrow), cyclical (broad → narrow → broad → narrow) or incremental (broad → narrowing → narrow). These studies lead to the conclusion that teachers do not always notice classroom events in the same way, but may follow certain patterns over time. Importantly, it seems that video clubs may provide a context for open discussion of multiple dimensions of noticing in classroom interaction, from the actors and topics involved to the teacher's perspective and focus.

However, one question that arises is whether participation in video-based professional development actually influences teaching. This issue was addressed in another report that viewed video clubs as a forum for learning to notice (Sherin & van Es, 2009). Here, classroom observations augmented the data from video club meetings and pre–post noticing interviews. These videotaped observations were conducted at the beginning and end of the year with seven teachers who joined a video club. The classroom data were analyzed to identify evidence and counter-evidence for teacher noticing (i.e. selective attention and knowledge-based reasoning) in response to student-initiated discussion about mathematical ideas. While the results showed evidence for and against noticing of student thinking throughout the year, there was a shift, exhibited by all teachers, toward more noticing at the end of the year. This is an important finding because it suggests that teachers can apply the noticing skills they acquire in video clubs during instruction. Nevertheless, it should be noted that this study lacked a control group, so it is not clear that the increase can be attributed solely to video club participation.

It is noteworthy that throughout their work Sherin and van Es regard teacher noticing as closely connected to professional vision, or ways of seeing and understanding key aspects of their work shared by members of a certain profession (Goodwin, 1994). The core idea is that vision is constructed through professional discourse, using various practices, including coding, highlighting and producing representations of domain-relevant phenomena. In a video club context, this vision is enacted with other teachers, who share an understanding based on co-membership. In a classroom context, vision is enacted in front of students who, it is assumed, can also become adept at recognizing what and how teachers notice (Wells, 2017). The idea, from the teacher education literature, that students observe and learn about the teaching profession from their early education (i.e. their apprenticeship of observation, Lortie, 1975, cited in Borg, 2015) lends some validity to this assumption. In both cases, the noticing that teachers do, based upon joint attention and shared reasoning, may thus be seen as an instantiation of norms, of either professional development or classroom instruction.

Teacher noticing is a topic of intensifying research focus as the number of studies grows. Beyond the domain of mathematics education, this literature now includes studies on teaching biology (Russ & Luna, 2013), music (Ankney, 2016) and second languages (Jackson & Cho, 2018). Meanwhile, investigations in mathematics have considerably expanded in their scope (see the chapters in Schack *et al.*, 2017; Sherin *et al.*, 2011b). This work is in keeping with trends in education that seek to refocus teachers away from content delivery and toward student thinking. As Ritchhart *et al.* put it, as teachers, 'we need to draw on our understanding of what thinking is and the types of thinking we seek to foster so that we can name, *notice*, and highlight thinking when it occurs in class: recognizing a student who puts forth a new point of view, offers up a nascent theory or conjecture, proposes an explanation, makes a connection, sees a pattern, and so on' (Ritchhart *et al.*, 2011: 29, emphasis added). As such, teacher noticing and professional vision are important to research on language teacher development. This raises a number of interesting issues, some of which are considered next.

Issues raised by teacher noticing research

This discussion raises two issues relevant to the construct definition of teacher noticing. The first issue is that clearly there are multiple definitions of teacher noticing. These definitions, however, all consider noticing to be multifaceted. At present, there seems to be a consensus that attention and interpretation are essential components. Some studies have added a third component by including decision-making (see Philipp *et al.*, 2017; Sherin, 2017, for discussion). This component is important to understanding how teachers respond to learners during engagement. Of course, it is possible that a teacher may attend to and interpret an event and then delay or even forgo a response, but this too constitutes a decision. Essentially, attention, interpretation and decision-making are distinct but connected processes; like other cognitive processes, they can be characterized by continuity in their temporal dynamics and they are intricately linked to action (Spivey, 2007). Thus, the triad of attending, interpreting and deciding how to respond (Philipp *et al.*, 2017) can offer a fuller account, while it should be acknowledged that meaningful noticing (especially for teacher development) might also occur based primarily on attending to and interpreting classroom events.

The second issue, which I will return to in Part 2, regards measuring teacher noticing. Astute readers will have already noticed that the empirical work reviewed in this section has used noticing outside the classroom (i.e. during video clubs or written reflections) as a proxy for classroom noticing. Yet, methodological advances have yielded recent studies of in-the-moment teacher noticing, based on wearable cameras (Russ & Luna, 2013; Sherin *et al.*, 2011). Using this approach, Colestock and Sherin (2016) instructed teachers to tag key moments of continuously recorded video that showed student thinking, and then elicited the teachers' explanations of these moments during an interview session, in which they reviewed the tagged clips. This helped to ensure that the teachers had adequate access to the context, over the duration of the noticing episode, and that their own rationales for what they had observed were related to lesson goals.

Where	In class	←——————→	Outside of class
When	At one time-point	←——————→	Across time
How	Individually	←——————→	Collectively

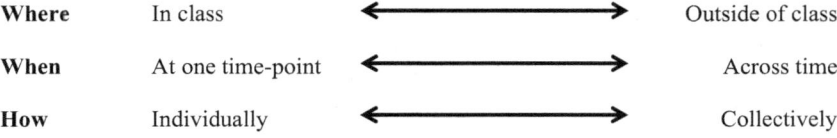

Figure 3.1 Continua for observing teacher noticing in practice

Acknowledging these issues, Sherin (2017) commented on the difficulty of observing noticing during student–teacher interaction, and suggested that investigations of noticing need not be restricted to classrooms. In theory, it is useful to bear in mind the orthogonal distinction between observing noticing inside or outside the classroom and individual or group noticing. The where, when and how of capturing teacher noticing, for research purposes, may involve several continua, as depicted in Figure 3.1.

The studies reviewed here seem to have gradually progressed toward having teachers mark off their noticing during the act of teaching, with the availability of new technology (see Colestock & Sherin, 2016). There is a subtle, yet important, difference between this approach and studies in which teachers are asked to identify episodes of noticing after the fact, as in Jackson and Cho (2018), for example, who found a significant difference in the number of comments teachers made based on the length of time between their teaching and recall sessions. There were fewer noticing instances as time went on. There is also quite a difference between asking teachers what they noticed in private and asking them this during a group session with peers, as in the video club studies described above. In the latter case, social expectations may influence reporting. Finally, the duration of noticing is a key, under-addressed matter, as it regards how long teachers sustain a single instance of noticing during a lesson, and also its development over weeks or years (see van Es & Sherin, 2008, for one longitudinal study). Digging even deeper into measurement practices, Jacobs (2017) cautioned that there are numerous choices to be made in selecting stimuli and eliciting teacher noticing, and also pointed out the influence of analytic lenses, which can include theoretical frameworks, learning goals and novice–expert comparisons. As she concluded, 'norms for measuring noticing are still emerging' (Jacobs, 2017: 278).

Language Teacher Noticing

Is language teacher noticing any different from mathematics teacher noticing? Based on the previous section, the answer is yes, insofar as separate discursive practices for talking about and representing language and math exist. It should be remembered that teacher noticing is mediated by language and enacted through discourse; if the discourse changes, the resources employed change as well. Later in this book, pre-service teacher

(PST) noticing will be described in greater detail, in the context of a task-based study with teachers-in-training in Japan.

In the first attempt to define this construct, Jackson and Cho (2018: 30) stated that 'L2 teacher noticing refers to teachers' awareness of features of second language classroom interaction that may influence student learning'. Here I expand on that statement, in light of the definition at the outset of this chapter, and the discussion so far. This involves further specification of selective <u>a</u>ttention, <u>i</u>nterpretation, <u>d</u>ecision-making and <u>e</u>ngagement, which lends itself to the mnemonic, AIDE. These dimensions can be recalled by reminding oneself that the teacher is an aide to students.

Attention

One problem with the Jackson and Cho (2018) definition is that although it referred to interaction, it did not directly address the issue of joint noticing. To remedy that, Figure 3.2 is adapted from Tomasello's (2003: 29) model of joint attention. A crucial component of this model is the inclusion of intention. Teacher noticing without learner noticing is indicated by Line 1 and learner noticing (Schmidt, 1990) without teacher noticing is indicated by Line 2. Lines 3 and 4 show an intention for the teacher or learner to attend. In the words of Tomasello and Carpenter (2007: 121), 'joint attention is not just two people experiencing the same thing at the same time, but rather it is two people experiencing the same thing at the same time and knowing together that they are doing this'. Thus, teacher–learner joint noticing is indicated by Lines 5 and 6 in the

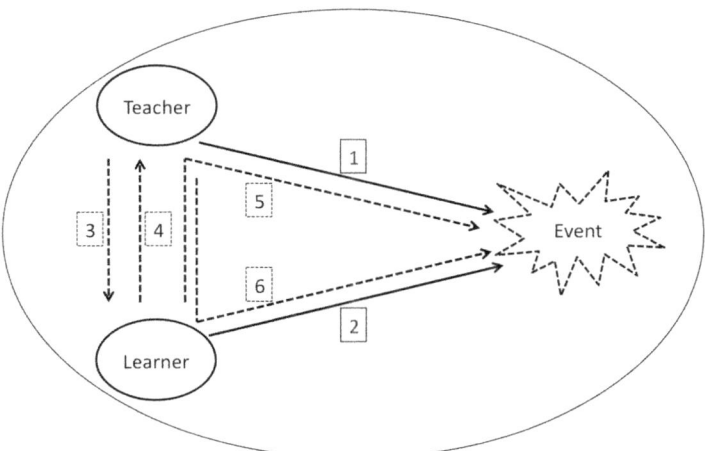

Figure 3.2 Individual and joint attention in noticing
Source: Adapted from Tomasello (2003).

figure, which differ according to whether the teacher or learner initiates the noticing by conveying intention. For instance, Line 5 denotes joint noticing initiated by the learner. Dotted lines indicate shared cognitions and solid lines indicate private ones.

More could be said regarding the nature of joint attention. Eilan (2005) traces the discussion of this phenomenon in child developmental psychology and philosophy. A key assumption, which also arises in the literature on teacher noticing of student thinking, is that our minds are at times transparent. There is, furthermore, a mutual awareness in joint attention. For Eilan, this raises intriguing questions, including what kind of mutual awareness might arise within joint attention (the epistemological question), what kind of understanding of attention a child needs in order to engage in episodes of joint attention, which occur much earlier than the development of a theory of mind (the concept question), and what kind of social interactions give rise to joint attention and mutual awareness (the social question). The idea being developed in this book is that social interactions during language teaching are potential sites of teacher–student noticing, or mutual awareness, which are driven by joint attention.

In another account, Gallagher (2011) also points out that joint attention involves social cognition. It joins primary and secondary intersubjectivity, where the former involves sensorimotor abilities used to gauge intentions conveyed through bodily means, and the latter involves how these means are used to stage actions. Teachers and learners use such embodied understandings during interaction, as well as their understanding of pragmatic norms. According to Gallagher, joint attention involves abilities that 'start out and continue as sensorimotor, perceptual, and action-oriented and are made more subtle and sophisticated via communicative and narrative practices' (Gallagher, 2011: 301). Due to its embodied nature, multimodal analyses (Mondada, 2016) of teacher noticing may be especially revealing. Noticing, when understood as a form of social cognition, is fundamentally multimodal.

Interpretation

Teacher noticing can be regarded as skilled viewing, or situation awareness (Miller, 2011). Beyond perception, it involves comprehension of meaningful events. To understand how teachers comprehend their work, Sherin and Russ (2015) identified interpretive frames based on attention and reasoning, grouping them into six types: *narrative* (storytelling or finding causal relations); *normative* (assessing performance or considering alternatives); *personal* (perspective-taking or affective responses); *expectation* (noticing familiar events, anomalies or omissions); *associative* (using metaphor or comparison to understand events); and *abstraction* (generalizing across contexts or applying teaching principles). This dimension of teacher noticing is specific to teachers' backgrounds and experiences and it is highly contextualized. Teachers in foreign language versus second language contexts, at various levels within educational systems and with more or less familiarity with the learners' L1 will, of course, interpret events differently. Some of the factors potentially influencing this level of noticing, including individual characteristics (Gurzynski-Weiss, 2017) and expertise (Tsui, 2009), are described later. The possibility that teachers may misinterpret classroom events should also be kept in mind.

Decision-making

As interpretation potentially leads to comprehension, so does decision-making potentially lead to action. Events unfolding during in-the-moment classroom interaction were conjoined to actions in Woods' (1996) ethno-cognitive model of teachers' decision-making. This cyclical model involves: (1) classroom actions/events; (2) planning/expectation, which originates prior those events (akin to the expectation frames noted above); and (3) understanding/interpretation, which is informed by beliefs, assumptions and knowledge (BAK). Under this view, actions carried out during a lesson may also subsequently inform future decision-making processes in a recursive model that spans across hierarchal units of teaching (Woods, 1996: 139). In describing interactive processes of classroom teaching events, Woods raises the point that teachers' BAK influences their perceptions of events, and also illustrates how teachers' actions may or may not be consistent with their beliefs. To add to this, building on general education research, Tsui (2003) noted that pedagogic decision-making may be reflective, immediate or routine (automatic). These types of decisions suggest that how novice and experienced teachers respond to the events they notice may fundamentally differ. In these ways, events that teachers experience may be linked to changes in their performance, eventually leading to expertise. Moreover, Tsui's research on the nature of expertise, interestingly, led her to the conclusion that it is not tacit but involves reflection, deliberation and constant engagement (Tsui, 2003: 277).

Engagement

As noted above (Table 3.1), one distinguishing feature of teacher noticing is that it happens in contexts of engagement with learners. The construct of engagement is a useful bridge between teacher noticing and student involvement/participation. Engagement includes cognitive, behavioral, emotional and social facets (Baralt *et al.*, 2016; Mercer & Dörnyei, 2020; Philp & Duchesne, 2016). For Mercer and Dörnyei (2020), student engagement entails active participation and affective–cognitive involvement in classrooms. Although Philp and Duchesne referred mainly to learner engagement during tasks in their review, they pointed out that teachers who observe their students are aware of differences in engagement. Furthermore, teachers themselves should be considered to be part of classroom engagement. In Figure 3.2, the oval encompassing teacher and learner noticing represents engagement. This in turn makes it possible to situate these processes within a broader model of the embedded nature of language teaching and learning put forth by the Douglas Fir Group (2016: 25), within which 'individuals engaging with others' occupies the centermost position in a series of concentric circles described as the micro level of social activity, the meso level of sociocultural institutions and the macro level of ideologies.

Following on from this, it can be argued that teacher noticing may encompass learners' use of language, their social identities and their values, each of which has important consequences for L2 teaching and learning, as long as those levels are evident during engagement. Such nested layers of groups, cultures and communities, comprising a wider ecological view, are likewise regarded as influential to the psychology of language teaching and learning by Williams *et al.* (2016, see their Figure 2.1).

This view of engagement as the context of teacher noticing is taken up again in the next chapter, in order to illustrate how PST noticing in the study was embedded within the expanding contexts of task, program and community. Furthermore, the operational definition of noticing (see Appendix B) incorporated engagement (Philp & Duchesne, 2016). That is, this study did not use all of the teacher cognitions reported, but instead focused only on those that occurred during participation in social, cognitive, emotional or behavioral dimensions of student–teacher interaction (see also Jackson & Shirakawa, 2020).

Summary

This chapter has proposed a definition of language teacher noticing and reviewed work on language teacher cognition, reflective practice and teacher noticing (in math and language education). It has also elaborated on the definition provided in order to illustrate how each dimension makes sense in light of other constructs. It appears that no other construct exists in the language teaching field to describe the amalgamation of these factors in teachers' *in situ* thinking. It therefore seems valuable to consider how a focus on what teachers find significant during their interactions with learners might uncover aspects of teacher cognition that have not been previously highlighted. In fact, this was part of Breen's (1985) motivation when he argued that the social context of teaching was neglected. More than 30 years on, it is unfortunate that the sociocognitive context of classroom language teaching, as seen by the teacher and learners, has received so little attention.

To recap, language teacher noticing is a conscious process that unfolds during classroom practice, whereas other teacher cognitions may less consciously, or even unconsciously, influence teaching (Borg, 2015). It invokes reflection, and therefore can form the basis of reflective practice in teacher development groups (Crookes, 2003), as well as potentially enhancing the overall quality of reflective practice (Walsh & Mann, 2015). Returning to the mnemonic, AIDE, it entails processes of selective attention to identify meaningful events, interpretation of these events and decisions regarding how to act upon them, which aligns it with research outside the field of language teaching (e.g. Philipp *et al.*, 2017). Lastly, it occurs during engagement with learners in classroom instruction, which situates it within cognitive, behavioral, emotional and social contexts at multiple, embedded levels (Douglas Fir Group, 2016; Philp & Duchesne, 2016). This last point is necessary in order to provide a preliminary answer to the question: What do language teachers notice? From a holistic viewpoint, it would be limiting to assume that they only notice language use. Teachers may notice anything that is evident to them in their engagement with learners. Having said that, their capacity and freedom to act upon their noticing is shaped by a multitude of other cognitions.

The question can be posed as to whether language teacher noticing is an instance of 'the same things, done differently', as Freeman (2016) put it. This refers to an overall trend in L2 teacher education of importing constructs from other domains of teaching, such as decision-making or teacher cognition. By now, the nature of language teacher noticing as an exogenous theoretical construct is clear: it draws heavily on educational research into how math teachers develop the capacity to notice students' thinking. Yet how it might be reshaped, or done differently, in language education largely remains to be seen. The observational research carried out by Jackson and Cho (2018) offered one example of how this construct might inform language teaching, while the research reported in the next section of this book offers another perspective.

Part 2

A Study of Pre-Service Teachers

4 Contextualizing the Study

The Psychology of Language Teaching

There are various approaches to the topic of psychology in language teaching and learning. For instance, some researchers draw primarily on cognitive psychology (e.g. Granena *et al.*, 2016) and focus their studies on language aptitude, working memory and other learner-internal mechanisms, in order to investigate their roles within second language acquisition (SLA), in laboratory or other settings. Another approach draws on educational psychology (e.g. Mercer *et al.*, 2012) and encompasses the aforementioned mental processes, as well as motivational and affective considerations arising in educational settings. Research in this vein has been promoted by the International Association for the Psychology of Language Learning and its biennial conference (see https://www.iapll.com/), as well as the present book series.

Earlier chapters drew heavily on educational research on teacher noticing, which places this book in the latter camp. To further strengthen this connection, this chapter describes how frameworks adopted in the field of the psychology of language learning and teaching (PLLT) influenced the present study. Teacher noticing is a system embedded within social contexts of education. This chapter describes the context of the study, gradually narrowing the focus to the psychological context of teacher noticing.

The traditional distinction in human psychology between cognition, motivation and affect has often guided researchers interested in the psychology of language learning (Dörnyei & Ryan, 2015). Lists of individual differences, including aptitude, motivation, learning styles, learning strategies and emotions, such as anxiety, informed much of the early writing in this field. Recent approaches to PLLT have engaged with these earlier-identified constructs, while seeking to explore new directions. In general, this field has problematized earlier research approaches, which offered insight into psychological constructs but did not often extend to external influences, temporal dynamics or the role of self.

In particular, the field has turned toward complex dynamic systems theory (CDST) as an approach offering insight into not only an individual's stable traits, but also their adaptations to particular states, and related meaning-constructing narratives (Dörnyei, 2017; see also Gregersen &

MacIntyre, 2017; Mercer, 2018; Mercer & Kostoulas, 2018a). According to Larsen-Freeman (2017), CDST seeks out the interconnections between dynamic systems, or entities that function as a whole, which are both embedded in larger systems and comprised of subsystems. CDST-informed studies may take on a range of different methodologies. These focus on distinct aspects of the overall concept.

In terms of its relevance to teacher noticing, scholars have recently drawn on CDST to emphasize new avenues for research on teacher cognition. Namely, Kubanyiova and Feryok (2015) proposed three shifts, which included: (1) highlighting the social aspects of teacher psychology by 'studying cognition as emergent sense making in action' (Kubanyiova & Feryok, 2015: 445); (2) focusing on intentionality, or purposeful actions within the ecology of practice (cf. the model of joint attention in teacher noticing in Figure 3.2); and (3) acknowledging the role of large-scale social influences beyond the research context. Building on these suggestions, the present study attempted to consider teacher noticing during social action in tasks, while focusing on how intentions were conveyed by embodied and verbal means. As for the role of social influences, its institutional context, described in this chapter, is important to understanding its findings.

One goal of this chapter is to suggest that the theme of influences on teacher noticing may be approached from macro, meso or micro contextual levels. As an example, the research in this book focused on the micro level. This chapter sets the stage for readers to more fully understand the results by explaining both the meso and micro levels of the context in detail. The reason for including the meso level is to acknowledge the role of larger social influences (Kubanyiova & Feryok, 2015). Chapter 5 then considers methods of researching teacher noticing, again referring to the present study as an example. For readers less interested in the technical details provided in the following chapter, the contextual background offered here should allow for a sufficient understanding of the findings reported later.

The Context of Noticing: From Meso to Micro Levels

This study took place within the context of a teacher education program at a private Japanese university. This section frames the study using multi-level, nested views of the social context of language learning and teaching (Douglas Fir Group, 2016; Mercer, 2018; Williams *et al.*, 2016). The Douglas Fir Group (2016) offered a description of language learning and teaching comprised of three levels: the macro level of ideological structures, the meso level of sociocultural institutions and communities and the micro level of social activity. Based on this ecological perspective, teacher noticing in this book is seen as embedded within (a) the institution/community, (b) the teacher education program and (c) the task-based study reported on in this section. This description of the context spans the meso and micro levels. The investigation itself concerned influences on teacher noticing at the micro level.

It would be possible to consider other levels of context. The cultural level (Williams *et al.*, 2016) is beyond that of the institution/community because it concerns norms for communication that are shared across many institutions. It seems certain that the cultural practices teachers engage in must shape what they notice. One interesting example of this is lesson study. During lesson study, teachers collaboratively develop a lesson, which they then observe being taught. They then discuss it together. This practice of lesson study has spread from Japanese schools to educational contexts worldwide. Research on teacher noticing has been conducted in math lesson study contexts, such as Lee and Choy's (2017) comparative study of teachers in the United States and Singapore. At present, the influence of specific cultural practices of language teacher development on their noticing remains a highly neglected area of investigation. Although arguably important, the influence of the macro level, including not only cultural but also political and religious values, fell outside the boundaries of the present study.

Figure 4.1 illustrates the levels addressed in this chapter, with noticing at the center. The following sections elaborate on each level of the context shown in the figure. This view of teacher noticing as a system nested within other systems suggests its size and scope relative to other systems (Mercer, 2018). It does not entail any certain influences but acknowledges that various influences permeate it. Because the potential influence of task on teacher noticing was a focus of this research, it is described in greater detail than the other levels.

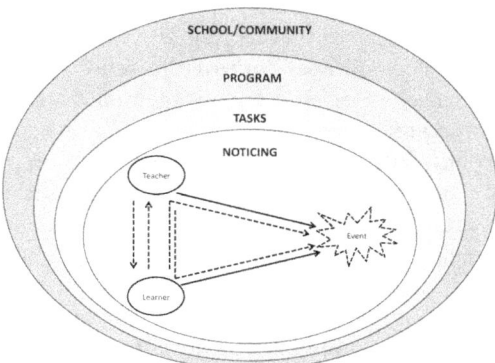

Figure 4.1 Multi-level framework depicting the embedded context of teacher noticing

The School and Community

The university where this research was conducted is a member of the Consortium of Foreign Studies in Japan, a group of universities whose curricula focus on providing foreign language education and training to enter the global workforce. This resonates with the Japanese Ministry of Education's longstanding emphasis on internationalization (Fujita-Round & Maher, 2008). The school itself is a private university in the Kanto region, established in the late 1980s. At the time of this writing, nearly 4000 undergraduate students were enrolled across all departments, with English being the most popular major. This university also houses a number of research centers, one of which provided an institutional grant to support this project.

The educational philosophy of the institution is expressed as, 'languages are the foundation to link the world in peace'. This reflects the school's identity as a foreign language university. Furthermore, it is consistent with an understanding of Japan as a nation that has renounced war and embraced peace. Specifically in regard to English language learning, the curriculum has placed emphasis on four principles (KGAA, 2011): independence, interdependence, interaction and individualization. For example, a typical day in the life of an English major might involve discussing an independent study plan with a learning advisor, cooperating with peers to prepare for a group presentation, interacting with classmates and teachers during lessons and individually choosing a topic of interest for an essay assignment. These principles are applied within and beyond university curricula.

Such principles and their associated practices are the focus of research by faculty and students at the university. Two examples are described here, although they are by no means the only ones (see also Mynard *et al.*, 2020). However, these cases concern teacher development and are thus appropriate choices. The initiatives to promote community-based teaching described next come from Murphey (2017) and Shirakawa (2018). These innovations were independent of the school's teacher education program, but nonetheless offered encouragement to those interested in potentially becoming teachers.

Firstly, Murphey (2017) described a study based on positive psychology that viewed teaching as a form of altruism. The author was a faculty member in the English Department. This study pointed out that, ironically, it is often teachers who learn the most in a classroom. The innovation, implemented in the author's courses, aimed at providing students with the opportunity to share what they learned, based on pro-social, communal teaching tasks done inside and outside the classroom setting. In order to make this possible, the students were asked to teach familiar cultural material using English (sayings or songs that displayed blending, use of gestures and/or word stress anomalies). A survey was given to three separate classes to determine their engagement with in-class and out-of-class teaching and their opinions of it. Quantitative results indicated that students generally agreed that teaching is a necessary skill for a range of professions, that they learned from having classmates teach them and that they learned material better when teaching it. Further qualitative results revealed that many students enjoyed teaching songs and found new ways to make their teaching public and communal. Murphey concluded that the use of teaching as a form of learning in this context may help students become passionate about teaching as a career and may also benefit their teachers because it promotes active learning, social engagement and helping others.

Secondly, Shirakawa (2018) contrasted with the previous study in that it described an out-of-class peer tutoring program organized by the Academic Success Center at the university. In this program, students volunteer to become tutors for their peers. The tutoring offers assistance in basic English, as well as preparation for TOEFL and TOEIC examinations. The author was an undergraduate student and a peer tutor. One goal of this research was to extend notions of teacher–learner autonomy (e.g. Smith & Erdoğan, 2008) to language tutors. A total of 11 tutors participated in semi-structured interviews. The investigation focused on their tutoring experiences, including perceptions of difficulty, the amount of preparation involved and personal development resulting from tutoring. In their comments, the tutors reported noticing that tutees sometimes looked nervous. Another challenge they mentioned was gauging tutees' level of comprehension of the material. Tutors extensively prepared for their sessions. Regarding personal development, two themes emerged: improvements to language skills (especially grammar) and increases in motivation. Similar to the findings from Murphey (2017), the tutors in this study felt teaching to be a motivating experience. Shirakawa (2018) discussed these results in terms of language tutor autonomy, which he situated between teacher and learner autonomy. In particular, adopting the tutor role made participants feel that they were responsible, self-regulated and improving in their own capacity and motivation.

These two studies illustrate how the four principles above (independence, interdependence, interaction and individualization) have gone beyond the curriculum to permeate the community. They show that many students at the school view their roles as dynamic. Many of them are willing to help others and they appreciate the value of engaging in teaching or tutoring as a means of learning. To be clear, these features are not entirely unique to the present context (see Lassegard, 2008, on peer tutoring at four national universities in Japan). Nor did all of the participants in these studies aim to become professional teachers upon graduation. Some of them did, however. Thus these studies can serve as a bridge to understanding the teacher education program.

The Teacher Education Program

Participants in the present study were recruited from the teacher education program at the university. This program assists students in obtaining teaching credentials. It is taught by faculty affiliated with the English Department. These instructors have extensive experience in Japanese public school settings. Consistent with their role as faculty members associated with this program, they may conduct workshops for in-service teachers in Japanese schools or write textbooks used by them. Students who wish to become eligible for a teacher's license must earn the required number of credits through the program. The participants in the study were all enrolled in courses to prepare them to teach English in junior and senior high schools. Students interested in the teacher education program learn about it through information sessions on campus. Those who join it typically complete most of the related coursework in their third and fourth year.

The program content focuses on knowledge and skills relevant to teaching English in the context of Japanese schools. One required course, English Language Teaching Methodology I, is held for two consecutive semesters. During this year, students are introduced to the Course of Study, which functions as the curriculum for kindergarten through senior high school (e.g. MEXT, 2017). Students learn how to create lesson plans in Japanese that adhere to established conventions. They learn how to teach the four language skills (speaking, listening, reading and writing) and evaluate materials from published textbooks. These activities promote interdependence through collaborative work aiming to encourage teacher development. Other course topics include classroom discourse, SLA and language assessment. Finally, students conduct video-recorded demonstration lessons for their teacher and peers based on plans they have written. Self-assessment rubrics and reflection papers are then used to promote reflective practice based on microteaching (Yoshizumi, 2018). This course provides the foundation for further study of English language teaching methods in subsequent years.

Another key program element is the Teaching Practicum, which is required in order to obtain a teaching license. The practicum provides further opportunities to apply pedagogic knowledge and skills learned through coursework (Yamasaki, 2016). In the practicum, pre-service teachers (PSTs) are assigned to a school and learn what it is like to teach there by interacting with its staff and students. This fosters independence as students gain further opportunities to develop their teaching competence by designing lessons and teaching them to actual students under the supervision of a school teacher. Three weeks of teaching are required to obtain a junior high school license and two weeks are required for a high school license. Students are excused from attending classes during this time and may travel some distance to their assigned school, which is often the high school that they graduated from. This sets the teacher trainees apart from their peers who are not in this program, because most undergraduates need not show this level of commitment to any particular job until they are ready to graduate.

Some students may perceive the teacher education program as challenging due to expectations regarding English proficiency. A TOEFL ITP® score of at least 550 (or the equivalent) is required prior to completing the program. The maximum score on this test, for intermediate to advanced users of academic English, is 677. For some, this may be difficult to obtain without studying abroad. Doing so, however, might make it difficult to complete the required coursework for the program within four years.

As implied earlier, completion of the teacher education program is no guarantee that an individual will obtain a teacher's license. To do so, those eligible must follow the procedures determined by the board of education in the locality in which they hope to teach. The following details give a clear indication of program participants' commitment to teaching as a career. During the academic year ending in March 2020, 51 graduates of the program received their teacher's license. Of these, 31 (61%) had secured part-time or full-time employment in schools by April.

The eligibility criteria for the study were that participants were (1) currently enrolled at the university, (2) in their third or fourth year and (3) taking part in the teacher education program. In practice, these criteria meant that their academic English proficiency was intermediate to advanced. It also meant that they had shown a commitment to the teacher education program, which requires coursework, including English Language Teaching Methodology I, prior to the third year. Participants' biodata were gathered using a survey (see the following chapter for detail).

The Tasks

The tasks used were an important context for this study. TBLT has influenced language education in Japan. It therefore seemed valuable to offer students in the teacher education program exposure to it. In turn, TBLT can also potentially inform the question of influences on teacher noticing, as a research issue within PLLT. In this way, the study focused on teacher noticing against the backdrop of task-based interaction, under the larger umbrella of teacher psychology. The following sections elaborate on this backdrop. In this study, participants, in pairs, completed a series of direction-giving map tasks with one participant in the teacher role and the other in the student role.

Tasks in Japanese schools

The Japanese education ministry's objectives for foreign language instruction at the senior high school, junior high school and elementary school level emphasize the foundation and development of communicative abilities, cultural understanding and positive attitudes toward communication (MEXT, 2010a, 2010b). Despite such apparently clear objectives, controversies remain regarding the amount of curricular emphasis to be placed on proficiency versus communication, as well as the role of such learning in supporting internationalization versus multiculturalism (Yamada, 2015). As an approach situated between strong and weak communicative language teaching (East, 2012), TBLT may promote linguistic development, communicative abilities and cultural understanding. Given its rising popularity in Asian contexts (Butler, 2011), it is not surprising that TBLT research in Japan has demonstrated its benefits for two primary stakeholders: teachers and learners.

In the case of teachers, classroom research by Jackson (2012) has explored the extent to which undergraduates enrolled in a TESOL course at one private Japanese university, who participated in a sequence of teaching-related tasks (i.e. lesson planning, teaching demonstrations, observations and debriefings), showed gains in practical knowledge, or the knowledge teachers accrue from reflection on practical experience (Meijer *et al.*, 1999). This study furthermore illustrated how this knowledge was co-constructed during discussions with a teacher development group, and reported generally positive attitudes toward TBLT based on a survey. In-service teachers in Japan, as well, have benefitted from task-based instruction designed to enhance their communicate abilities (Moser *et al.*, 2011).

More research has been carried out on the effects of tasks on learner development in Japan. These studies demonstrate the flexibility of TBLT to foster multiple dimensions of communicative language ability within junior high school or high school contexts. A few of the potential outcomes investigated have included: global and specific measures of complexity, accuracy and fluency in oral production (Mochizuki & Ortega, 2008; Sasayama & Izumi, 2012); accuracy, structural complexity and lexical complexity in written production (Ishikawa, 2007); and dialogue concerning major social issues, such as bullying and coping with academic pressure (Konoeda & Watanabe, 2008). These and other studies with younger learners (Shintani, 2015, 2016) generally show that TBLT has much to offer English learners in Japan.

Persistent questions remain about the abilities of teachers to implement TBLT, especially in light of the highly interactive roles they are expected to take during task-based lessons (Samuda, 2015; Van den Branden, 2016; Willis & Willis, 2007). For instance, surveys of Japanese elementary school teachers have revealed that they do not possess their desired levels of competence in the domains of oral or written English skills (Butler, 2004). However, TBLT involves holistic use (Samuda & Bygate, 2008) of multiple skills. Therefore, the challenges facing teachers may be considerable. Regarding expectations to teach English in English, teachers doubt their own productive abilities and question their students' comprehension skills (Machida, 2019). The following commentary by Butler pinpoints a much-needed area of teacher development which is relevant to the implementation of tasks in Japanese schools:

> ... conversation breakdown often occurs in EFL classrooms. Students might be unable to understand their teacher's English-language instructions or to use English to respond to their teacher's questions. To compensate for these breakdowns, *teachers need strategic knowledge of English and the ability to use it*. (Butler, 2004: 270, emphasis added)

The present study aimed to facilitate the development of such knowledge and abilities among pre-service English teachers. To do so, a series of communicative tasks were designed, as described in the next section.

Task features

The task materials used in this study are shown in Appendix A. Tasks such as these are intended to promote interaction and foster communicative competence in the target language. The choice of direction-giving map gap tasks was made with reference to specific language use situations (i.e. 'Asking and giving directions') and specific functions ('Facilitating communication') which are described in Ministry of Education, Culture, Sports, Science and Technology (MEXT, 2010b) guidelines for foreign language teaching at the junior high school level. Because this study focused on developing teaching competence, the tasks were intended to resemble materials that are used in Japanese school contexts. A perusal of ministry-approved English textbooks (Sano *et al.*, 2006) confirmed that the communication tasks used in this study are among the types of pedagogic materials that teachers are likely to encounter. For further commentary on the extent to which junior high school English textbooks contain materials that meet the definition of tasks, see Fukuta *et al.* (2017).

Samuda and Bygate (2008: 13–16) offered a useful list of eight features of a task. These features are listed in Table 4.1 along with brief comments regarding how they were instantiated in the direction-giving map gap tasks.

Simple and complex tasks

In addition to the features noted in the previous section, simple and complex versions of the tasks were developed, based on the Triadic Componential Framework for task design (Robinson, 2001, 2007, 2011, 2015). *Complexity* here refers to the cognitive complexity inherent in the task's design, which is distinct from the *conditions* under which it is implemented and the subjective *difficulty* experienced by the learners. Robinson's framework offers a guide to these distinctions and lists relevant task design variables.

Table 4.1 Samuda and Bygate's (2008) features applied to the tasks used in the study

Task feature	Instantiation in the map tasks
Holistic language use	As determined by the teacher and student roles
Meaningful outcome	To arrive at a specific location via a given route
Input material	Teacher (route-marked) and student map versions
Individual and interactional processes	See later chapters
Task phase	See later in this chapter
Target of the tasks	Spoken English vocabulary, motion constructions, locative prepositions
Task conditions	See later in this chapter
Use of the tasks	To simulate a portion of an English lesson

The present study drew upon the Triadic Componential Framework to manipulate three design variables. Planning time, number of elements and familiarity were chosen. Specifically, pre-task planning time was varied across simple and complex versions by giving the teacher participants three minutes to look up and jot down any words or phrases they thought might be useful, before the task phase for the simple tasks. An English–Japanese electronic dictionary was provided. On the other hand, no planning time was allowed prior to complex tasks. The number of map elements (e.g. buildings, doorways, staircases) was increased from the simple to the complex tasks, as was the intricacy of the route needing to be followed. Lastly, the simple task materials showed familiar locations, including the university campus and a local train station nearby, whereas the complex task materials showed locations that were not drawn to resemble any specific locations, but rather showed a generic shopping center and a museum area.

Given its focus on teachers, this book makes an additional, supplementary claim regarding the Cognition Hypothesis. Namely, it is crucial to comprehend not just the design features that underpin complex tasks and how they influence learner production, interaction, noticing and processing/retention but, in addition, how they may affect teacher cognition. According to one view, tasks are spaces within which both the teacher and the learners jointly operate. For instance, studies have shown how teachers work with design specifications when making in-the-moment decisions about how to transform a prospective workplan into a dynamic workplan (Samuda, 2015). Thus it is possible that design elements, which include various dimensions of task complexity, influence teacher noticing, or teachers' awareness of ongoing interaction.

In fact, studies have begun to look into how language teachers experience task complexity. For instance, a case study of two in-service teachers probed the issue of task sequencing based on complexity at the level of teachers' beliefs and planning (Baralt *et al.*, 2014). These researchers found that the teachers drew on their pre-existing knowledge of lesson objectives and classroom issues when integrating principles of task complexity into their repertoires. Thus, experienced teachers may situate perceptions of task complexity within a wider array of cognitions about their teaching (see also Révész & Gurzynski-Weiss, 2016). The present study builds on this important line of research by raising the question of how task complexity influences PST noticing.

Noticing Based on Video

The tasks provided a context for interaction in teacher versus student roles. Video-recordings of these interactions, another component of the study materials, provided another, separate context for the teachers' immediate reflections. Data on what they noticed were collected using stimulated recall methodology, as described later. Notably, the context for their reflections was systematically altered, in the following way. The video-recorded study materials depicted the task interaction from either a field or an observer perspective.

Psychologists, particularly those interested in perspectival memory, point out that the visual experience of recalling an event can be from a field or an observer perspective (Nigro & Neisser, 1983, cited in McCarroll & Sutton, 2017). In the former, one recalls the experience using a first-person viewpoint, that is, according to their field of vision at the time when the experience initially occurred. In the latter, one recalls the experience from a third-person viewpoint, as if they were an outside observer who had witnessed the experience. In their discussion, McCarroll and Sutton (2017) considered perspectival memory to be related to how visual perspective influences genuine memory. They summarized studies on the effects of these perspectives as follows: '[f]ield perspectives seem to be related to remembering the emotional details, feelings, or psychological states associated with an event; in contrast, observer perspectives tend to include less sensory and affective detail but more information related to concrete, objective details' (McCarroll & Sutton, 2017: 114; see also Libby *et al.*, 2005; McIssac & Eich, 2002). McCarroll and Sutton went on to note that one can, during the recall of an episode, switch between these two perspectives, such that both perspectives are used to reconstruct a memory. Yet, in their view, the differences that may emerge when one or the other perspective is used constitute no less than contrasting representations of the self and a reconfiguration of space. There is debate as to whether observer perspectives can be considered genuine memories, as they differ from initial encoding of events. However, for present purposes I regard both field and observer as being functionally similar in that either perspective could, based on the methodology adopted here, facilitate the recall of teacher noticing. The issue then becomes: does an outside, or observer, perspective invite the teacher to see the task through a student's eyes? By contrast, does the field perspective yield more attention to the teacher's own prior mental and affective states? And, based on this, what changes might occur in the reporting of teacher noticing?

Indeed, Miller (2011) has argued that perspective may make a difference when training teachers to notice. In this case, teacher noticing is considered a form of situation awareness (Endsley, 2000) that involves perceiving, understanding and monitoring key classroom events. Miller suggested that this wider frame of attention is needed for skilled viewing. To promote it, classroom recordings that use a field perspective, or teacher-perspective videos as he calls them, may be useful, in opposition to the traditional, observer perspective relying on video-recordings from the back of the classroom. He illustrated this point using the example of an experienced teacher reading in front of a classroom. It turns out that this activity involves a great deal more distributed attention than the act of reading itself does, which observer perspectives may not reveal (Miller, 2011: 60–61).

Concerning this study's methodology, no second language (L2) studies using stimulated recall, to my knowledge, have attempted to use stimuli that afforded field versus observer perspectives, although this could arguably influence what teachers recall having noticed. In considering the implications of stimulated recall for studying language teacher cognition, Ryan (2012: 149) problematized the fact that often, 'participants view themselves from a perspective that is very different from their original experience of the actual event'. It is not clear, however, that this does pose problems, or whether it makes little difference. Therefore, to enhance study validity and, moreover, to gain insight into whether different perspectives do in fact yield different types of recall comments (as reported in the literature reviewed by McCarroll & Sutton, 2017), the current study presented teacher participants with recordings of their task performances that alternated between field and observer perspectives. This was achieved by having the participants switch seats during the task performances, which were recorded by a stationary camera that faced either the teacher or the student. Admittedly, one potential limitation of this approach is that, as noted, the teacher's memory recall may in practice combine both perspectives, regardless of the stimuli.

In a practical sense, this distinction between perspectives may be relevant to second language teacher education (SLTE). A study by Kalaja and Mäntylä (2018) with Finnish PSTs found that participants' own annotated visual depictions of an ideal English class varied according to environments, activities and roles. This finding underscored the multimodal nature of PST cognition and the richness of language learning environments, as well as influences from coursework and education ministry initiatives. The authors concluded that PSTs further along in their training and/or those with more teaching experience produced more complex visual narratives. In a similar study, Mäntylä and Kalaja (2019) reported a content analysis of future teachers' visual narratives, which highlighted the roles of language in interaction, language use situations, metalinguistic knowledge, language and content learning and language as a discrete system. The field versus observer perspective, which relates to the use of video in SLTE, might also be linked to how teachers visualize their future classes. For instance, use of a wider range of camera angles during practice teaching might foster multimodal narratives that more closely reflect the complexities of L2 classroom teaching. Finally, in experimental psychology, memory recall from these perspectives has been shown to influence assessments of personal change. In this research, participants believed they had changed more when prompted to visualize a past autobiographical event from the perspective of an outside observer than from the original field perspective they had during the event (Libby *et al.*, 2005). Miller's (2011) claim concerning the importance of the field perspective in teacher education notwithstanding, field and observer videos could perhaps both be used for different purposes in SLTE. Research is needed to better understand these purposes.

A final justification, as well as a caveat, now needs to be stated. The most important reason to explore the use of video in this study was because it may assist PSTs in becoming better at noticing. It should be acknowledged that teacher noticing is likely enhanced through experience. Professional teachers need to make many extremely quick and efficient decisions on a daily basis and they have many more hours of practice compared to the participants in this study. One difference may be that expert noticing is more uniform than that of novices. For instance, in Jackson and Cho's (2018) study of eight novice teachers, the percentage of comments coded as noticing ranged widely, from 16% to 52%. That is, about half or more of their comments were unrelated to features of interaction important to learning.

It may be the case that experts notice less overall, albeit more of what matters. In other words, expert teachers' noticing may be more economical in proportion to other interactive thoughts (Anderson, 2019). Perhaps experts do not notice more; instead, they notice better. The aforementioned indicator – the percentage of comments that contain noticing – could perhaps be used to chart progress in language teacher development. To enhance their noticing, video-based training for PSTs could seek to provide deliberate practice, where they are motivated to perform teaching tasks beyond their current ability (but which can be mastered with practice), they are provided immediate feedback, and they move gradually from assisted to unassisted performance over time (Bartels, 2005). A major limitation of this study was its cross-sectional design, which probed the influence of task and perspective at a single point in time. Nonetheless, such studies are needed to better understand what influences interventions meant to foster language teacher development.

Summary

The psychology of language learning and teaching can be approached from internalist or externalist perspectives. Studies in the latter camp broaden the focus of scholarship to the educational and social contexts of learning. They may approach psychological constructs as complex systems, which are characterized by various interconnections and environmental adaptations and their importance to an individual's sense of self (Dörnyei, 2017; Larsen-Freeman, 2017). The case has been made for language teacher psychology as a complex, dynamic system (Borg, 2015; Feryok, 2018; Mercer, 2018; Mercer & Kostoulas, 2018a). One key implication of looking at teacher psychology this way is that the role of the social context needs to be acknowledged (Kubanyiova & Feryok, 2015). In this chapter, the levels of school/community, teacher education program and task were considered.

At the level of the school/community, social activities were described that encourage teaching as a form of learning that promotes interconnection and autonomy. These are consistent with principles of independence, interdependence, interaction and individualization. The teacher education program extends these tenets to professional training, which can lead to a teaching license. The program is a major commitment for undergraduates as it actively encourages professional development through coursework, as well as reflective practice based on microteaching and practical experience in the school setting in which participants eventually hope to teach.

In seeking to understand which aspects of the context influence PST cognition, the present study focused especially on the role of tasks, owing to their perceived value in promoting communicative language teaching, as well as linguistic and social development, in Japanese schools (Butler, 2011; Jackson, 2012; Konoeda & Watanabe, 2008; Mochizuki & Ortega, 2008; Moser *et al.*, 2011; Sasayama & Izumi, 2012; Shintani, 2016). Features of the tasks used in this study were described in Table 4.1 and the motivation for using simple and complex tasks (Robinson, 2015) was presented. This study aimed, in part, to contribute to research on the potential effects of task complexity on teacher cognition (Baralt *et al.*, 2014; Révész & Gurzynski-Weiss, 2016).

In addition, video-based reflection is a major component in teacher education (Yoshizumi, 2018; see also Calandra & Rich, 2015; Hüttner, 2019; Knight, 2014; van Es & Sherin, 2006, 2008). This study built on the suggestion in Miller (2011) that teacher competence in perceiving and understanding classroom events may be fostered by the use of teacher-perspective videos, or those displaying teaching situations as originally seen by the teacher. Findings from research in the psychology of pre-service language teacher development, too, have revealed the complexity of visual narratives and their valuable role in professional development

(Kalaja & Mäntylä, 2018; Mäntylä & Kalaja, 2019). However, there is scant research into the ways in which different camera angles employed during video-based stimulated recall might influence PSTs' perceptions of their practice teaching.

Hence, the experimental design at the core of this study involved two factors: task complexity and recall condition. Further description of their role in the study and their potential influence on PST noticing is presented in Chapters 5 and 6. This core design offered room for expansion. Chapters 7 and 8 focus on PSTs' noticing of the intentions conveyed through embodied and verbal resources, which served to flesh out the ecology of practice during the process of implementing the tasks (Kubanyiova & Feryok, 2015; Samuda, 2015). Of course, this is not to deny that other influences, at the macro, meso and micro levels, exert influence over PST noticing. Yet, the roles of tasks, video and communicative intentions formed ample boundaries for the present investigation.

5 Researching Teacher Noticing

Challenges in Researching Noticing

This chapter elaborates on the innovative mixed-methods study reported in this book. A distinction can be made between multimethod research versus mixed-methods research, where the latter includes consideration of the purpose of mixing methods (Brown, 2014), which here was to offer an integrative perspective on teacher noticing. The use of 'innovative' means that the primary motivation for seeking to combine quantitative and qualitative methods was epistemic pluralism (Riazi, 2016). This study was designed with such concerns in mind. After considering methodological options, this chapter describes the present study's design and methods. Subsequent chapters in Part 2 focus on results, including the influence of task design and recall conditions on noticing instances, as well as verbal and nonverbal resources used by the pre-service teachers (PSTs). The remainder of this section outlines some challenges in researching noticing.

The challenges involved in researching teacher noticing are in some ways akin to those of researching learner noticing (see Chapter 2). This introduction refers back to those discussions in order to frame the issues surrounding investigations of language teacher noticing. Here as well there are concerns regarding appropriate research methodology. There are matters of the practical significance of the construct at hand and there are also puzzles regarding its theoretical significance. Although some of the issues are discussed elsewhere in this book, here they are recast in terms of the problem of identifying suitable analytic approaches. This chapter will argue that, for various reasons, mixed-methods research (MMR) constitutes a viable approach to understanding pre-service language teacher noticing. MMR has been defined generally as research that 'combines elements of qualitative and quantitative research approaches ... for the broad purposes of breadth and depth of understanding and corroboration' (Johnson *et al.*, 2007: 123).

Psychological processes such as teacher noticing are largely inaccessible. Even although new technologies such as wearable cameras (Russ

& Luna, 2013) afford considerable advances in classroom research methodology, the access problem remains because teacher commentary on the events filmed is still retrospective. Due to concerns regarding forgetting and fabrication in verbalization (Ericsson & Simon, 1984), time is of the essence when asking individuals to report their noticing. Looming large as well is the concern that the manner in which one tries to observe a teacher's noticing will alter it. These issues, along with practical considerations faced by new teachers, make attempting to observe PST noticing in actual classrooms (e.g. during their practicum) difficult. The stance adopted here is that it is reasonable to use a laboratory setting as a proxy for classroom practice, as long as the tasks and procedures bear a resemblance to those encountered during actual teaching. Previous research with second language (L2) learners has found that differences across laboratory and classroom settings may depend more on the tasks employed than on the setting (Gass *et al.*, 2005).

Next, researchers need to have a firm grasp on what participants may actually notice. This issue has led to controversy in discussions of the noticing hypothesis (see Schmidt, 2001). In the present context, too, it is necessary to have a solid understanding of what the developing teachers in this study might possibly have noticed. Is it their own or their partners' grammar, pronunciation or lexis? Is it the repair strategies used to facilitate communication? Is it the overall task performance or the affective responses that it arouses? The pedagogic tasks used in this study offered some parameters, as described in the previous chapter (see Table 4.1). Yet task blueprints cannot predict what teachers will notice about the architecture of pedagogic spaces (Samuda, 2015).

Another concern regarding teacher noticing research is that (again, like learner noticing) it may not be possible, nor is it necessary, for one to have conscious awareness of everything that is detected. This issue, however, seems more relevant to expert teachers, whose automatic reflexes and attentional capacities have been sharpened by countless hours of classroom practice (Tsui, 2003). In this respect, one might anticipate finding more noticing among teachers with less experience, such as those recruited for this study.

The last challenge faced in teacher noticing research, and perhaps the most difficult, is its relationship to theory. As indicated earlier, noticing as described by Schmidt has become a mainstay of cognitive-interactionist second language acquisition (SLA) theory. Yet, to foster commensurability, SLA theorists now seek to bridge several divides between: (1) psychological versus social explanations, (2) abstract versus situated views of knowledge and (3) product-oriented versus process-oriented approaches (Douglas Fir Group, 2016; Ortega, 2011). Elsewhere, I have argued for an approach to classroom-oriented research that encourages theoretical complementarity (Jackson & Burch, 2017). In this book as well, I suggest that a pluralistic view of teacher noticing as a sociocognitive construct under the umbrella of teacher psychology is valuable. MMR, as a pragmatic approach, may contribute to achieving this balance.

Methodological Options

There are various methodological options to consider when conducting research on noticing. In the second language literature, studies have used diaries, interviews, questionnaires, stimulated recall methods and other retrospective means of probing what participants might have noticed. In contrast to these retrospective measures, concurrent measures such as think-aloud protocols may be used; however, this online method seems less common due to the perceived complications of speaking while performing a learning task. Recordings of reaction times and eye movements are also concurrent (or online) measures that have recently been used in L2 studies into the role of awareness.

In teacher noticing studies, too, a wide range of methods has been applied. The norm is to employ retrospective approaches, including written reports, video clubs or stimulated recalls. In one qualitative study with language teachers, Lengeling *et al.* (2020) utilized participants' journals, written reflections (after live and video-recorded observations), ethnographic notes, an end-of-term questionnaire and a focus group. It is also possible to involve teachers in capturing their own noticing as it unfolds during instruction, through the use of wearable cameras (Colestock & Sherin, 2016). Real-time methods of documenting teacher noticing are underused in language teaching research and thus constitute a major avenue for future development.

In light of previous research, some preconditions can be established that may enhance the validity of methods of investigating teacher noticing. This discussion focuses on self-report measures (e.g. questionnaires, interviews, video clubs, stimulated recall methods) as these have been used widely. The first consideration involves timing. The measurement should occur while, or as soon as possible after, noticing occurs. Using stimulated recall methods, studies have reported a decline in teacher noticing instances after two days (Jackson & Cho, 2018). To avoid the risk of forgetting, data on noticing should be collected as soon as it is possible to elicit the teacher's interpretation. This is typically not feasible during a lesson. The second precondition is that the method should focus on distinguishing noticing from other thoughts. This means directing the investigation toward the teacher's attention, interpretation and decisions while engaged with students. Teachers should be informed of this focus and asked to report only past thoughts. Researchers should employ procedures to ensure that only data concerning noticing are used and that their coding of noticing is reliable. Finally, and especially in the case of language teachers, language background needs to be considered. Steps need to be taken to ensure that participants' language proficiency does not get in the way of reporting their noticing. Ideally, they themselves should choose the language in which they report their noticing, as researchers cannot know which language they are more comfortable with. Note as well that language choice here is also a matter of professional identity. Teacher agency should of course be emphasized throughout the research process, and this can begin with giving them total freedom to say what they noticed in any language(s) they wish. Any study needs to strike a balance between teacher agency, teacher development and these three preconditions. For additional commentary, see Borg (2015), Gass and Mackey (2017), Jackson and Shirakawa (2020) and Ryan (2012).

Research Design and Questions

This section offers a bird's-eye view of the overall research design. It addresses the question of how the use of the aforementioned design and sources constituted MMR (Brown, 2014; Creswell & Plano Clark, 2011; Johnson *et al.*, 2007; Mertens, 2007; Onwuegbuzie & Johnson, 2006; Riazi, 2016, 2017). From its outset, this project was envisioned as bringing together quantitative and qualitative strands, with the purpose of using these distinct approaches to complement each other. Technically speaking, methodologists have referred to this complementarity as legitimation (Brown, 2014; Onwuegbuzie & Johnson, 2006). I will return to the concept of legitimation when later summarizing the results of the study.

I have chosen to describe the specific MMR design used here as embedded, based on the discussion in Creswell and Plano Clark (2011). In their words, an investigator using such a design, 'collects and analyzes both quantitative and qualitative data within a traditional quantitative or qualitative design' (Creswell & Plano Clark, 2011: 71). The fundamental design deployed in this study was a traditional quantitative design, namely a factorial experiment, with the factors: task (simple versus complex) and perspective (field versus observer). This was a repeated measures, counterbalanced (Latin squares) design, with each teacher facilitating a task and performing a subsequent recall under all four conditions. One commonly noted strength of this design is that it allows investigation of the main effects of the factors, but also permits exploration of interactions between them (see Chapter 6).

Considering the fact that little research on teacher noticing has been conducted, this approach allowed for a cautious empirical test of the potential influence of task and perspective. This was the reason why the factorial design was chosen. However, the data collection procedures allowed for a supplementary qualitative strand to enhance the quantitative study. As noted by Creswell and Plano Clark (2011: 73), embedded MMR designs can be used for the purpose of obtaining a richer understanding of an experimental study, allowing for a focus on both process and outcomes.

In practice, there were several phases of research built around the core design, each of which sought to answer related but separate questions (see Figure 5.1). The initial, quantitative phase of the study first probed potential effects on teacher noticing, relying on the factorial design to investigate the influence of task complexity and recall perspective on instances of language teacher noticing. These results are provided in Chapter 6. Afterwards, the study took a qualitative turn. During this phase, the focus shifted to the interactional resources surrounding teacher noticing. Thus, participants' noticing of embodied versus linguistic resources are dealt with in Chapters 7 and 8, respectively. The last phase of the research focused on forming an integrated, pluralistic understanding of language teacher noticing based on the overall mixed design. The QUANT-QUAL strands of the research are drawn together in Chapter 9.

These phases utilized the data sources in different ways, in accordance with strategies for MMR data analysis (Creswell & Plano Clark, 2011). The QUANT phase of the study drew primarily on the coded stimulated recall interviews. These interviews were transcribed, translated and coded for instances of noticing. As such, even this phase should not be seen as purely quantitative because scoring and analyses involved decisions that went beyond merely tallying results, as described later. The possibility that the effects of task and perspective are mainly qualitative is also considered.

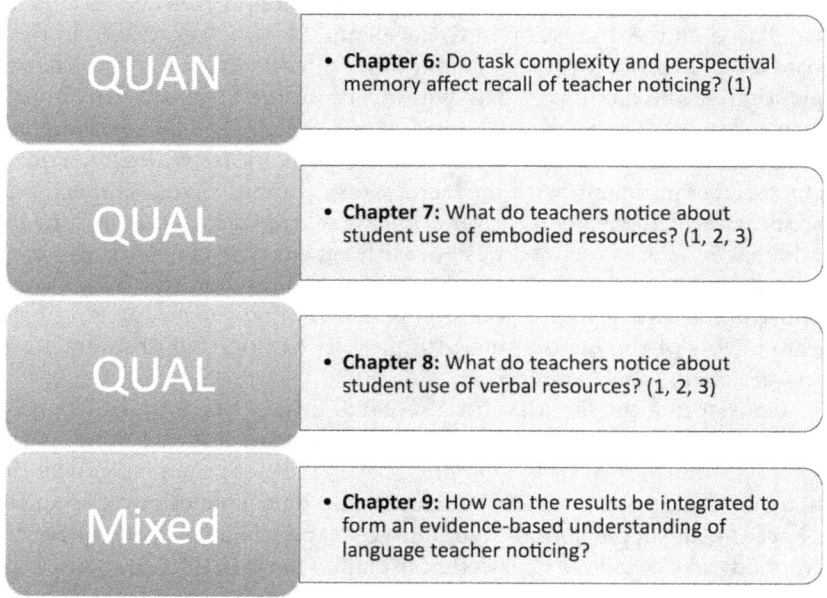

Figure 5.1 MMR design with the research questions and data sources. Notes: (1) = stimulated recall interviews; (2) = task-based interactions; (3) = scored task materials

Additional sources relied on during the QUAL phase were the transcriptions of the task-based interactions and scored task materials. During this phase, strategies of consolidating and comparing sources were employed. This was thought to be a judicious use of the data to address the research questions posed by the study.

Participants

Thirty-two PSTs joined this study in pairs. Their ages ranged from 20 to 22 years ($M = 20.91$; $SD = 0.65$). A majority had some teaching experience, as private tutors or cram school instructors. Additionally, because it might influence their willingness to communicate, they were asked to rate their familiarity with their partner, on a scale ranging from 0 (*I met the person today*) to 5 (*I know the person well*). Results for this item ranged from 0 to 5 ($M = 3.19$; $SD = 1.79$). Further participant characteristics are summarized in Table 5.1.

Table 5.1 Participant characteristics ($N = 32$)

Characteristics	n	%
Gender		
Female	19	59.38
Male	13	40.63
Year		
Third year	21	65.63
Fourth year	11	34.38
Major		
English	26	81.25
Ibero-American studies	4	12.50
Intercultural communication	2	6.25
Intended workplace[a]		
Junior high school	18	50.00
High school	16	44.44
Elementary school	2	5.56
Teaching experience		
Yes	23	71.88
No	9	28.13
Study abroad		
Yes	22	68.75
No	10	31.25

Note: [a] More than one answer was allowed for intended workplace.

Table 5.2 Data sources in the study

Data sources	Participant roles
(1) Video-recordings of task performances	Teacher and student
(2) Maps with the route marked as explained by the teacher	Student
(3) Audio-recordings of the stimulated recall sessions	Teacher

Data Collection and Procedure

The study used data from all participants to focus primarily on those participants assigned to the teacher's role. As shown in Table 5.2, there were three main sources of data in the study. This section explains the use of these sources. According to Brown (2014: 20), triangulation refers to 'gathering and interpreting data from multiple viewpoints'. The collection and use of the data for this study can be described as data triangulation. Each source provided the opportunity to explore a distinct perspective on the interaction between the participants. Furthermore, the sources were balanced in order to try to gather a range of insights, from participants in both roles.

The remainder of this section provides specific details concerning each data collection method.

Video-recordings of task performances

A Panasonic high-definition video camera mounted on a tripod was used to record the participants while they interacted to complete each of the four tasks. These videos were used in two ways. Firstly, they served during the data collection as stimuli for the recall interviews (see below). Secondly, they were later transcribed to analyze the participants' language production and interaction during the tasks. The transcription conventions were based on those utilized in conversation analysis (Lee & Burch, 2017; see also Hutchby & Wooffitt, 2008). Additional detail is provided on the analysis of these transcripts in the subsequent chapters in this section.

Maps with the route marked

Task instructions were given to the participants. There were separate instructions depending on the participants' assigned roles. They were written in English as follows (a Japanese translation accompanied both sets of instructions). The instructions to those in the teacher role were: 'Tell your partner where to go. He or she needs to follow the route marked on your map exactly. He or she should start at the place marked START and finish at the place marked FINISH. Describe the route to your partner, in English, as carefully as you can. Check to make sure your partner understands. Do not show your partner your map or look at your partner's map.' The instructions in the student role were: 'Your partner will tell you where to go. You need to follow his or her directions and mark the route on your map exactly (draw a line on your map to show the route). You should start at the place marked START and finish at the place marked FINISH [this location was unmarked on the student maps]. Listen carefully while your partner describes the route in English. Check to make sure you understand. Do not show your partner your map or look at your partner's map.'

Four maps were given to each participant, in the counterbalanced order determined by the study design. The teacher versions had the route marked (see Appendix A). As reported below, two researchers scored the completed student versions of the maps, based on established coding practices (Révész, 2012).

Audio-recordings of the stimulated recall sessions

As in previous research on language teacher noticing (Jackson & Cho, 2018), stimulated recall methodology was used to probe the teacher participants' noticing. These recall interviews were conducted after each task in the same 90-minute session. Following recommendations in Gass and Mackey (2017), clear instructions were prepared and translated into Japanese, along with a video-enhanced example of a teacher performing a recall, accompanied by a transcript. These instructions made clear that participants should: (a) use the video to recall the task performance, (b) say aloud precisely what they were thinking at the time and (c) use the video as an example of how to report their thoughts. Additional guidelines stipulated that: (d) they could pause the video, if necessary, (e) the researcher would listen quietly during the recall and (f) the researcher would prompt them to speak, if they remained quiet for more than one minute while watching the video. The following examples were provided as things participants should not comment on: impressions that occurred after the task performance (e.g. *I wish I had done that differently*); reactions to seeing or hearing themselves on video (e.g. *Wow, I look tall*); and actions that occurred during the performance without thinking (e.g. *I didn't know I was doing that*). The purpose of these examples was to constrain the teacher's reports to in-the-moment noticing, as much as possible. They were further reminded that the purpose of the activity was not to evaluate whether their teaching was good or bad but instead to elicit thoughts they had during the interaction. This information was included in a PowerPoint file used to conduct a training session prior to the first recall. During training and recall, only the researcher and teacher participant were present in the room; the student participant was momentarily excused. The researcher established rapport by using some Japanese to check that the teacher understood the instructions. Participants were encouraged to use Japanese or English during their recall (most used Japanese, their L1). Once these preliminaries were completed, the participants watched each video on a MacBook Pro laptop computer while wearing headphones, and talked aloud as their speech was recorded on an Olympus Linear PCM audio-recorder placed on the desk nearby. A paid research assistant, who is a Japanese native speaker with advanced English ability, later transcribed and translated these recordings into English. Afterwards, they were coded by two researchers for instances of teacher noticing (see Chapter 6).

Procedure

To recap, this section details the procedures carried out for each data collection session. Volunteers were recruited to join the study through announcements in several sections of the English Language Teaching Methodology course and by word of mouth. Upon contacting the research assistant, two participants were scheduled to join each 90-minute data collection session at a mutually convenient time. These sessions began with the researcher greeting the two participants at his office and having them read and sign a consent form explaining the study's purpose and procedures. Then the biodata survey was administered. After collecting these documents, participants were assigned to the roles of teacher and student using a coin toss. They were then asked to read the task instructions pertaining to their specific role: teacher or student.

The participants then carried out the first of four map tasks, seated across a large table from one another, while their performances were video-recorded. Then the researcher excused the student participant, transferred the video data to a computer, and invited the teacher participant to sit at the desk with the computer. The teacher participant was trained to carry out the stimulated recall and began their first of four recalls. Upon completion of the recall, the student participant was called back in and the participants repeated the aforementioned sequence for the three remaining tasks (except for the recall training). At the end of each session, the researcher asked if there were any questions, thanked the participants and gave them information regarding payment for the study.

The data analyses for each of the quantitative and qualitative strands in the study are described in their respective chapters.

Validity and Reliability

The distinction between simple and complex tasks was important to this study's claims. However, this distinction cannot be taken for granted. It is primarily a matter of the task design, or blueprint. How tasks play out in the hands of users is instead a matter of process, or implementation. Several approaches have been developed to evaluate the validity of simple versus complex L2 tasks (Baralt, 2013; Robinson, 2001; Sasayama, 2016). Here, validity was assessed in terms of factors that are primary concerns for teachers using tasks, i.e. the degree to which the tasks were successfully completed and the amount of time taken to do them.

Task completion

Task completion has been asserted to be 'more important than any other feature of task performance' (Sample & Michel, 2014: 30). To score the map task performances, a customized scoring rubric was created that incorporated both accuracy and completion (see Table 5.3). Two trained raters used this rubric to independently score 25% of the completed maps, resulting in strong inter-rater agreement ($r(14) = 0.94$, $p = 0.00$). A single rater scored the remaining data.

Based on this scoring, Table 5.4 gives descriptive statistics for each of the four tasks. As can be seen, the task with the highest average score was the Shops task ($M = 4.56$), while the task with the lowest score was the Museum task ($M = 2.56$). Each task elicited the full range of possible scores (i.e. 1–6).

Regarding the mean scores, inspection of histograms and results of the Shapiro–Wilk test indicated that the score distributions were not normal. Thus, the non-parametric Friedman's ANOVA was used to test the overall effect of task design on completion scores. This test revealed that the mean scores were significantly different ($\chi^2(3) = 9.29$, $p = 0.03$). To further investigate these differences, tests of pairwise comparisons were carried

Table 5.3 Scoring rubric for direction-giving map tasks

Descriptor: *The student has ...*	Score
... completed the route and made no errors	6
... completed the route and made corrected errors	5
... completed the route and made uncorrected errors	4
... not completed the route, but made no other errors	3
... not completed the route and made corrected errors	2
... not completed the route and made uncorrected errors	1

Table 5.4 Task completion scores for each map task

Design	Task	Min	Max	Mean (*SD*)
Complex	Shops	1	6	4.56 (1.63)
Simple	Campus	1	6	4.50 (1.93)
Simple	Station	1	6	4.19 (1.80)
Complex	Museum	1	6	2.56 (1.71)

Table 5.5 Task completion scores: Mean differences across simple versus complex tasks

Simple	Complex	Mean diff.	p-value	Effect size (d)	BCa 95% CI	
					Lower	Upper
Campus	Museum	1.94	0.01	0.76	0.12	1.41
Campus	Shops	−0.06	n.s.	−0.03	−0.57	0.49
Station	Museum	1.63	0.03	0.63	0.06	1.31
Station	Shops	−0.38	n.s.	−0.20	−0.80	0.38

Note: n.s. = non-significant.

out using the Wilcoxon test. The Wilcoxon test results are given in Table 5.5, alongside bootstrapped effect sizes (LaFlair et al., 2015).

Taken together, these results indicate that participants' completion scores were higher on the simple tasks than on the complex Museum task. As Table 5.5 shows, the mean differences between the Museum task and both simple tasks (Campus and Station) were significant. The effect sizes for these differences were $d = 0.76$ and 0.63, respectively, indicating small to medium effects (Plonsky, 2015). Thus, for the Museum task, the design appears to have resulted in a more challenging task relative to the simple tasks. On the other hand, the complex Shops task was not harder than either simple task to complete. Contrary to expectation, it had the highest average completion score among the four tasks. This may be due to its design having contained fewer difficult-to-navigate landmarks than the other tasks. It also may have been generally more familiar to the participants, because it showed a generic shopping area.

Time on task

Participants were informed that they would have no more than five minutes to complete each task. An electronic timer with an alarm was used to enforce this time limit. Inevitably, some participants completed certain tasks in a shorter amount of time than allotted. This, of course, constrained not merely the amount of language produced and the degree of interaction engaged in, but also the length of the stimuli used in the stimulated recall sessions, during which participants watched a video of the task performance in its entirety. For these reasons, a full understanding of the outcomes of this study requires consideration of time on task. Times reported here are based on the length of these video-recordings, which corresponded to the task performances. As indicated by Figure 5.2, the complex tasks tended to take longer on average to complete than the simple tasks.

Using Friedman's ANOVA, the overall means were significantly different ($\chi^2(3) = 17.49$, $p = 0.00$). Thus the Wilcoxon test was used to

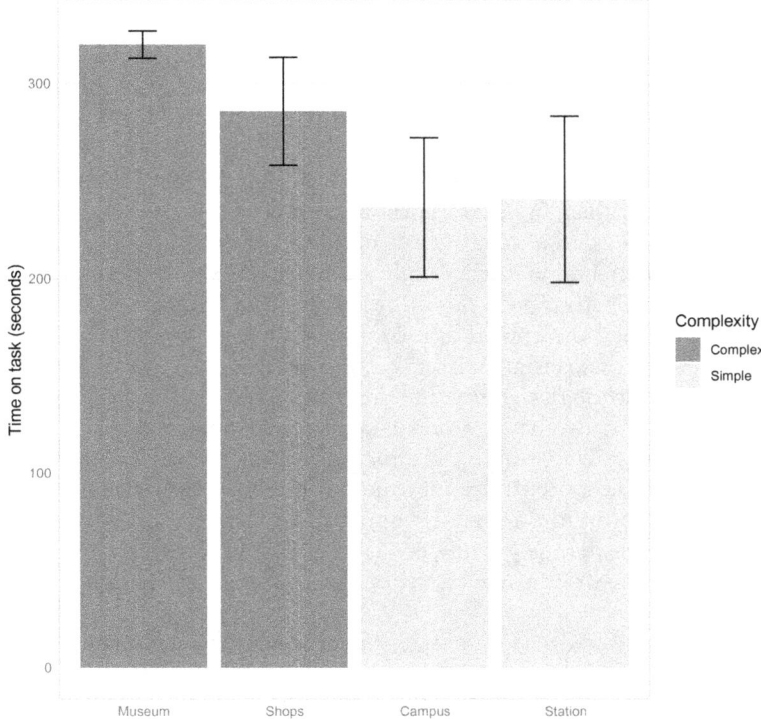

Figure 5.2 Bar plot of time on task

perform pairwise comparisons, which are reported in Table 5.6. These results confirm the effect of task on the length of time taken. The Museum task took significantly longer than both the Campus and the Station task. The effect here can be seen easily as the mean difference is expressed in the number of seconds. On average, the Museum task took over a minute longer to complete than either of these tasks. These effect sizes are in the medium to large range (Plonsky, 2015).

Table 5.6 Time on task: Mean differences across simple versus complex tasks

Simple	Complex	Mean diff.	p-value	Effect size (d)	BCa 95% CI	
					Lower	Upper
Campus	Museum	82.81	0.00	1.31	0.87	1.99
Campus	Shops	48.94	n.s.	0.57	−0.00	1.05
Station	Museum	78.63	0.00	0.99	0.54	1.49
Station	Shops	44.75	n.s.	0.47	−0.05	1.03

Note: n.s. = non-significant.

Summary

To conclude this chapter, the potential benefits of MMR in this study can be described in terms of its specific design, its potential for legitimation and its social value. As pointed out by Riazi (2016), MMR studies can be described as eclectic, principled eclectic or innovative. The present study relied on a specific, embedded MMR design. It also acknowledged the need for pluralism in its conceptualization. For these reasons the study can be regarded as an innovative use of mixed methods (Riazi, 2016).

As for its benefits, firstly the embedded design (1) afforded an efficient approach to collecting both quantitative and qualitative data simultaneously, (2) retained the appeal of a conventional experimental design and (3) augmented this design with a qualitative phase (Creswell & Plano Clark, 2011). Although the initial design originated in a quantitative tradition, the data can also be regarded as qualitative in nature. The quantitative phase recognized this by building on the analyses to probe cases illustrative of the potential experimental effects, while the qualitative phase sought to build on analytic approaches that blend conversational and introspective data (e.g. Polio & Gass, 2017). This recognizes the complex nature and varied dimensions of the construct of language teacher noticing.

Secondly, based on its mixed design, a key component of this study is legitimation, which has been proposed as a more neutral term for what quantitative researchers call *validity* and qualitative researchers call *credibility* (Brown, 2014; Onwuegbuzie & Johnson, 2006). At the heart of legitimation is the issue of how MMR balances the strengths and weaknesses of these traditionally separate research paradigms. That is, how does the study as a whole come to represent more than the sum of its parts? Several possibilities can be considered, including convergence, divergence, elaboration, exemplification and clarification (Brown, 2014). These are distinct ways of integrating QUANT and QUAL findings.

A third potential benefit of this approach relates to Mertens' view of MMR as a transformative paradigm. According to her, such a paradigm requires an awareness of social realities, researcher–participant dialogue (which helps to define the problem statement) and an ethical stance founded on respect, beneficence and social justice (Mertens, 2007: 216). While I cannot claim to have met these criteria to the degree I would have hoped for, it is true that this project arose out of my recognition of the social importance of English teacher education in Japan. Furthermore, a good number of the PSTs who volunteered to participate in this study were past or present students of mine. Therefore, I hoped to conduct research that could potentially benefit them. Despite having received solid education and training, these individuals would likely face numerous professional challenges, not least of which is marginalization as non-native English speaking teachers (NNESTs; Crandall & Christison, 2016). This is a problem, because more important than when or how they learned English is their ability to use it in teaching, which includes noticing their students' use of it.

A related change that this book is intended to promote is a move away from circumscribed views of language teaching as primarily a matter of learner psychology and toward those that encompass teacher psychology as well (Mercer & Kostoulas, 2018a). There is already a rich tradition of research on teacher cognition (Borg, 2015) and teacher reflection (Farrell, 2015) in TESOL; in addition to this work, language teacher educators have begun to cite work on teacher noticing (Borg, 2019; Hüttner, 2019; Jackson & Cho, 2018; Jackson & Shirakawa, 2020; Lengeling *et al.*, 2020). New ways of thinking about psychology in language education may help us better understand the daily challenges teachers face.

This book also views pluralism as an advantage in research methodology (Riazi, 2016). As for the specific methods used, which are revisited in later chapters, language teacher cognition has recently been investigated using stimulated recall methods and conversation analysis, but these are not often combined with the explicit goal of nurturing pluralistic conceptualizations of key phenomena. More than simply combining such tools, the use of MMR here, it is hoped, addresses the challenges in researching language teacher noticing by encouraging readers to see it as social, cognitive, situated and dynamic in nature.

6 Influences on Teacher Noticing

Issues and Hypotheses

The present chapter focuses on the first research question posed in the study: 'Do task complexity and perspectival memory affect recall of teacher noticing?' The data reported here were collected via stimulated recall interviews carried out after each of the tasks was completed. This chapter provides key quantitative details of several aspects of the study, including how noticing was distinguished from other comments, how much noticing occurred and whether experimental conditions impacted the amount of noticing. For readers less interested in these details, subsequent chapters explore the qualitative nature of noticing and the results of both strands are summarized in Chapter 9. In addition to addressing the aforementioned research question, reasons for including the procedural details found in this chapter were to aid understanding, foster transparency and guide future studies.

To refer back to the methodological options presented in the previous chapter, the choices described in this chapter represent but one example of how teacher noticing can be investigated. Written (versus oral) reports of noticing should be considered too (Lengeling *et al.*, 2020). Video-based techniques that allow the teacher to initiate recordings (Colestock & Sherin, 2016) are also a feasible option, which has yet to be employed in second language (L2) studies. This chapter demonstrates how considerations related to timing, distinguishing noticing from other cognitions, and language background informed this study. Later, in its conclusion, the chapter elaborates on how establishing certain research standards may facilitate a better understanding of teacher noticing across groups and over time.

A fundamental concern in using stimulated recall data is that one cannot step in the same river twice. This adage has been attributed to the Greek philosopher, Heraclitus. It relates a seemingly universal feeling that any subjective experience (including a teacher's cognition) is transient and cannot be revisited in precisely the same form. This has implications for those using stimulated recall methods with language teachers (e.g. Anderson,

2019; Gkonou & Mercer, 2018; Gurzynski-Weiss, 2016; Jackson & Cho, 2018; Loewen, 2019; Mann & Walsh, 2017).

It was assumed that what teachers in this study noticed during the recall procedure existed in their memory, and yet that assumption itself poses unique challenges. In modern terms, episodic memory is a complex construct characterized by multiple criteria, including (1) conscious recall, (2) the past occurrence of what is recalled, (3) a contextualized event which is the focus of recall, (4) automaticity of encoding (rather than encoding via repeated exposure), (5) a retrieval process, (6) dependency of retrieval on associated internal or external cues, (7) fallibility (i.e. forgetting) and (8) a reconstructive nature (Gallo & Wheeler, 2013).

This study's reliance on memory recall raises two fundamental issues: veridicality and reactivity. The first of these, veridicality, refers to the degree to which the river stepped into during recall is actually the same. To improve the truthfulness of recall, it is recommended (Gass & Mackey, 2017) that researchers: (1) provide stimuli that will facilitate recollection of the processes engaged in (e.g. video), (2) train participants to reduce interference from intervening thoughts and focus them on past events, (3) conduct recalls in temporal proximity to the event and (4) consider carefully issues arising from the language of the recall, particularly if using an L2 may impede verbalization. These suggestions were kept in mind and, as described previously, video-based, consecutive stimulated recall in the L1, with explicit L1 training, was used in this study.

The second issue, that of reactivity, refers to the possibility that the cognitive processes being studied may be altered by participants' having to verbalize them. Here it is important to note the study's repeated measures design. The teacher participants completed a series of recall interviews, i.e. one after each of the four tasks. Doing these recalls might have led to changes in the thinking processes recruited when performing subsequent tasks or recalls. This is why the Latin squares design was used. Although this does not solve the problem, it means that each condition was as susceptible as any other to potential reactivity effects. Another related problem is that prior recalls might contaminate the content of later ones (i.e. participants may recycle memories from previous recalls). To limit this possibility, the recall sessions were interspersed between the tasks. Finally, as Gass and Mackey (2017) point out in their discussion of the issue, the assumption that reactivity will occur is not a given; validation studies have yielded mixed results (see Gass & Mackey, 2017: 125–129).

The issues described above are familiar ones in the research literature. In designing this study, they led to two further considerations related to the use of video-based stimulated recall in the context of pre-service teacher (PST) education. The first of these concerns the perspective from which the interaction was recalled, while the second offers a different take on reactivity.

Firstly, this study goes beyond the issues raised above to consider yet another methodological issue, regarding perspective. A useful definition of this comes from McCarroll and Sutton (2017: 4): 'Perspectives can be cognitive, embodied, emotional, or evaluative in nature; they occur in many domains, including imagination, perception, and memory; and they can be first-, second-, or third-personal.' This research adopted a cognitive approach to perspective, grounded in perception, memory and noticing. The field and observer perspectives used here can be glossed as first- and third-person perspectives, respectively. Based on this, and by changing the participants' position relative to the stationary video camera used throughout each session, the study systematically created two distinct viewpoints on the participants' teaching or, essentially, different routes to reconstructing teacher noticing (Miller, 2011).

Secondly, in this study change was regarded as a desirable outcome of verbalization. From the perspective of sociocultural theory, Swain (2006b: 110) has argued that verbal protocols, including data from stimulated recall sessions, entail 'a process of comprehending and reshaping experience'. Under this view, rather than being neutral brain dumps, recalls should be considered a source of learning and development. In contrast to earlier accounts, which claimed that 'cognitive processes are not modified by these verbal reports' (Ericsson & Simon, 1984: 16), Swain observed that verbalization may mediate learning. This is so for three reasons: it transforms thought and selectively focuses attention; it yields observable artifacts that may then be thought about or reconsidered; and it can ultimately lead to the internalization of such new artifacts (Swain, 2006b: 101). The position that recalls constitute an offloading of stored information is already challenged by the focus, adopted throughout this book, on memory as reconstructive (McCarroll & Sutton, 2017). Also, Swain's view is particularly appealing if the mental process being examined can be regarded as helpful to the participant's development, which is certainly true here. As mentioned earlier, Mann and Walsh (2017) have made the case for stimulated recall as a valuable tool for encouraging reflective practice among language teachers. This issue is taken up again in Chapter 9.

Based on the foregoing, in the remainder of this chapter two quantitative hypotheses are examined:

- **Hypothesis 1**: The means for recall comments and noticing instances will be higher for complex tasks than for simple tasks. This hypothesis is grounded in the assumption that, in line with the Cognition Hypothesis (Robinson, 2015), complex tasks make cognitive demands on attention beyond those of simple tasks. These demands arose, in the present study, from the decreases in planning time and map familiarity and the increase in the number of map elements.

This may seem counter-intuitive. Based on Tsui (2003), expert teaching involves not attending more, but attending less overall while directing focused attention onto what matters. However, the participants in this study were not experts. Hypothesis 1 is not necessarily expected to hold for experienced teachers, whose expert cognition and noticing might be less susceptible to the influence of the task-as-workplan (Breen, 1989; see Samuda, 2015, for related evidence).

- **Hypothesis 2**: The means for recall comments and noticing instances will be higher using the field perspective than when using the observer perspective. This hypothesis assumes, following Miller (2011: 61), that teacher (or field) perspective videos reveal 'a far more complex and dynamic scene than that captured by traditional [or observer] video' and also shift the focus of the recall away from the teacher and toward engagement with the student, which was incorporated into the definition of language teacher noticing employed in this study.

Data Coding

The stimulated recall method used to train participants and elicit data was introduced in Chapter 5. This section picks up where that discussion left off, and describes how the data were transformed and analyzed for use in the study. The following steps were undertaken:

(1) The stimulated recall interview audio files were transcribed exactly as heard in the recording by a paid undergraduate research assistant who was a native speaker of Japanese (and also a proficient user of English), based on a set of transcription guidelines. These guidelines conveyed the instruction to list and number each utterance on a separate line whenever the topic changed, or after lengthy pauses (more than 5 seconds). In the case of speech in Japanese, standard Japanese orthography was used. For words or phrases spoken in English, which could constitute code-mixing, the English spelling was used. At the end of each utterance, in parentheses, a timestamp was added from the audio file to make it easier to refer to the original spoken utterance. After the timestamp, beginning on a separate line, an English translation was added. The transcription guidelines specifically noted that special attention should be paid to the accuracy of the translation, in particular its tense. The completed file contained four verbal protocols from each of the 16 teacher participants, for a total of 64 protocols, which were initially labelled using only the session and task number. Information about task complexity and perspective was masked during coding.

(2) After the transcriptions were checked, an initial meeting with a second rater was arranged. This rater, who held a Master's degree and was an English instructor at the university where the study was conducted, acted as the second rater, along with the researcher/author. An overview of the study, the coding job and the work schedule were provided at this point and initial paperwork concerning remuneration was dealt with.

(3) Next, coding guidelines for the recall data were prepared and sent to the second rater, along with a subset of the data. These guidelines included a definition and examples of language teacher noticing. The layout used, at this stage and later on, included both the transcription of the task interaction between the teacher and the student and, beneath it, the teachers' comments during each subsequent recall (including the original Japanese and the English translations). Based on recommendations in Gass and Mackey (2017: 26), the inclusion of these data sources in the coding sheet was intended to improve comprehensibility by providing further context related to understanding the teachers' verbal protocols.
(4) Both raters carefully reviewed the guidelines and worked through the data in order to ensure that they were easy to understand and use. That is, both raters independently coded the provided subset of the data (i.e. two protocols from different participants). In doing so, each separate comment was labelled as 'noticing' or 'not noticing' based on the definition included in the coding guidelines.
(5) The two raters then conducted a follow-up meeting to review and discuss their coding decisions. Based on this discussion, several suggestions emerged that are worth mentioning here: (1) the operational definition of teacher noticing could be extended to refer explicitly to the types of comments that should *not* be coded as noticing; (2) the number of examples, including comments which exhibited noticing as well as those that did not, should be increased; and (3) both raters agreed that focusing on the specific dimension of engagement (i.e. social, cognitive, emotional or behavioral engagement, either separately or in combination) would be useful in making final determinations about whether to code a comment as noticing or not. The researcher updated the coding guidelines to incorporate these suggestions (see Appendix B for an excerpt of these guidelines).
(6) To check the reliability of the finalized coding guidelines, 25% of the protocols, representing each study condition, were selected randomly (Révész, 2012). These co-rated protocols contained 114 comments in total, which amounted to 20% of all comments in the entire data set. Both raters used the final guidelines to code these data independently.
(7) Afterwards, the researcher used the co-rated data to compute the simple percentage agreement, which reached 90%. To account for chance agreement, Cohen's kappa was also computed. This was 0.80 ($p = 0.00$), indicating strong agreement. The researcher then individually coded all remaining data.

Descriptive Statistics

This section reports the total number of comments made by the participants during all of their recall sessions, as well as the subset of these comments that were coded as noticing. The former are referred to below as recall comments, while latter are referred to as noticing instances. Table 6.1 displays these results for each participant separately, followed by group statistics at the bottom.

It can be seen that, across participants, there were differences in the number of both recall comments and instances of noticing. On average, roughly half of the comments were counted as displaying noticing. Again, these data are treated separately in this chapter and elsewhere, as they afford a somewhat different insight into PST cognition. In addition, this table reveals a key difference across the teachers regarding their performances. Namely, a large amount of variation was observed in terms of the percentage of recall comments that were coded as noticing instances. This figure ranged from 30% to 67%, suggesting that certain participants' comments fit the description of noticing to a greater extent than those of others.

In Tables 6.2 and 6.3, the data were averaged to inspect differences in recall comments and noticing instances by task design and recall condition. Also included are measures of the dispersion. A few noteworthy differences can be seen in these tables.

Table 6.1 Stimulated recall results: Means for participants

Participant	Recall comments	Noticing instances	%
1	25	13	52.00
2	23	7	30.43
3	31	13	41.94
4	56	24	42.86
5	29	16	55.17
6	31	18	58.06
7	34	23	67.65
8	39	19	48.72
9	30	13	43.33
10	50	25	50.00
11	46	18	39.13
12	42	13	30.95
13	39	18	46.15
14	23	12	52.17
15	42	22	52.38
16	20	10	50.00
Mean	35.00	16.50	47.56
Min	20	7	30.43
Max	56	25	67.65
Range	37	19	38.21
SD	10.41	5.27	9.53

Table 6.2 Recall comments by task and perspective

Design	Perspective	M	SD	Min	Max	Range
Complex	Field	9.75	2.70	4.00	14.00	11.00
	Observer	9.50	3.16	5.00	16.00	12.00
Simple	Field	7.75	3.24	3.00	15.00	13.00
	Observer	8.00	3.33	4.00	13.00	10.00

Table 6.3 Noticing instances by task and perspective

Design	Perspective	M	SD	Min	Max	Range
Complex	Field	4.81	2.20	2.00	9.00	8.00
	Observer	4.25	2.79	1.00	10.00	10.00
Simple	Field	3.81	1.76	1.00	9.00	9.00
	Observer	3.63	1.89	1.00	7.00	7.00

In Table 6.2, firstly, the task design seemed to matter. The average number of recall comments in complex tasks was higher than those for the simple tasks. Additionally, when using complex tasks, the field perspective yielded slightly more comments. However, this pattern was reversed when using simple tasks. In that case, the observer perspective yielded slightly more comments.

Based on Table 6.3, the task design also seemed to influence noticing instances. That is, noticing instances were higher in complex tasks than in simple tasks. In this case, there appeared to be a more consistent effect for perspective. Namely, the field perspective resulted in more noticing across simple versus complex tasks. As a further visual representation, the plot in Figure 6.1 illustrates the differences in noticing across study conditions. This figure suggests clear effects for both factors, although the differences are in fact quite small.

Quantitative Analyses of Noticing

Based on the previous section, further analyses are reported here. The main issue addressed is whether task complexity and recall conditions measurably influence PST cognition, in terms of recall comments and noticing instances. If they do, then it would seem reasonable to suggest that such factors are worthy of closer consideration at the initial stages of language teacher preparation. This section presents the results for the two research hypotheses stated at the outset of the chapter. The analyses reported here were carried out using R software, Version 3.5.0 (R Core Team, 2018).

Prior to testing these hypotheses, the data were examined and found to be non-normal based on a histogram and the Shapiro–Wilk test.

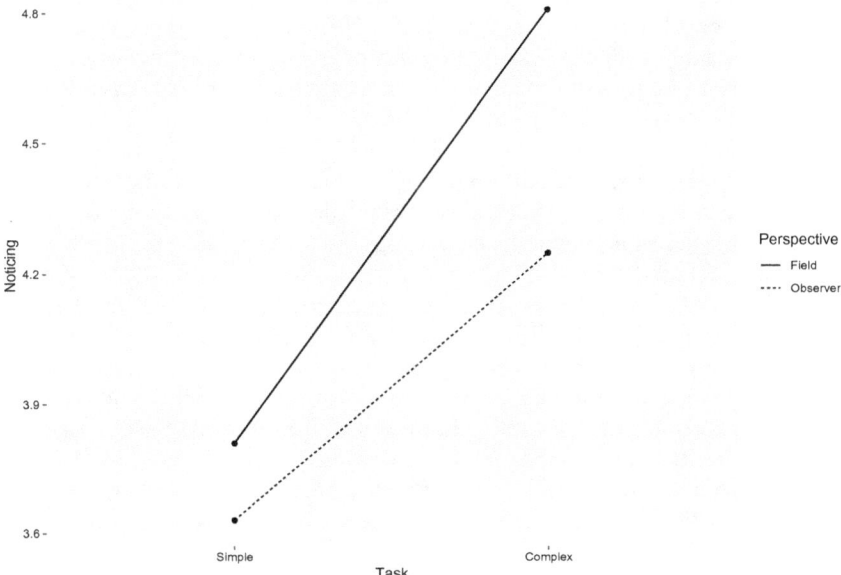

Figure 6.1 Plot of teacher noticing instances by complexity and perspective

Therefore, the choice was made to adopt non-parametric tests. As recommended by Feys (2016), the R package nparLD was used in light of the two-way, within-subjects design. The package function ld.f2 includes an ANOVA-type test, which was used here.

Regarding the analysis of recall comments, the main effect of complexity was significant, $F(1, 15) = 8.18$, $p = 0.00$. However, the main effect of perspective was not significant, $F(1, 15) = 0.01$, $p = 0.94$. Also, there was no significant interaction between complexity and perspective, $F(1, 15) = 0.58$, $p = 0.45$. Effect sizes offer additional insight to inform such results. The package bootES (Kirby & Gerlanc, 2013) was used to calculate within-subjects standardized effect sizes for each contrast. These were based on the difference scores for each participant. The number of recall comments from simple tasks was subtracted from those in complex tasks. Likewise, those associated with the observer perspective were subtracted from the field perspective. These difference scores were then used to compute effect sizes and bootstrapped confidence intervals for the effect of these two factors on the number of comments. For complexity, the effect size was small to medium, indicating the advantage for complex tasks, Cohen's $d = 0.73$, 95% CI [0.23, 1.13]. An effect size of zero was found for perspective, Cohen's $d = 0.00$, 95% CI [−0.59, 0.51].

As for the analysis of noticing instances, the main effect of complexity was not significant, $F(1, 15) = 1.74$, $p = 0.19$, nor was the main effect of perspective, $F(1, 15) = 0.80$, $p = 0.37$. There was no significant interaction between complexity and perspective, $F(1, 15) = 0.65$, $p = 0.42$. Again, the analysis included effect sizes and bootstrapped confidence intervals for the effect of both factors on noticing. For complexity, the effect was positive, Cohen's $d = 0.40$, 95% CI [−0.10, 0.89]. A very small, positive result was also found for perspective, Cohen's $d = 0.17$, 95% CI [−0.39, 0.98]. These effect sizes are consistent with Figure 6.1, which suggests that both factors influenced noticing slightly. However, they also conform to the non-parametric analyses that revealed a lack of significance, because the confidence intervals included zero.

Given these mixed results, little support can be claimed for the two hypotheses stated earlier. Hypothesis 1 was clearly supported in the case of recall comments, which were significantly greater in the complex task. However, there was no significant difference in the number of noticing instances across complex versus simple tasks. It is possible that the significant finding for the number of recall comments merely reflects the fact that the complex tasks took longer (see the previous chapter). Thus there is potential for more noticing in those tasks, but the participants in this study did not report noticing, as operationalized here, to a much greater degree. As there was a clear trend toward more noticing in complex tasks, additional research seems warranted. The question as to whether there were qualitative differences in noticing related to task design will be addressed later in this chapter.

Considering Hypothesis 2, the study offered less support. Recall comments and noticing instances did not significantly increase when a field perspective was used, although this does not rule out the possibility that the field versus observer distinction yields qualitative differences (see below). The means for noticing were, however, consistently higher when participants viewed the interaction from a field perspective. Future research could build on this finding. The lack of a significant interaction between the factors in this study can be taken to indicate that, for instance, complex tasks did not yield a greater difference in the number of noticing instances across field and observer perspectives, as suggested by Figure 6.1. That would be an intriguing possibility, with consequences for teacher education. Again, these results can only suggest that more work is needed to explore this possibility.

The remainder of this chapter will consider in detail how the two factors of complexity and perspective *might* at times influence teacher noticing, in the ways predicted, based on a closer examination of the data. As predicted, there was a small, significant increase in the number of comments when participants were recalling events that had occurred during complex tasks, as well as a non-significant increase in the amount of noticing. As the values reported here show, task design and recall conditions had small, positive effects on noticing. Based on the effect sizes and confidence intervals, there was a slightly larger and more precise effect for task complexity than for perspectival memory. The issue of significance may be related to the small sample of participants, but it is also important to recognize the limitations of null hypothesis statistical testing, to report results carefully and transparently and to pay primary attention to indicators of effect size rather than significance (Norris, 2015).

It is also clear that, in the face of these results, this study must look beyond experimental factors and quantitative outcomes in order to gain deeper insight. Considering the overall results, it seems plausible to assume that, in general, individual variation in language teacher noticing will be greater than that which is experimentally induced. This is particularly clear from Table 6.1, which indicated that the proportion of noticing instances to recall comments ranged from 30% to 67%. Such large differences among pre-service English teachers speak directly to language teacher educators, in that, even in a relatively small group of individuals whose L1 and educational background were similar, there is substantial variation in readiness to adopt the teacher's role during task-based interaction.

Fortunately, the mixed-methods approach adopted in this study incorporated a qualitative dimension to further probe the nature of noticing by these PSTs at an individual level. In the rest of this chapter, the mixed-methods research (MMR) strategy of exemplification (Brown, 2014) is adopted to offer examples, based on the qualitative data, of how task and perspective may at times influence PST noticing. The following sections give only a taste of what qualitative analyses can reveal. Subsequently, Chapters 7 and 8 more thoroughly develop the qualitative side of this study.

Taking Teacher Noticing to Task

To zoom in on the effect noted in the previous section, the difference scores used to compute effect sizes for task design were first re-examined. These scores were computed by subtracting the number of noticing instances in simple tasks from those in complex tasks. Thus, a larger number indicates a greater difference in noticing instances. The data showed that the highest difference scores were from Participant 7, who had a score of 9, and Participant 6, who had a score of 8. These participants were thus chosen as suitable cases to illustrate the potential effects of task complexity on teacher noticing. It can be noted that these individuals were also among those whose comments reflected an above-average proportion of noticing instances (see Table 6.1). This meant that their data contained sufficient examples to draw on.

For Participant 7, instances of noticing were fewer among the simple Campus and Station tasks than among the complex Museum and Shops tasks. Precisely, these amounted 16 instances in complex tasks (Museum = 6, Shops = 10) versus seven instances in simple tasks

(Campus = 6, Station = 1), resulting in, as already noted, a difference of nine instances. To begin with the simple tasks, particularly during the Campus task, the teacher's initial comment (which was not coded as noticing) simply asserted that the location was familiar and hence the task 'felt easy'. In this task, several noticing instances related to student questions as well as anxiety and then later, relief, concerning the student's understanding. Next, examples from the complex Museum task included those pertaining to a word search ('how can I say') for the lexical item, *roof*, which was resolved through mutual understanding with the student by referring to the building's 'top'. Another instance concerned how to explain that the student should enter the second door from the right, among four doors ('I felt anxious about whether or not my partner understood'). Yet another instance regarded how to navigate around a tree situated along the route. Here, the teacher reported that 'although I thought if I said "clockwise", my partner might go around in a full circle, I didn't know what else to say'. This teacher's recall interview based on the complex Shops tasks elicited comments regarding noticing of her use of techniques for checking understanding, including those that were verbal ('I checked where my partner was … because I didn't know if we saw the same thing') and nonverbal ('looking at her expression, my partner nodded a lot when she understood, so I could proceed confidently'). A final comment on the Shops task, which reflected noticing of collaboration with the student but indicated pressure due to the amount of time allotted, was as follows: 'we ran out of time at the end, and the part at the coffee shop was difficult, so I was anxious about whether I could properly convey that, and I thought I wanted to check more.'

The data for Participant 6 followed a similar pattern, wherein the complex tasks contained more instances (Museum = 4, Shops = 9) of noticing than the simple tasks (Campus = 3, Station = 2). There were eight more noticing instances in complex tasks. Commenting on the simple Campus task, this teacher reported noticing of mutual understanding and said that 'because there was little information, I added to it'. This comment confirms that the task design itself offered less detail to engage with. Intriguingly, it also suggests that the teachers themselves could have modified the complexity of these materials during the task-in-process. Further recall comments from the simple Station task, which were not coded as noticing because they did not refer specifically to engagement with the partner, included those indicating greater confidence and that the task was 'going smoothly'. While viewing the video of the complex Shops tasks, this participant again commented that the interaction was going smoothly, but this time noticed that 'both of us were surprised because it looked more difficult'. Another comment here, coded as noticing, was that 'maybe because both of us were anxious, I was explaining using gesture'. Later in this interview, there were further instances of noticing based on the need to confirm the directions and correct certain explanations that the student had not understood initially. The complex Museum task, as well, revealed a concern for communicating efficiently, an issue that did not seem to arise during the simple tasks. Here, Participant 6 noticed having to speak slowly and adjust to the student's pace, waiting for him to finish tracing the route on the map. This task again led the teacher and student to confirm their understanding. As the teacher reported, 'I was anxiously checking whether my partner understood'.

Taken together, these data, from participants whose performances showed the greatest differences across simple versus complex tasks, appear to reflect the task designer's intentions and to further corroborate the validity checks reported in Chapter 5. The complex tasks involved more elements, less familiar locations and no pre-task planning time. The foregoing examples suggest that these tasks consequently differed in terms of what some PSTs noticed, in several ways accounted for by the Cognition Hypothesis (Robinson, 2015). Namely, their conceptual and linguistic demands varied, as shown by examples concerning word searches (*roof*), gesture and spatial navigation. Also, the need for negotiation seemed to increase, as these teachers reported noticing episodes in which they confirmed landmarks and directions with their partner to a greater degree. In addition, there were instances of noticing based on a shared perception of difficulty that was in line with the task design ('both of us were surprised because it looked more difficult'). Other design features mentioned by these teachers were familiarity and time pressure. Based on these examples, in future research it may be possible to isolate certain task-related influences on teacher noticing.

Putting Teacher Noticing in Perspective

As in the last section, the potential influence of perspective was investigated by considering cases in which the predicted effect was evident. It should be noted again, however, that the hypothesis that the field perspective would generate more noticing was not supported. That hypothesis, perhaps, is more appropriate for contexts in which teachers are engaged with groups of students, which was not possible in the present study. However, it was felt that turning the camera lens on the student as in the field perspective, versus on the teacher as in the observer perspective, might alter what the teachers reported on in the stimulated recall interviews.

There could be more to attend to, interpret and decide when faced with stimuli depicting another person, simply because what is noticed then is much more a matter of conjecture, being based largely on attempts to understand the other person's thoughts, feelings and attitudes. There is also more unpredictability when encountering other minds (as almost any teacher knows). So, the field view offers a better window, perhaps, on interactional dynamics than does an observer view which shows the familiar image of the teacher who is doing the recall. The observer view is akin to looking in a mirror, wherein personal appearance and behavior come to the foreground and shared cognition, when considered at all, may be more tacit, less easily articulated and based more on internalized self-impressions than on engagement with the external environment. Ultimately, this seems more a matter of quality than quantity.

Participant 3 may shed some light on the issues. In this case, noticing instances were three times greater when viewing the interaction from a field perspective (10 instances) than an observer perspective (3 instances). Based on the study design, the field perspective was used during the complex Museum task and the simple Station task, while the observer perspective was used for the complex Shops task and the simple Campus task. Note that this fact may account for some of the variation observed here, as might the participant's own approach to the tasks and recall interviews.

In this particular case, the field perspective seemed to be associated with a greater concern with the student's orientation to the maps used. For instance, based on the Museum task, this teacher noticed that it was not clear 'whether my partner was looking at the map in a vertical way or a horizontal way' and then, during the Station task, she remarked that 'to check which direction each of us was looking at, I confirmed that there was a theater on the right'. These examples, although limited, suggest that the field perspective yielded more comments pertaining to noticing the student's thinking or, in particular, his mental spatial model, which underlies the act of giving directions. Mental models here are representations of the spatial environment, which may be conveyed by route (*as you leave the station, turn left toward the entrance to the park*) or survey (*the park entrance is located to the northwest of the station*) descriptions, and function to assist navigation through reference to specific landmarks and actions (Denis, 2018). In practice, the directions teachers gave typically involved route descriptions.

On the other hand, the teacher's comments while viewing the interaction from an observer perspective often concerned behaviors she herself undertook, along with self-evaluations of ability or confidence, rather than collaborative engagement, and were therefore not coded as noticing. Interestingly, reports of self-performed action, in the form, *I sat at the table*, were significantly greater under an observer condition than a field condition in the study of episodic memory by McIsaac and Eich (2002: 148). Similar comments from the current data included, 'when I said, "please go to the third floor", I was not sure if I could use "until"' and 'I used "most left side door" and "most right side door" without knowing if they were really correct'. These reported thoughts do not refer directly to student engagement. Instead they arose from the teacher's reflection on her own language use.

This does not mean that self-reflection on language use is unhelpful to teacher development; most likely the opposite is true. Yet, in this book, the emphasis is shifted toward teachers' noticing of student thinking in order to promote understanding of communicative language teaching, including its sociocognitive dimensions. The difference between a focus on student thinking versus one on self-evaluation is crucial to understanding and supporting PST development. In this regard, it seems relevant to consider carefully the optimal use of video stimuli in teacher education contexts, which includes how it portrays the teacher. When it comes to implementing tasks, beginning teachers should be encouraged to see themselves as orchestrating effective performance rather than exhibiting perfect competence.

Summary

This chapter focused on whether task complexity and perspectival memory affect recall of teacher noticing. It carefully considered the reconstructive nature of memory, methodological concerns with stimulated recall and interpretations of verbal reports. Multiple views were integrated, ranging from cognitive psychology to sociocultural theory, in order to address the choice of methodology adopted in this study.

The chapter then described the coding of noticing and provided descriptive statistics. The descriptive data revealed a large amount of individual variation in PST noticing, which was indicated by the range in the percentage of recall comments coded as noticing instances. Based on mean scores, some variation in these two outcomes seemed related to task design and, to a lesser extent, perspective. Then non-parametric statistics were used to test two hypotheses. The first of these, that task design may influence PST cognition, was supported, only in the case of recall comments. This could be due to time on task. However, neither task nor perspective significantly influenced noticing, although small effects in the predicted direction were found.

Subsequently, brief examples were given from the stimulated recall interviews. In some cases, the task design did seem to matter to teacher noticing. This is noteworthy, in particular because participants were not told beforehand that these tasks differed in complexity. Thus, teachers and researchers interested in follow-up studies might consider: (a) informing teachers of the differences in complexity, (b) examining these effects with more experienced teachers and/or (c) seeking to uncover effects by increasing the differential demands on a wider range of simple versus complex tasks, among other suggestions. The effects of the recall conditions, it was noted, are likely more a matter of quality than quantity (McIsaac & Eich, 2002). Based on these results, the study must look beyond factors such as task design or recall conditions. The following chapters therefore turn to more in-depth qualitative views of PST noticing.

Regarding the big picture issue of distinguishing teacher noticing from other teacher cognitions, this chapter may provide some practical insight.

The use of stimulated recall methods leads to a large amount of data, much but not all of which pertains to noticing. Although there are limitations to such comparisons, it might be informative to consider the percentage of participants' comments that constituted noticing across different studies. For instance, as noted previously, in Jackson and Cho (2018) this figure ranged from 16% to 52%, while in the present study it was from 30% to 67% (see Table 6.1). The earlier study, it should be noted, did not attempt to conduct the stimulated recall interviews immediately after participants taught. Perhaps this is one reason for the higher percentage range here. Although various factors complicate the interpretation of these diverging results, such as the participants' background and experience, efforts to standardize the measurement of noticing could potentially enable more valid comparisons across groups and time. Ultimately, this could have implications for understanding the relative effects of different types of interventions used in second language teacher education, as well as the longitudinal development of teaching skills within individuals.

7 Noticing of Embodied Resources

The Role of Embodied Resources

This chapter and the following one pair specific noticing instances with further analyses inspired by multimodal conversational analysis (CA). The goal is to provide a more detailed account of the task-based interactional processes noticed by these pre-service teachers (PSTs). As noted by Hall and Looney (2019) in the introduction to their edited collection, CA focuses on analyzing the resources participants use to organize action, which can be verbal (talk), embodied (gaze, posture, gesture) or multimodal (use of objects such as a chalkboard, a textbook or a map). Any use of these resources is closely intertwined. Hall (2019) offered this valuable description:

> Teachers must calibrate their language, facial expressions, gestures, body positions, and even the use of material artifacts such as a textbook or smart pad such that the pedagogical project is advanced, the shared attention of students is maintained, and individual student participation is promoted. (Hall, 2019: 47)

This coordination of multiple resources was also apparent in the experimental data gathered for this study. To look beyond the contribution of the tasks, here the focus shifts to resources that the teacher and student brought to these interactions – that is, to what the teachers themselves attributed significance to, and how it mattered to their interactions. Nonetheless, task features will occasionally be referred to in these chapters to contextualize these interactions. The question driving these chapters is: What do pre-service teachers notice about the use of embodied and verbal resources during language instruction?

Embodied interaction during tasks

To begin with a definition, embodied resources are 'nonverbal bodily means for taking action such as gestures, facial expressions, gaze, head movements, body movements and postures, and so on' (Hall, 2019: 85). A principal assumption in studying embodied interaction is that these resources for making meaning are not peripheral to communication but are instead closely intertwined with verbal resources (Streeck *et al.*, 2011). For example, language users regularly employ resources such as recipient nodding to convey their understanding. Another example is the use of ensembles of gesture and onomatopeia to elicit unknown lexical items, such as 'hammer' (Gullberg, 2011). Such resources are used to co-construct meaning.

A number of studies have described the use of embodied resources by language learners, a few of which, especially those focused on tasks, are noted here. Platt and Brooks (2008) examined embodiment and affordances in a sequence of tasks, including a map task, carried out in Swahili by participants unfamiliar with the language. Pointing, gazing and touching materials were among the embodied means found to assist with task completion. The authors noted that these resources functioned not only to establish and maintain communication, but also to focus the participants' own attention. Two further studies addressed these matters in the context of task-based lessons. Kunitz and Skogmyr Marian (2017) analyzed conversations among Swedish junior high school students during English lessons in which they made a poster. Among other findings, gaze was used to indicate the need for access to visual (or written) information and to call for the teacher's assistance when orienting to the spelling of a new word. In another CA study, Lee and Burch (2017) examined how university students collaboratively planned for a presentation. The inclusion of embodied interaction in their study served to show how these students used multiple resources (e.g. gaze, body movement and gesture) to nominate speakers and indicate who they intended to address. Some fundamental aspects of communication in task-based interaction, therefore, may be overlooked when analyses neglect embodied resources.

Teacher noticing of embodied resources

Teachers also notice student use of embodied resources. In one detailed study of such classroom behavior, based on observations from a content and language integrated learning (CLIL) class conducted in English in Finland, Käänta (2014: 86) defined embodied noticings as 'types of interactional events that are performed through different kinds of visibly intensified embodied and material practices'. The study investigated, in particular, student responses to a teacher's written answers to an exercise that were projected onto a screen. Where these answers were unclear, the students initiated repair by the teacher through embodied noticings. Such noticings can be regarded as social actions that promote joint attention and may express a stance toward what is noticed that others (including teachers) may align to or not. Following Schegloff (2007: 88–89), their performance is initially through bodily-visual means, which may or may not be subsequently accompanied by verbal behavior.

Drawing on CA, Käänta's (2014) study of embodied noticings adds depth to our understanding of language classroom interaction. It enriches the description of classroom events by shedding light on the undeniably situated nature of language learning and language use, which incorporates material and bodily semiotic resources. This study raises questions about when and how teachers attend to, correctly interpret and initiate decisions based on students' use of embodied resources to communicate.

Data from Jackson and Cho (2018) further illustrate how a teacher's noticing of students' embodied actions may be used in pedagogic decision-making (Example 7.1). This sequence occurred during a demonstration lesson on Chinese, in which students were explicitly taught vocabulary items for various activities (e.g. *singing, dancing, playing*). Subsequently, the teacher distributed to each student several sheets of paper with cartoons illustrating the activities and checked the students' comprehension by asking them to listen to the words again and hold up the appropriate picture. However, this proved challenging for the students, and thus the teacher went on to conduct a spontaneous review of the words. In the example, the teacher is standing and facing the students, who are seated at their desks.

Example 7.1

		Classroom interaction	*Recall comments*
01	T:	so, let's go over it again (.) repeat after me (.) I'm just gonna go through the list	
02	T:	dǎ qiú ((to play ball))	
03	Ss:	dǎ qiú	
04	T:	without the pictures (.) without looking +BH palms down	
05	T:	dǎ qiú	
06	Ss:	dǎ qiú	
07	S1:	play ball	
08	T:	+BA swings +yeah there you go play ball	
09	T:	tiào wǔ ((to dance))	
10	Ss:	tiào wǔ	
11	T:	+dancing motion	
12	S2:	+BA dancing motion	I was kind of happy [S2]'s getting super into this, and I was gonna use [S2] as um a way to get the rest of the class excited and into it.
13	Ss:	((laughter))	
14	T:	((laughs)) good job	

Beginning with Line 01, the teacher verbally initiates the review by instructing the students only to repeat. After eliciting the first word (Lines 02–03), he then clarifies that they should not look at the pictures, gesturing for them to put down their papers (Line 04, which has tiers for verbal and embodied action). He then repeats the first word, which the students repeat again. One student then offers a translation, which the teacher evaluates as correct (Line 08). Here, the teacher also swings both arms as if playing a ball game. The teacher introduces the next item for review, *tiào wǔ*, in Line 09, which the students repeat. Immediately thereafter, the teacher begins dancing in place and is followed by S2, whose exaggerated movement, in the context of being seated in the classroom, elicits laughter from the students and teacher. The teacher then positively evaluates S2's embodied response, and also shifts his body toward S2 while smiling (Line 14). As his comments in the right-hand column make clear, the teacher recalled this episode with satisfaction and reported an intention to use it to foster the students' affective engagement.

In the teacher's mind, particular attention was drawn to S2's active response (Line 12), which was interpreted as emotional engagement and resulted in the decision to use S2 get the rest of the class excited about the review. There is only a suggestion that the teacher did indeed use this student in the video-recorded data, where he can be seen turning toward and smiling at S2. Possibly, this action was deemed sufficient by the teacher, as the unfolding sequence of responses by the other students was also positive (as seen in their laughter in Line 13). The teacher seems to have been considering various options to organize or structure this brief, unplanned review, which after a slight misunderstanding by the students (see Line 04) was now evidently proceeding in sync with his intentions.

The remainder of this chapter will focus on similar instances of PST noticing. In these instances, the teacher participants attended to the student participants' use of embodied resources, such as facial expressions, eye contact and movement. The main focus will be on how the teachers interpreted nonverbal communication expressed by the students. The aim is to uncover how these teachers used their noticing to engage communicatively and to foster performance. The precise question addressed here was: In what ways did the teacher participants notice their student partners' facial expressions, gaze and movement during the interaction?

Method

In addition to the noticing instances, another data source drawn upon here was the video-recorded interactions between the teacher and student. These were the same videos used as prompts during the stimulated recall interviews previously reported on. As for the method, these recordings, which amounted to approximately five hours, were transcribed in their entirety, using conventions based on CA (Hutchby & Wooffitt, 2008; Mondada, 2016; Schegloff, 2007). Recent CA-for-SLA work (Kunitz & Skogmyr Marian, 2017; Lee & Burch, 2017) was also consulted, especially regarding the transcription of embodiment in tasks. In these excerpts, a plus sign (+) is used to denote the onset of embodied actions, which are described in italics (see Appendix C for the entire set of transcription conventions used in this study).

These transcripts offered a rich context for understanding the teachers' self-reported noticing during the stimulated recall sessions. They were used to support the interpretive analysis of the content of PSTs' noticing instances. The entire data set was reviewed carefully to identify possible themes emerging from it. The primary unit of analysis during this stage was the noticing instance. Using an inductive approach, it became clear that these instances could be classified into those primarily emphasizing noticing of embodied resources versus noticing of verbal resources. This is not to deny that the interactions involved coordination of these resources, aptly characterized as multimodal gestalts by Mondada (2016). However rough and binary, this classification seemed to offer a credible solution to the problem of organizing the large amount of data gathered in this study.

Further analysis involved revisiting the video-recorded interactions and the task materials (i.e. the students' completed maps) to better understand the context of these noticing instances. Lastly, closer inspection of the data revealed subcategories that were repeated across multiple teachers and tasks. From these subcategories, selected excerpts are analyzed in detail in this chapter and the next one. The subcategories identified under the theme of embodied resources included use of facial expressions, gaze and movement. Only after the content of their noticing was established did I attempt to deductively apply the attention, interpretation and decision-making during engagement (AIDE) framework to describe the process of noticing.

Facial Expressions

These examples show how teacher participants noticed their student partners' facial expressions, detailing the context of these interactions. As for their presentation, the task interaction appears on the left, while the recall comments are on the right. All of the teacher comments presented in this chapter and the next were coded as noticing instances. The timestamps from these media guided the alignment of the two columns.

The teacher in Excerpt 7.1 intended to work at a junior high school or high school after graduating. He had not yet taken the practicum course (one of the required courses for the teacher training program) and had no other teaching experience. He and his partner were somewhat familiar with each other. This exchange occurred during the Station task, which was scored as a 4, meaning that the student had completed the route and made uncorrected errors.

98 Part 2: A Study of Pre-Service Teachers

Excerpt 7.1 Noticing a facial expression as miscomprehension (Session 1, Station task, Field perspective)

		Task interaction	*Recall comments*
27	T:	okay (.) and go go towards	
28	S:	crosswalk	
29	T:	okay	
		and when you across you you	
		should go +diagonal	
		+RH pointing up	
30	S:	di?	

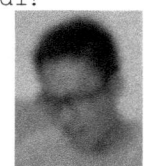

At that moment, I looked at my partner's face and thought he didn't understand the expression 'diagonal', so I was trying to come up with an alternative expression.

31	T:	diagonal = +diagonal line	
		+RH pointing	
32	S:	diagonal line means um like	
		+this shape right?	
		+BH perpendicular gesture	
33	T:	[so so the center	
		of +straight and rightways	
		+RH gesture backwards	

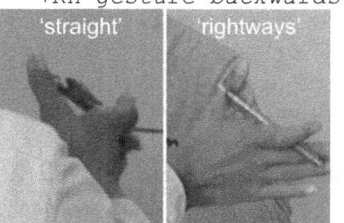

		(.) diagonal	
34	S:	okay	
35	T:	diagonal	
36	S:	diagonal	
		+GZ up	
37	T:	that means so forty-five	
		degrees	
38	S:	aaah okay (.) I understand	

In Excerpt 7.1, the teacher was instructing the student to change direction slightly to arrive at the finish point. In Line 29, he uses an appropriate expression for this (*go diagonal*), and also gestures with his right hand. However, the student, who was looking at his map, did not notice this gesture. Subsequently, in Line 30, the student begins to repeat the word *diagonal*, pausing (with his mouth agape) after the first syllable. This constitutes a student-initiated repair, which is accomplished through segmentation and facial expression. The teacher then seeks to elaborate, first using *diagonal line* in Line 31. After this, the student gestures with both hands in Line 32, indicating imprecisely the intended meaning. The teacher then continues to explain, using the expressions *the center of straight and rightways*, in Line 33 and *forty-five degrees*, in Line 37. In Line 33, the teacher's gesture is also depicted, where he can be seen quite noticeably bending his right hand backwards (while holding a pen) to illustrate the two directions, simultaneously verbally indicating the intended path at the center of these two directions. He then goes further, referencing shared knowledge of geometry, in observing that a diagonal line intersects two lines at a 45-degree angle. It is not until after the student verbally claims understanding (Line 38) that the teacher resumes giving directions. This excerpt illustrates how facial expressions, as embodied misunderstanding, can be noticed and acted upon, reciprocally, through embodied and verbal communication. To revisit the AIDE mnemonic, in his recall comment, the teacher confirmed that he attended to the student's facial expression, interpreted it as a lack of understanding of *diagonal*, and sought to address the issue through his decision to reformulate his expression. Here, his alternate expression was not merely a synonym but the use of a complex, diverse, and sophisticated communicative repertoire (Hall, 2019).

Regarding the next excerpt (Excerpt 7.2), the teacher hoped to teach at a junior high school upon completing her studies. She had not taken the practicum course but had some teaching experience. The teacher and student in this case were familiar with each other. The following exchange occurred during the Shops task. This task performance was assigned a perfect score of 6 to indicate that the student had marked the entire route on her map without error.

Excerpt 7.2 illustrates how complex nonverbal routines can shape instruction. Here, the teacher was explaining the map route, which led from the student's present location on the sixth floor of one building across and down to the fifth floor of an adjacent building via a walkway. In Line 07, the teacher attempted to orient the student to the new building by using *there are five stairs*, and indicated a target location within it (*the bank*). The student, who appeared to be listening carefully, showed understanding by nodding. Line 08 shows that this movement was aligned with the word *bank* in the teacher's instructions. The teacher then explained, in Line 09, to go down one flight of stairs from the current position, but phrased this new location as *four*, then after a lengthy pause, *line*. The student did not immediately respond to this, even though the teacher was looking directly at her, which led the teacher to then laugh in Line 10. In Line 11, the student gazed back down at the map, which could be understood as a problem with the instructions. Then, in Line 12, the teacher repaired her previous utterance by counting the stairs, while tapping her map on the table, and ended on *five*, this time correctly indicating the fifth floor. The student then nodded again to convey her understanding in Line 13. This teacher's comment implies that she noticed her student's

Excerpt 7.2 Noticing a facial expression as comprehension (Session 7, Shops task, Observer perspective)

		Task interaction	*Recall comments*
07	T:	and there are five stairs (.) right so you can go (.) and then you can see the (.) place of maybe +bank right?	
08	S:	+nodding	
09	T:	and then you can go there (.) and then (.) go down one stairs=only one stairs and then so now you can (.) you stay four (1.2) line +right? +GZ at S	
10	T:	((laughs))	
11	S:	GZ down at map	
12	T:	+one two three four five (.) FIVE five +tapping map with finger	While looking at my partner's face, when my partner understood she nodded a lot so I could proceed while feeling relieved.
13	S:	+nodding	

embodied noticing of her inaccurate description of the route. Indeed, elsewhere she reported that *because I thought what I was saying was wrong, I saw that my partner was confused*. Her comment adjacent to Line 12 addresses the student's use of nonverbal communication to convey understanding, which she considered a relief.

Gaze

The next two examples help to show how the teachers noticed and understood their partners' gaze. The teacher in Excerpt 7.3 aimed to teach at a junior high school. She had some teaching experience but had not done the teaching practicum course yet. The teacher and student in this example were unfamiliar with each other. These data come from the Station task, which was scored as a 6, as the student had marked the exact route with no errors.

Excerpt 7.3 Noticing comprehension via gaze (Session 3, Station task, Field perspective)

		Task interaction	Recall comments
22	T:	and when you are in front of café	
23	S:	+mm +drawing line on map	
24	T:	you go straight	
25	S:	mm-hm	
26	T:	toward movie	
27	S:	+movie +drawing line on map	
28	T:	ah (.) and you see the movie on the right side	To check which direction each of us was looking at, I confirmed that there was a theater on the right.
29	S:	mm-hm	

In Excerpt 7.3, the teacher was explaining the directions to the student, who was gazing down at his paper and intermittently tracing the route with a pencil. She first oriented the student to the desired location in Line 22. The student confirmed verbally and marked the route to this location in Line 23. Then she indicated a direction (*you go straight*) in Line 24, and then, after a brief backchannel response by the student in Line 25, she indicated a target location, *toward movie*, in Line 26. The student continued to acknowledge by repeating *movie* and marking his map, as indicated in Line 27. Then the teacher used the token *ah* along with the expression *you see the movie on the right side*, evidently to check the direction of his movement with respect to the theater (Line 28). This expression, like *in front of café* in Line 22, employs a spatial frame of reference (Levinson, 2003). Yet, they are distinct in that *in front of* is an intrinsic frame of reference (i.e. it uses a landmark as the point of reference) whereas *on the right side* employs a relative frame of reference (i.e. it uses the listener's viewpoint as the frame of reference). This interpretation is clear from the teacher's use of the construction, *you see*. In these ways, the teacher relied upon linguistic systems embedded in gaze to ensure proper communication. Her comment establishes that this was intentional. Her attention here seemed to be on the direction of the student's gaze and his progress, while her interpretation of the task and materials led to the decision to add further spatial information to her instructions.

In Excerpt 7.4, the teacher role was assigned to a participant who aimed to teach in a junior high school context, as did her partner. They knew each other prior to the study. Neither had taken the practicum course. The exchange shown here took place during the Shops task. The task was carried out perfectly by the participant, and thus received a score of 6.

Excerpt 7.4 Noticing two options for conveying directions via gaze (Session 8, Shops task, Field perspective)

		Task interaction	*Recall comments*
47	T:	okay so then could you go back to stairs and down to the +ground?	
48	S:	+drawing line on map	
49	T:	okay and then the two door	
50	S:	yes	
51	T:	and could you (1.1) go to the left (.) left side?	
52	S:	left side?	
53	T:	which is (.) yeah (.) out the building from the left side[door	Well, from the view of someone on the stairs, it was right, but from the view of someone looking at this paper, it was left, so I said left a little anxiously.
54	S:	[°okay°	
55	T:	okay?	
56	S:	okay	

In Excerpt 7.4, the teacher had successfully guided the student to the bottom floor of a building that had two exits (Lines 47 and 48). She then paused and commented on the location in Line 49 (see also Figure 7.1). The student acknowledged this in Line 50 without any other action. Continuing with her explanation, the teacher paused but then clearly instructed the student to exit the door on the left (Line 51).

The student then initiated a repair sequence by repeating this instruction (Line 52) and the teacher followed up, again somewhat haltingly, with a further, more detailed explanation in Line 53, *out the building from the left*

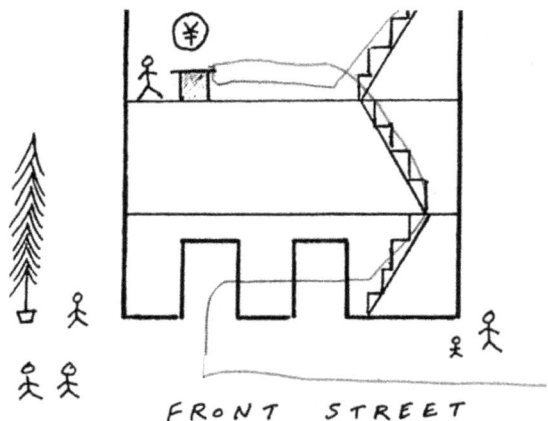

Figure 7.1 Detail of the Shops task map (student version)

side door. Her comment during the interview indicated that she was aware that the student's perspective might have been either that of someone on the stairs or that of someone looking at the map, which would entail different directions, when using the relative frame of reference (Levinson, 2003). There was clearly potential for confusion here. Her hesitation and choice of words during this episode seemed to have been based on this consideration. In Lines 54–56, the teacher and student confirmed the instructions.

Movement

Bodily movement, including nodding and gestures (Stam & McCafferty, 2008), conveys a wide range of meaning. To illustrate that these are not peripheral but rather central modes of communicating (Streeck *et al.*, 2011), the final two examples demonstrate the role of nodding and specific gestures in the teacher participants' awareness.

The participants in Excerpt 7.5 were the same as in Excerpt 7.2. Here, though, the data come from the Shops task. Again, the student's map was completed without errors, and thus the performance was assigned a 6.

Excerpt 7.5 Noticing presence of recipient nodding (Session 7, Shops task, Observer perspective)

		Task interaction	Recall comments
19	T:	and then you can see Front street +right? 　　　　　　　+nodding	While I was consciously making eye contact with my partner, I checked again and again my partner nodded.
20	S:	+GZ up at T +nodding	
21	T:	so::: please use street Front street and then go go coffee shop	

This interaction, despite its brevity, contains several features that turned up in other exchanges elsewhere in the data. Line 19 contains the construction, '*you can see* + noun', which was frequently used by the teachers to orient their students to a particular place. This line ends with the comprehension check, *right*. To this utterance, the teacher also added a quick nod, as if to answer her own comprehension check affirmatively. At this point, the student turned her gaze upwards and, seeing the teacher's expression, also nodded (Line 20). As Aoki (2011: 103) has observed in Japanese contexts, '[t]hrough the use of head nods while recipients' gaze is secured, speakers not only attempt to regulate recipients' actions, but also monitor their current understanding of the activity-in-progress'. In Line 21, the teacher resumes giving directions, beginning with the long utterance (*so:::*), which functions here as a continuer.

The teacher's comment reveals three things about her noticing, which are again analogous to AIDE. Firstly, she was aware of making eye contact (*I was consciously making eye contact*), which secured her partner's gaze and implicitly acknowledged that her partner's response to her could be nonverbal. Secondly, she noted clearly that her purpose was to check the student's understanding, and that this was a repeated action (*I checked again*). And thirdly, she noticed her partner's nodding, which confirmed their understanding and thus fulfilled the goal of her own preceding utterance-final nod. This comment highlights especially how nonverbal communication is nonetheless available for verbal report.

Excerpt 7.6, involving the same participants as the previous excerpt, follows up on this teacher's interpretation of nodding by the student. Here, though, the data come from the Museum task. As noted previously in Chapter 5, average scores on this task were significantly lower. Notwithstanding, in this case the student successfully followed all of the teacher's directions without any mistakes. Their performance was scored as a 6.

Excerpt 7.6 Noticing absence of recipient nodding (Session 7, Museum task, Field perspective)

		Task interaction	Recall comments
23	T:	and then go back the stairs and go down one floor go down one floor (.) okay?	
24	S:	+mm +drawing line on map	Although my partner nodded up until now, because she didn't nod this time I kept going, thinking anxiously that maybe she didn't understand
25	T:	okay?	
26	S:	okay	
27	T:	and so you are in second floor now	
28	S:	+mmm +nodding	

Line 23 of this interaction shows that the teacher provided instructions to traverse from the present location back to the stairs and then to the bottom of those stairs, one floor down. The student partner briefly signalled that she heard these instructions in Line 24, and immediately traced the line on her map. The teacher used a comprehension check to ensure that the student understood in Line 25 (*okay?*) and then continued, not with further directions, but instead with another check to make sure that the student had arrived at the second floor. Interestingly, the teacher attended to the absence of nodding, which is marked in dyadic interaction. She reported that her partner had nodded prior to this point, but did not here. She thus interpreted the omission as significant to their interaction. It is possible that the student did not nod because she was focused on drawing the line on the map. It seems also that the teacher's noticing and subsequent anxiety may have led to her decision to check in with the student, in Line 25, and then to seek confirmation of her location, in Line 27, after which the student did nod once more. This again reveals AIDE to be a useful set of processes for accounting for noticing. Although the teachers in this study were able to notice the students' writing on the maps, they apparently did not always interpret such action as signalling comprehension and (as here) relied on other cues as well.

Tasks and Embodiment

The excerpts provided above demonstrate noticing of a variety of nonverbal aspects involved in task performance. These were based on a one-way, listen-and-do type task, involving the participant in the teacher role giving route directions to a listener in the student role. At some level, this task is already quite familiar to the participants, who have spent their entire lives navigating complex physical spaces and interacting with others in order to do so. Nonetheless, there were inherent challenges in using English to communicate all of the directions, the maps were designed to be more or less complex, and time pressure was often a factor.

These results confirm those of previous studies examining embodied interaction in task performance. Previous work had shown that embodiment is used alongside affordances such as task materials (Platt & Brooks, 2008) in multimodal ensembles (Mondada, 2016). In several of these excerpts, nonverbal messages were closely connected with material affordances made available by the seating arrangement and the maps. This was shown in Excerpt 7.6, in which the student audibly drew a line on her map, without nodding, and the teacher subsequently noticed and followed up on this action. The teachers also produced affordances, such as when one teacher audibly tapped on her map (on the table) while counting the stairs to confirm in Excerpt 7.2.

Students in a task may use gaze in the direction of their materials to show that they need to access visual information (Kunitz & Skogmyr Marian, 2017). Interestingly, this option was discouraged by the experimental setup used here; the teacher held the map containing the marked route, and was asked to verbally convey the route to the student, who sat across the table with a small screen between them. Notwithstanding, in Excerpt 7.3, the teacher sought to orient to her students' gaze toward the map, and noticed it as a way of checking comprehension. The teacher in Excerpt 7.4 also clearly indicated the complexities of understanding gaze in task-based interaction. In that example, it occurred to the teacher that the student might have imagined the task as a guided tour through the map buildings, instead of a description of where to draw the line on her map as per the task instructions. In this case, gaze toward the map formed the foundation for deeper noticing of student thinking, which has consequences for language use in interaction. Namely, if a student's gaze implies viewing the physical map as the point of reference, then the expression *go out the door on the left* is appropriate. However, if the student's gaze entails navigation of a different mental model held in the imagination, then *go out the door on your right* is acceptable, too (see Figure 7.1). A consideration of gaze was thus necessary, but hardly sufficient, for effective communication in these tasks.

Finally, the use of several embodied resources simultaneously has been observed during multi-party task-based classroom talk (Lee & Burch, 2017). The present data showed that teachers noticed students' use of ensembles of nonverbal signals. In Excerpt 7.2, the student employed a sequence of gaze – up from the map directly toward the teacher, then down again toward the map – to convey miscomprehension, and after the teacher noticed this and corrected herself, the student nodded to signal understanding. It is noteworthy that this student's completely silent sequence of actions served to initiate a correction by the teacher. Käänta (2014) described such embodied noticing, or visible embodied practices, to perform this function in content and language instruction in the Finnish context. More research is needed to explore students' nonverbal signals in TBLT settings, as well as teacher noticing of these signals.

Summary

Those in the teacher role in this study often attended to their students' use of embodied resources, including facial expressions, gaze and movement. In the latter case, the non-use of recipient nodding was also noticed. These features of communication are familiar enough that PSTs, within the context of a meaningful task, relied on them to interpret the ongoing interaction and make spontaneous decisions. These analyses appeal to the fuller meaning of language teacher noticing, involving attention, interpretation and decision-making. All occurred during engagement. The examples highlighted noticing of:

- a facial expression as miscomprehension
- a facial expression as comprehension
- comprehension via gaze
- options for conveying directions via gaze
- presence of recipient nodding
- absence of recipient nodding

The PST cognitions described here also included actions to convey or clarify intentions in order to support task completion. In this chapter and the next, the analyses consider meaning making within these dyads, whose familiarity may have helped them to communicate. Thus, it remains for future studies to examine how teachers who lack familiarity with their students notice nonverbal signals.

Task-based studies on embodied interaction (e.g. Kunitz & Skogmyr Marian, 2017; Lee & Burch, 2017; Platt & Brooks, 2008) are few and far between, yet they have provided a valuable literature to frame the present findings. As noted above, there is much more to communication than linguistic production, and nonverbal meaning may inform teachers' decision-making during the task-in-process (Breen, 1989; Samuda, 2015) if noticed and interpreted as significant. Another intriguing aspect of these data is that the majority of these excerpts, chosen because they best illustrate the teachers' recall of their noticing of nonverbal resources used by students, were based on video stimuli taken from the field perspective. In this way, perspectival memory seems to have influenced the quality of recalled noticing. Lastly, several of the examples in this chapter came from the same teacher (Excerpts 7.2, 7.5 and 7.6). This teacher seemed to be particularly aware of how facial expressions, eye contact and nodding benefitted her communication with the student. This raises the prospect of sensitivity to embodied communication as a candidate variable in future studies of individual differences among novice language teachers.

8 Noticing of Verbal Resources

Meaning and Usage-Based Learning in Tasks

The construction of meaning during language use is a psycholinguistic process embedded in social interaction. This forms a large and significant part of the psychology of communicative language teaching. Language tasks can be designed to make certain meanings more relevant (Loschky & Bley-Vroman, 1990); however, the task-in-process (Breen, 1989) involves social context, personalization and cooperation, which shape outcomes beyond any designer's control. This chapter first explores several assumptions about meaning making in usage-inspired approaches to language teaching (Tyler & Ortega, 2018), including task-based language teaching (TBLT). The learning opportunities tasks offer include acquisition of constructions, which develops semantic knowledge, and participation in usage events, which constitutes pragmatic knowledge. Then, examples are presented and discussed to demonstrate how pre-service teachers (PSTs) noticed the verbal resources used to convey meaning in tasks.

As in the previous chapter, the data-driven, qualitative analysis uncovered subcategories used by multiple teachers. Here, those subcategories were related to addressing issues in the use of a second language (L2) and engaging in social actions approximated by the task. The specific verbal resources most often used concerned how to (1) explain the meaning of language used and (2) engage in relevant social actions. Some theoretical background is provided to frame this chapter, key constructs are applied to an example, and then several data extracts are analyzed in detail. The chapter concludes with a discussion of the relationship between tasks and language.

The research question was: In what ways did the teachers notice the students' comprehension of semantic (i.e. language usage) and pragmatic (i.e. landmark descriptions and route directions) meaning during interaction?

Meaning in usage-based language learning

The value of tasks for language teaching is often described in terms of their emphasis on meaning (e.g. Bygate *et al.*, 2001; Jackson & Burch, 2017; Prabhu, 1987). However, some applied linguists, who distinguish between semantic and pragmatic meaning, have lamented that the use of the term *meaning* in TBLT is imprecise (Widdowson, 2003: 125). According to this critique, tasks present presumably authentic, pragmatic contexts for language use in the classroom, under the assumption that 'this will activate the acquisition of semantic encoding' (Widdowson, 2003: 128). This assumption deserves closer scrutiny and, indeed, how learners will come to encode meaning in novel forms is a major point of contention. On the one hand, some scholars have consistently argued for brief interventions to focus on form at the point of need (Long, 2015; Long & Robinson, 1998) as a means by which to encourage acquisition of difficult features of the L2. Others suggest, contrary to this, hybrid approaches that incorporate structural syllabi into a task-supported curriculum (R. Ellis, 2018).

In the present study, tasks were viewed as opportunities to comprehend and produce language in a manner that simulates real-world usage. By doing so, it is assumed that learners gradually build knowledge of how to create meaning in the L2, along a continuum of semantic to pragmatic understanding. Several current assumptions are examined next to set the stage for a fuller account of how tasks focus on meaning.

Meaning can refer to the semantic distinction brought about by a single morpheme, such as the negative prefix *a-* in adjectives like *atypical*, *apolitical* and *asymptomatic*. Traditionally, it can refer to the dictionary meaning of such words as *loquacity*, or the characteristic of being extremely talkative. More recently, in cognitive semantics, meaning is instead viewed as encyclopedic. This view asserts that: (1) meaning (i.e. semantic knowledge) is inseparable from usage (i.e. pragmatic, social or cultural knowledge); (2) word knowledge is organized as a network of associations; and (3) encyclopedic and contextual meanings are distinct (Evans & Green, 2006).

Each of these three assertions warrants further attention. The first one posits a continuum between word knowledge (semantic knowledge) and knowledge of use (pragmatic knowledge). Instances of language can thus be analyzed in terms of meaning or use. The recurring construction '*you can see* + noun' from the study data usefully illustrates this point. In terms of word knowledge, viewing this construction schematically, words within the same categories, including '*you will see* + noun' or '*I can see* + noun', are also possible. Semantic knowledge provides distinct understandings of these meanings. Alternatively, the construction can be regarded as a useful formula for assisting another person when giving directions. Any change to the words that comprise it may then imply different contexts of use, but the basic function stays the same. This chapter considers such distinct construals based on what the teachers noticed. It does not seek to separate meaning from use a priori.

Furthermore, the organization of word knowledge is assumed to be built upon associations. Empirical studies by N.C. Ellis *et al.* (2016) offer a sophisticated account of how learning and representation are driven by mechanisms sensitive to association, including chunking, categorization and contingency. Chunking refers to language users' sensitivity to the probability of a sequence of sounds, letters or words occurring. Chunks are often described as bigrams (e.g. *go to* …) or trigrams (e.g. *go to the* …). These are the basis of fluent language performance. Categorization involves comparing new material to instances stored in memory and determining their degree of similarity. For instance, the verb *go* was frequently used in this study to express motion, and it is likely that participants compared other verbs used (e.g. *walk, proceed*) to this one, which may strengthen the representation of newly encountered items. Finally, contingency means that cues vary in how reliably they predict outcomes. N.C. Ellis *et al.* demonstrated this in two ways: constructions may predict verbs and verbs may predict constructions. That is, given the construction 'verb *across* noun', one can predict that the frequent verbs *go* or *walk* will appear. Note that these verbs occur in many different constructions, so they do not reliably predict this construction. However, given the verb *skid*, one can be more certain that the construction 'verb *across* noun' will occur (e.g. *skid across the road*). More predictable associations are easier to learn (Ellis *et al.*, 2016: 91–92). One role of the teacher in TBLT is to provide language input to activate these processes.

Based on Evans and Green's third assertion, context guides understanding in the case of several possible meanings. For example, in the utterance *go through the building*, the speaker's intended meaning can be either (a) to continue on a trajectory leading into and outside of (past) the building, or (b) to continue on a path that leads to another (here, unnamed) location within or attached to the building. Context reduces ambiguity. The task materials used here, as part of the context, served to constrain such interpretations. Note, too, that alternate constructions contain nuances, as in *make your way through the building*, which conveys a sense of creating a path and moving along it toward a desired goal, based on the *way* construction (Goldberg, 2019). This example illustrates how language users may offer various construals of the actions inherent to tasks.

To summarize the argument so far, in TBLT and other usage-inspired approaches to language teaching (Tyler & Ortega, 2018), semantic and pragmatic meaning are closely linked, although learners, teachers and researchers may choose to explicitly focus on one or the other, at different times. How learners come to encode meaning in ways that are relevant to communication in an L2 during tasks may depend as much on their exposure to rich input and the activation of cognitive processes (through chunking, categorization and contingency learning) as it does on negotiation of meaning (through clarification requests, confirmation checks and comprehension checks) or teacher-initiated focus on form (through recasts or metalinguistic explanations). Furthermore, task materials subtly constrain the meaning of various constructions (Eskildsen, 2008; Goldberg,

Table 8.1 Usage-based L2 learning opportunities within meaning-focused tasks

Learning metaphor	Linguistic category	Knowledge type
ACQUISITION	Constructions	Semantic
PARTICIPATION	Usage events	Pragmatic

2006) that offer multiple interpretations. The use of semiotic resources as well, such as maps, is essential to understanding meaning making (Hall, 2019). Task roles indelibly shape the social construction of meaning in which learners participate, and so, naturally, these too must be considered as a factor influencing choices used to encode meaning. From these perspectives, the emphasis on meaning in tasks can be more clearly articulated and understood.

The usage-based framework adopted here is particularly helpful because it invokes two distinct metaphors for learning: acquisition and participation (Ortega, 2011; Sfard, 1998). As Langacker argued, language learners need 'sufficient exposure to representative use of a given unit ... in the context of meaningful exchanges approximating socially and culturally normal usage events' (Langacker, 2008: 81; see also Eskildsen, 2008). Tasks provide a context for acquisition of the units, or L2 constructions, as well as enabling participation in usage events. Furthermore, researchers have lauded usage-based approaches as a means of acknowledging the complementarity of cognitive processes and social practices in L2 learning (Eskildsen & Cadierno, 2015). These are inextricably involved in the accumulation of semantic and pragmatic knowledge (see Table 8.1).

Prelude to the excerpts

This section builds directly on the previous one, but focuses more tightly on concepts and definitions that are specifically relevant to the data analyses presented after it. The examples in this chapter show how the teachers attended to learner comprehension during attempts to construct mutual understanding of language usage, landmark descriptions and route directions. The first of these categories concerns instances in which the participants were concerned with co-constructing semantic meaning, while the second and third clearly exhibit pragmatic meaning, in the dual sense of how language is used to perform its social function of giving directions but also of how teachers may be called upon to model such knowledge.

The semantic knowledge encoded in language depends on a detailed representation that includes mappings between form and meaning (or constructions), as well as connections between words. These connections may occur as collocations, associations, synonyms or antonyms. On the other hand, pragmatic knowledge enacted through language is a matter of doing things with words, which from the teacher's point of view includes explaining language and using it to facilitate completion of a task in an appropriate way.

As an example, the following data from Jackson and Cho (2018) are presented. This example occurred during a classroom demonstration of a task in which groups of students each analyzed a portion of the lyrics from the song 'A Whole New World', featured in the Disney film *Aladdin*.

Example 8.1

		Classroom interaction	*Recall comments*
01	T:	okay, so Section C, if there's any (0.7) or, what kinda things (came up in your discussion)?	
02	S1:	um:: he's actually thinking he: you know, he wants to see: he wants to explore the world together (.) like he kinda knows that there's stuff out there and he wants to spend (his life) together and then(.) um (.) the red letter part?	
03	T:	mm-hm	
04	S1:	um (2.7) I just think maybe it's like he's just saying everything's great and	
05	T:	[yeah do you know what red letter do you do you guys know what red letter means? What she means by red letter?	
06	S2:	+*shaking head* 'no'	One of the students
07	T:	so red letter is I forget which um: which people (it started with) but it refers to like important days on the calendar, like Christmas, Thanksgiving, anything, any like significant and important days	pointed out the red letter the red letter phrase and so I asked the students if anyone knew I assumed no one knew and they didn't so I explained to them what it was so that they kinda understood.

The teacher here was focused on explaining the meaning of 'Every moment red letter', in the song, which is a lyrical usage of the phrase 'a red-letter day'. The interactional moves he used positioned him as having epistemic authority (Gray & Morton, 2018) to guide the analysis and offer deeper explanation. It shows the teacher first eliciting more, via the continuer *mm-hm* (Line 03), then checking whether intervention is called for

(Line 05), and only after Student 2's embodied confirmation (Line 06), proceeding with the explanation (Line 07). Importantly, this practice of leading the task from behind (Samuda, 2001) relied on the teacher's semantic knowledge of this construction in the target language and in these lyrics. To achieve this, the teacher relied on his own proficiency, experience and confidence regarding the task content (which he himself chose) and procedures.

In contrast to the teacher above, the PSTs in this study were somewhat less prepared. In the following sections, semantic mappings are the focus of Excerpts 8.1 through 8.4, while pragmatic aspects are the focus of Excerpts 8.5 and 8.6. For an overview of the method, see the previous chapter and Appendix C (Transcription Conventions).

Constructional Meaning

By definition, tasks emphasize meaning (Bygate *et al.*, 2001). This emphasis comes about through, for example, the requirement to exchange meaningful information. In cases where meaning is not fully understood, tasks create a space for negotiation to understand relevant form–meaning mappings, or constructions (Goldberg, 2006). Interactional processes occurring within tasks therefore promote acquisition of lexis and grammar (Keck *et al.*, 2006). The kinds of constructions that teachers and students notice, and their relevance to the communication, may make task-based interaction selectively facilitative of acquisition (Sato, 1986). This section examines several aspects of constructions that were problematized during the task-in-process, from the perspective of teacher noticing. These included introducing new constructions and repairing ambiguous or infelicitous ones.

Beginning with Excerpt 8.1, it is not uncommon for non-native English speaking teachers (NNESTs) to express concern over the plausibility of communicative teaching due to their perceptions of their own abilities in the L2 (Machida, 2019). Such concerns may be partly offset by considering how teachers self-repair as part of their repertoire when conveying task-essential meanings. In this case, the teacher's future goal was employment at a junior or senior high school. At the time of the study, he was a 4th year student in the English Department. He had not taken the practicum course but had some teaching experience. The teacher and student in this example were somewhat familiar with one another. This excerpt comes from the Campus task. Their performance on this task was given a score of 5, which means that the student had completed the entire route, making errors that he subsequently corrected.

The excerpt focuses on a portion of the interaction during which the teacher guided the student through a building. The teacher's utterance in Line 15, particularly the usage of *farest*, seemed to give rise to his noticing of the student's miscomprehension. Yet, even if *farthest* had been used here, it is possible that further negotiation may have been required for the

Excerpt 8.1 Noticing miscomprehension of one's usage (Session 1, Campus task, Observer perspective)

	Task interaction	Recall comments
15	T: so go through the building toward far(est) entrance	
16	S: uhh (maybe) there's three entrance, right?	
17	T: umm no there is there're one two three four entrance (except) you you entered the entrance which you entered so left side left side go over there and (just right side is below the entrance) go the opposite side from entrance you entered you can see some trees and kind of garden, I think	My partner didn't really understand the expression I used there, so I looked for a different expression, and I had him look at how many doors there were on one side, and I explained using the number
18	S: mm-hm	

student to fully grasp the intended meaning. This can be seen in Line 16, where the student postponed the direction-giving activity by seeking confirmation of the number of entrances (rather than asking for clarification of the meaning of *farest*). This presented the opportunity for the teacher to elaborate in much greater detail, in Line 17. After this detailed explanation, which links the student's previous position to the updated goal, the student replied *mm-hm* to indicate understanding.

This teacher's comment put the initial focus on his own usage, however. In this comment, the teacher assumed that his partner had not understood the expression he used and he thus sought an alternative means of conveying the directions. This entailed enumerating the entrances, which might have been sufficient to explain. There is additionally a further shift in the meaning resources deployed, from the intended *go through the building toward the farthest entrance* to *go [to] the opposite side from entrance you entered*, which situates the goal with respect to the starting point of the movement, locating it specifically as the opposite entrance (see Eskildsen & Wagner, 2015). This utterance is not more target-like because it omits the path marker *to*, but it does frame the goal with respect to a previous, known location. In this way, it assists the student's comprehension. Also helpfully, the teacher goes on to describe a nearby landmark (the garden). In combination, these semantic elements seem more than sufficient to guide the student. To summarize using AIDE, the teacher, upon attending to his usage and interpreting this as problematic for the student's comprehension, subsequently decided to focus on providing a more elaborate description of where to go. Under a usage-based account, this responsiveness could benefit student acquisition.

Noticing of Verbal Resources 115

At other times, teachers may be concerned that students will not understand even usage that is perfectly accurate. This is a reasonable concern but, if the task is viewed as a process, it poses more opportunities than obstacles for learning. In Excerpt 8.2, the teacher was a 3rd year student in English whose career aim was to teach in a junior high school setting. She had no practicum experience but had some outside teaching experience as well as study abroad experience. Her partner was a 4th year English student with whom she was not familiar. Here, they were working on the Station task, which they performed perfectly, leading to a score of 6.

Excerpt 8.2 Noticing usage of a new form for an understood meaning (Session 3, Station task, Field perspective)

```
           Task interaction                    Recall comments
01  T:  so (.) please go straight
        and go through the
        crosswalk
02  S:  cross
03  T:        [crosswalk um white       Because I looked up
        +white lines                    'crosswalk' in
        +RH 'line' gesture              advance, I knew but
                                        because my partner
                                        didn't know, at first
                                        I wondered how I
                                        should explain
```

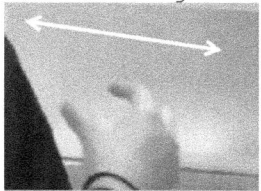

```
04  S:  white lines
05  T:  yes white lines
06  S:  yes
07  T:  and go toward train station
08  S:  from right?
09  T:  yeah turn right go into
        train station
10  S:  okay
```

At the beginning of the Station task, the materials depicted a crosswalk, through which the route proceeded. This referent is commonly understood, although few teacher participants (three out of 16) used the word *crosswalk*, despite being encouraged to look up any useful lexical items during the planning phase for this simple task. In two cases when it was used, the students understood the word immediately. In this excerpt, however, the student did not, as the teacher noticed. Their conversation opened in Line 01 with the teacher's instruction, which the student responded to in Line 02 by segmenting her utterance (*cross*), which initiated a repair sequence. The teacher then repeated the word, paused and described the referent as *white lines*, also gesturing with her hand to indicate their spatial characteristics (see Line 03). The student then repeated this part of the teacher's utterance, which the teacher confirmed (Lines 04–05). In Line 06, the student said *yes* to show his understanding.

The teacher's comment on this episode showed, to once again refer to AIDE, that she paid explicit attention to her use of *crosswalk*, having looked it up during the planning time. In the comment, she provided the interpretation that the student did not know the word, and noted that this required a decision regarding how to explain it. Her use of *um* as a filler in Line 03 suggests that she paused to consider this decision briefly before using two strategies in synchrony. One was to use circumlocution, essentially describing the crosswalk in terms of its physical features: white lines painted upon the road. Another was an iconic gesture (Kendon, 2004) that, as depicted in the excerpt, represented the orientation and length of the lines. It is not clear, however, that the student saw her gesture, because it was partly concealed behind the screen. Besides, the student continued looking downward at his map during this exchange. Nonetheless, the combined deployment of these strategies, as well as her intention to use the word, suggest a flexible communicative repertoire (Hall, 2019) that can be adapted for the purposes of task-based interaction in classroom settings. Such usage can drive meaning acquisition (Eskildsen & Cadierno, 2015; Tyler & Ortega, 2018).

In contrast to Excerpt 8.2, the next excerpt shows how usage is not simply a matter of mutually understanding referents via a common set of linguistic resources. Instead, Excerpt 8.3 reveals how, given the inherent ambiguity of form, joint attention to context across dialogue fosters the co-construction of meaning. The two participants were both female 3rd year English majors. The teacher sought to eventually teach high school and had some teaching experience but had not completed her practicum course. They indicated that they were slightly familiar with one another. Here, they performed the Campus task, which they completed without error in the allotted time. The section of the map they were discussing is shown in Figure 8.1.

The teacher's instructions in Lines 21–25 appear to be clear and precise. The student signals her understanding twice while listening to them (Lines 22 and 24). Then, in Line 25, when the teacher asked the student to exit the building, it prompted a repair by the student in Line 26, where she asked, *from the door?* The teacher repeated this utterance, as if simply confirming that having the student exit by the door was her intention. In Line 28, the student then appeared to seek confirmation of the position of the door, by asking whether the teacher had construed the map as depicting one or two buildings. The teacher confirmed that it was two buildings (in reality, they are two separate buildings connected by a walkway) and, after pausing, began to explain where to go. This explanation was completed by her partner, in Line 30, who was quick to confirm her

Excerpt 8.3 Noticing ambiguous usage of a form–meaning mapping (Session 5, Campus task, Observer perspective)

		Task interaction	Recall comments
21	T:	enter this and walk through the building	
22	S:	mm-hm	
23	T:	until the end	Here I said 'end' to indicate the last building of two buildings, but it seemed it was understood by my partner as 'until the end of one building'
24	S:	alright okay	
25	T:	okay and get out from the building	
26	S:	from the door?	
27	T:	from the door	
28	S:	is there one or is there two buildings?	
29	T:	two buildings (.) and go	
30	S:	[okay so I can go this whole way?	
31	T:	yes	
32	S:	into the other one?	
33	T:	yes and get out	
34	S:	from the side which close to the carve ((curve))	
35	T:	yes and you get out	
36	S:	[okay	

understanding that she was to go through both buildings. The student also seemed to attend to the two exits in the building on the left-hand side, by confirming that the teacher intended for her to take the exit close to the curved wall of this building (see Line 34 and Figure 8.1).

The teacher's comment again provides support for the AIDE framework: she paid attention to the student's interpretation of her use of *until the end* in relating these directions. She had clearly meant for it to indicate the end of the conjoined buildings, but was correct in interpreting the interaction as involving some additional work. As shown, her decision to offer further explanation set off a sequence of several student-initiated repairs. Teachers occasionally omitted details when explaining where to go, perhaps because they saw the directions marked on their materials, or simply because they assumed student familiarity. However, the students did not see any of the route information and thus had to rely on the

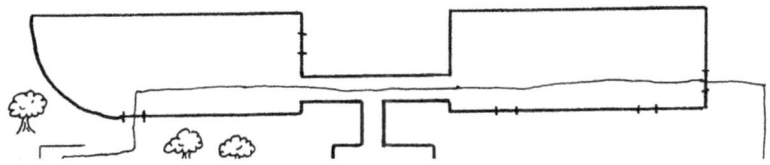

Figure 8.1 Detail of the Campus task map (student version)

teachers, as well as context cues from their materials, to gradually build a mental map of the directions while listening. This might have made them seem cautious to the teachers. In this light, the teacher's initial instructions (*walk through the building ... until the end*) were doubly ambiguous. The preposition *through* can be interpreted as either meaning *through the building to its other side* or *through the building to the next building*. Also, *the end* (in contrast to *its end*) may mean either the end of the building or the endpoint of the path one is moving along. The solution that was adopted here was to resolve this ambiguity through student–teacher interaction. This enabled both participants to share closer attention to the context (i.e. the spatial arrangement of map elements), which facilitated understanding.

As seen in the previous excerpt, forms can have multiple meanings. Conversely, several forms exist for very similar meanings. This is something that PSTs should take note of during task-based interaction, as Excerpt 8.4 illustrates. In this example, two female teachers-in-training, both of whom were 3rd year undergraduates in the English department, carried out the Campus task. They were familiar with one another. They had not done the practicum, but the teacher had some paid teaching experience. Despite having struggled with some of the other tasks, they performed this task well, and it was scored as a 6. Relevant to this example, they had performed the Museum task, which had the word *path* written on the teacher and student maps, just prior to the Campus task described here.

Excerpt 8.4 Noticing usage of two forms for one meaning (Session 11, Campus task, Observer perspective)

		Task interaction	*Recall comments*
42	T:	go out at the ((laughter)) right left side door (.) and maybe you can see some trees or flowers and please walk on the street. You can see this street?	
43	S:	besides the tree and flowers?	Getting out, when I said 'please go through the street', the word 'path' didn't come to mind so I said 'street', but it helped me when my partner said 'path'
44	T:	yeah, yeah, yeah (.) in tree and flower? I don't know. Maybe you can see the shape of the square street	
45	S:	ah the little path?	
46	T:	yeah mmm and go straight and ple:ase	

In Line 42, the teacher directed the student to exit a building, and in doing so referred to a part of the campus as a *street*. This section of the actual campus, which both participants were likely familiar with, would be more aptly described as a *path* or *walkway*, owing to its size and the fact that it is open only to pedestrian traffic. In Line 43, the student initiated a confirmation of the location, using another landmark, which the teacher seemed to recognize in Line 44, although she may have misheard slightly, judging by her use of *I don't know*. She then continued to describe the area as a *square street*, seemingly making an effort to be more precise. Then the student, in Line 45, used *ah*, a change of state token (Schegloff, 2007), and added the description, *the little path*, with rising intonation. The teacher confirmed this description in the next line.

During the recall interview, the teacher commented on this episode. She first admitted to having trouble recalling the word *path* for this location, implying that she had attended to and was aware that *street* was not the ideal word choice but instead an approximation of the precise referent. She then offered an interpretation, noting that it helped her that her student partner used *path*. Here, the decision to use *path* emerged from the interaction; it was not entirely her own. This suggests that processes underlying AIDE may be co-constructed by the student(s) and teacher. Furthermore, the interpretation here seemed to occur after this decision, which should be taken as an indication of the dynamic nature of teacher noticing.

As noted, they had encountered the written word *path* in previous task materials. Then, the teacher had used it in constructions such as *going to the path* and *turn at the corner of the path*. To some degree, she had associated it with other location words such as *road* and *street*, but had not used it in other constructions. For instance, she did not say, by analogy with her utterance in Line 42, *walk on the path*, at any time. This points to the need for greater exposure through extended usage leading to the activation of mechanisms such as categorization (Ellis *et al.*, 2016) to support usage-based learning by PSTs. If these individuals can foster their development through usage-based approaches, they should become more likely to believe that their future students can, as well.

Landmark Descriptions

In usage-inspired approaches to language instruction, including TBLT, pragmatic meaning is invoked through explicit reference to learner participation in contextualized social practices (Eskildsen & Cadierno, 2015; Tyler & Ortega, 2018). TBLT accomplishes this goal by employing pedagogic tasks corresponding to target tasks, or things people do in relevant social contexts outside the instructional setting, such as making travel reservations or hiring foreign workers (Long, 2015). In this chapter, the term *usage event* was introduced earlier to refer to meaningful communication that arises in connection with social and cultural norms (Langacker, 2008). Notably, a usage event may typically evoke certain constructions and it can occur either inside or outside a classroom; that is, it is a linguistic rather than a pedagogic construct.

120 Part 2: A Study of Pre-Service Teachers

The specific usage event (or target task, if one prefers to hew to TBLT jargon) examined in this study was giving street directions. Essentially, this event involves conveying one's mental model for the purpose of establishing joint attention to spatial features germane to navigation (Denis, 2018; Tomasello, 2003; Tomasello & Carpenter, 2007). In the abstract, such events may be constituted by means of various semiotic resources, such as whistling, wayfinding, coordinate systems or digital maps – human culture is replete with examples of navigational resources. Thus, the present study constituted only one culturally situated approach to direction giving. The teacher explained the route to the student using a printed map. The reason for this was that English teachers in Japan are likely to encounter direction-giving map tasks in the form presented to them here in textbooks. Furthermore, the explicit conventions adopted by these participants followed from the task instructions to use English to convey the directions, which led the teachers to notice pragmatic features of their task performances that can be generally classified as (1) landmark descriptions and (2) route directions. This section focuses on the former, while the next section covers the latter.

Direction giving often involves describing landmarks. As noted, the tasks here varied according to the participants' familiarity with the landmarks, with consequences for the quantity of information needing to be conveyed. Excerpt 8.5 comes from a female teacher who was a 3rd year English major interested in teaching at the high school level. She and her

Excerpt 8.5 Noticing of landmark details (Session 15, Campus task, Observer perspective)

	Task interaction	*Recall comments*
15 T:	and go to building four, which is the very left and above	
16 S:	you go through +narrow? +LH pinch	

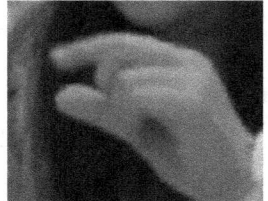

17 T:	um yeah you can go through	Then, the narrow, I noticed that I forgot to mention the narrow path. Then, I had her pass through, and had her get out of Building four
18 S:	Building four?	
19 T:	yeah (.) and then turn left and go out building four	

partner were somewhat acquainted. The teacher had no study abroad experience, although the student had some. The data here reveal an instance of a student and teacher collaboratively noticing landmark details. This data come from the Campus task, which was scored as complete with no errors (i.e. a score of 6).

In Line 15 of this excerpt, the teacher gave her directions using precise language consisting of a locally recognized conventional expression for the location, *Building 4*, and its position relative to the campus as depicted in the materials (it was shown in the upper-left corner of the map). In Line 16, the student initiates a repair using both verbal and nonverbal means. Specifically, she related this to the teacher as *you go through narrow*, combined with an iconic gesture to depict the location she was referring to. This area is situated along the usual route one would take when going from Building 1 to Building 4 (see again Figure 8.1). The student's gesture was clearly visible from the teacher's side of the table. In Line 17, the teacher repeated the student's use of *through*, which implies a narrow space, using the modal construction *you can go through*, to confirm. Afterwards, the student checked that Building 4 was indeed the goal, and the teacher confirmed this and proceeded with her directions.

The teacher referred to this episode in her comment, stating that she herself had forgotten to mention the narrow pathway. It is interesting that this teacher chose to construe this as a matter of forgetting, when one could assert that such small details as pointed out by the student here are not entirely necessary. Yet the student did make the information relevant using both verbal and embodied resources. Part of the issue may have been the means to refer to this location in English. The teacher's original comment used a generic word in Japanese (*michi*, or *path*) which neither the student nor the teacher used in their dialogue. The English noun *path* was avoided entirely, as it could be understood from the context and the student's gesture. As for the teacher's decision-making process, she followed up in the same comment by noting how the navigation proceeded after the student was guided to Building 4, thus keeping the focus strictly on getting the task done. Although not entirely clear, it is also possible that the teacher noticed a gap (Schmidt & Frota, 1986; Swain, 2000) in terms of her ability to describe the path, which the student effectively conveyed via multimodal communication.

Route Directions

In addition to landmark descriptions, another key aspect of direction giving is describing routes. The final excerpt in this chapter concerns this aspect. In Excerpt 8.6, the difference between the spatial cognition, or mental models, of the teacher and participant is again the focus. Both participants were male, 3rd year English majors, who intended to teach high school. They had some practical teaching experience but had not

Excerpt 8.6 Noticing of alternate routes (Session 10, Museum task, Observer perspective)

	Task interaction	Recall comments
03 T:	and then you're standing museum area please enter the museum	
04 S:	okay	
05 T:	and please go up the stairs to third floor	
06 S:	okay but there are two entrance maybe	When I was asked 'there are two entrances but which should I go in?' I was surprised like 'oh you ask that point'. I didn't expect that. Then I was like 'how can I say the front side?' and I said 'nearest one' and my partner said 'first one', so I thought 'oh that's okay'.
07 T:	okay please go to (1.5) the nearest one	
08 S:	+RH head scratch +nearest one?	
09 T:	yeah	
10 S:	ah first one?	
11 T:	yeah first one	
12 S:	first one and go to ah third floor	
13 T:	third floor (.) yeah	
14 S:	okay	

entered the practicum phase of the program. They were familiar with one another. This excerpt comes from the Museum task, which they did not score well on (1 out of 6).

In Line 03, the teacher used an expression to confirm his partner's location (*you're standing museum area*) and directed him to enter the museum building (see Figure 8.2). The student acknowledged this as the goal in Line 04. The teacher then went on to ask the student to go to the third floor (i.e. the roof), in Line 05. The student then initiated a repair sequence in Line 06, by noting that there were two entrances. The teacher replied to this in the next turn, pausing before identifying the correct

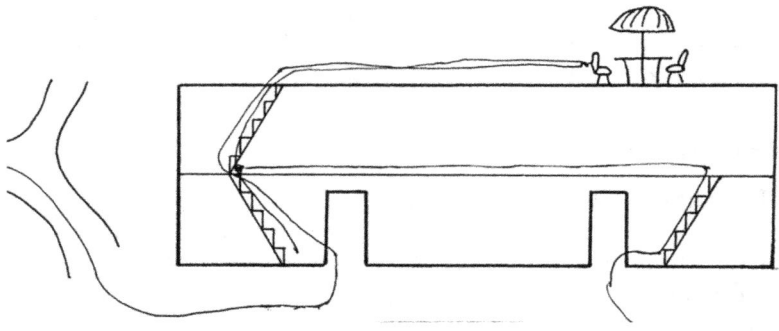

Figure 8.2 Detail of the Museum task map (student version)

entrance as the *nearest one* (Line 07). This segment of the teacher's utterance was then repeated with rising intonation by the student in Line 08, accompanied by a head scratch that the teacher did not seem to notice because he was looking down at his map. The teacher then affirmed his word choice. In Line 10, the student used a change of state token, then an equivalent expression: *ah first one?* The teacher confirmed this in Line 11 and then the student resumed the activity of navigating the building in Line 12.

The teacher's useful but arguably imprecise confirmation of the student's location (*the museum area*) may be partly to blame for the repair sequence in Lines 06–12. Furthermore, the teacher's use of *the nearest one* in Line 07 is indeterminate. It can be understood as the nearest entrance to the front side of the building (see recall comment) or the nearest entrance to the stairs leading all the way up to the rooftop (see Line 05). If interpreted as the nearest entrance to the front, then ambiguity arises as to which end of the building is to be regarded as the front. Also, *nearest one* could have been intended to refer to the entrance nearest the student's location on the map as understood by the teacher. In any case, the student's questioning of this information in Line 08 was clear enough. The teacher's recall comment indicates that, returning once more to AIDE, he paid attention to the student's question, interpreted the question as a chance to consider alternative spatial expressions to improve comprehension and decided, based on the student's suggestion, that *first one* and *nearest one* were equally acceptable.

Tasks and Language

By applying a usage-based approach, this chapter considered how tasks facilitate acquisition and participation through the lens of PSTs' noticing of constructions within usage events. It was recognized at the start that tasks are more than just blueprints. Task processes emerge from social interaction between teachers and students. Usage-inspired language teaching approaches, such as TBLT, share the idea that learning comes from engaging in language use in interaction. During these tasks the teachers attended to and understood as relevant a range of interactional processes. In response, they executed principled actions to support the student. Only when the teacher and student are experiencing the same thing at the same time, and they know together that they are (Tomasello & Carpenter, 2007: 121), can teachers effectively intervene to focus on language or offer procedural assistance.

Firstly, some things they noticed concerned form–meaning mappings. Excerpt 8.1, which dealt with noticing one's own usage, showed how self-repair functions as a response to miscomprehension, whether it is due to error (i.e. *far(est) entrance*) or ambiguity (i.e. the precise number of entrances). Excerpt 8.3, dealing with a motion verb, showed how the ambiguity of the entire motion verb construction (*walk through the building ... until the end*) led the teacher to notice the student's misunderstanding, resulting in further discussion. Semantic elements including the aforementioned ones, as well as certain lexical items (*crosswalk, path*), were considered first in this chapter. This evidence suggests that tasks may provide contexts for the acquisition of semantic encoding (Widdowson, 2003) via interactional processes stemming from teacher noticing.

Secondly, this chapter went further to consider pragmatic aspects. In these tasks, the teachers were asked to give directions, which is a cognitive and social activity broadly relevant to the goals of the participants in this study. The teachers thus noticed aspects of the activity toward the other side of the semantic–pragmatic continuum as well. These included gaps in the description of landmarks and routes. Excerpts 8.5 and 8.6 illustrated how interaction with the students provided feedback to the teachers on their ongoing performance of the task. This may reflect its authenticity. Such participation in usage events, which evokes but does not predetermine language usage, is fundamentally different from leading drills or doing exercises. These PSTs shared insights into this difference. In general, their comments conveyed the need for continuous monitoring and ongoing adjustments during the task-in-process, which cannot be accomplished without the teacher's close attention to how students think and act.

Lastly, Excerpt 8.5 also raised the fascinating possibility of overlapping teacher noticing and the noticing of gaps in L2 performance (Schmidt & Frota, 1986; Swain, 2000) by the same individual. In the present study, this possibility is consistent with the participants' hybrid identities as both learners and PSTs of English.

Summary

To summarize, teachers need to work with contingencies that arise from the task-in-process to enhance the effectiveness of tasks (Samuda, 2015). This chapter was based on analyses of the task interaction, focusing on how teachers noticed students' understanding of semantic and pragmatic meaning. Usage-based linguistics provided a helpful theoretical perspective owing to its affinities with task-based approaches. These include: a primary focus on meaning; a recognition of active use of language as a key developmental mechanism; and equal weight on the importance of acquiring constructions and participating in usage. The data excerpts in this chapter brought to light the psychological realities of PSTs' concerns with making meaning, in the case of:

- miscomprehension of their own usage (*farest*)
- a new form for an understood meaning (*crosswalk*)
- ambiguous form–meaning mappings (*walk ... until the end*)
- two forms for one meaning (*street* versus *path*)

They also noticed pragmatic issues arising from the map gap tasks, in particular:

- landmark details
- alternate routes

In closing, because it involved using the language, the task-in-process was emergent. Throughout their engagement in this experience, the teacher and student together became aware of constructions and usage relevant to their shared goal. Such awareness builds knowledge of semantic or pragmatic features and enables learning by doing.

9 Noticing and Pre-Service Teachers

Overview of the Main Findings

In this chapter, I will revisit the research questions, seek to integrate the findings reported in previous chapters and suggest implications within the context of the study. In doing so, I will be looking back again. As noted earlier, revisiting prior thoughts naturally involves lapses and distortions in perception. Yet, when teachers reflect on their noticing, they may also better understand their students, develop their own identities or find ways to manage their emotions. Likewise, revisiting the results of this mixed-methods study presents an opportunity for positive transformation.

In this section, the main findings will first be reviewed. Then, in the next section, the integration of these findings will be considered in order to reflect on the nature of language teacher noticing. This chapter will also begin to address the theoretical issue of whether the idea of teacher noticing, as a multifaceted construct involving (1) attending to key aspects of teaching situations, (2) carefully interpreting the details of such interactions and (3) making decisions that potentially further learning and/or participation (Philipp *et al.*, 2017; Sherin, 2017; van Es & Sherin, 2002; see Chapter 3), can advance research on the psychology of language teaching, alongside views on teacher cognition and reflection. This issue is taken up again in Chapter 10. As a reminder, the mnemonic AIDE is used to specify these processes and their to link to engagement.

Do task complexity and perspectival memory affect recall of teacher noticing?

In Chapter 6, the teachers' stimulated recall data were used to quantify the number of recall comments and noticing instances. Noticing instances were coded by two trained raters based on a careful operationalization of the construct. Two hypotheses were put forward to inform the research question stated above. For the sake of convenience, they are repeated here:

- **Hypothesis 1**: The means for recall comments and noticing instances will be higher for complex tasks than for simple tasks. This hypothesis is grounded in the assumption that, in line with the Cognition Hypothesis (Robinson, 2015), complex tasks make cognitive demands on attention beyond those of simple tasks. These demands arose, in the present study, from the manipulation of planning time, the number of map elements and the familiarity of the map locations.
- **Hypothesis 2**: The means for recall comments and noticing instances will be higher using the field perspective than when using the observer perspective. This hypothesis assumes, following Miller (2011: 61), that teacher (field) perspective videos reveal 'a far more complex and dynamic scene than that captured by traditional video' and also shift the focus of the recall away from the teacher and toward engagement with the student, which was incorporated into the definition of language teacher noticing employed in this study.

Hypothesis 1 was supported in the case of recall comments. These were significantly greater in complex tasks. However, there was no significant difference in noticing instances between complex and simple tasks. As for Hypothesis 2, no statistical support was found for either recall comments or noticing instances. As shown in Figure 6.1, the mean scores were in the hypothesized direction, and they seem to suggest the possibility of an interaction whereby the effect of perspective may be larger in complex tasks.

What do teachers notice about students' use of embodied resources?

Chapter 7 used the map, interaction and stimulated recall data. The approach was inspired by multimodal conversation analysis (CA; Mondada, 2016). Data excerpts were selected to illustrate how teachers attended to students' use of nonverbal resources for constructing meaning. Each excerpt consisted of a noticing instance and a transcription of the interaction that prompted it. Based on a comprehensive review of the data, it was shown that teachers noticed how students used facial expressions, gaze and nodding, which are aspects of embodied interaction, to communicate. The teacher participants reported noticing of:

- a facial expression as miscomprehension
- a facial expression as comprehension
- comprehension via gaze
- options for conveying directions via gaze
- presence of recipient nodding
- absence of recipient nodding

The conversational data lent further support to these instances of noticing by contextualizing them in tasks. The AIDE model, originally developed within the math and science literature to account for teacher noticing, was supported in the case of these pre-service teachers (PSTs). For instance, Excerpt 7.1 revealed that the teacher participant attended to his partner's facial expression, interpreted it as a lack of understanding of the word *diagonal* and reformulated the expression, which suggests that he was acting upon the knowledge that comprehensible input is necessary for second language (L2) learning and performance (e.g. Long, 2015). His reformulation also used a hand gesture, highlighting the role of embodied communication in language teacher discourse (Hall & Looney, 2019).

The focus on such discourse features addressed a gap in the studies of how language teaching depends heavily on nonverbal resources. By examining whether and how PSTs attend to and use such cues, one can glean information about strategies for managing the task-in-process (Breen, 1989). Evidently, these PSTs used a wide array of nonverbal strategies to understand students' thinking. These were coupled with language, as in the case of Excerpt 7.3, where a teacher used the utterance *you see the movie on the right side* to check that the student's gaze was directed to the appropriate map location. It was also noted in this chapter that most of the excerpts were based on video stimuli taken from the field perspective. It can thus be suggested that video stimuli may influence teacher noticing in terms of its quality. It seems obvious that field perspectives may orient one to students' nonverbal messages because it is only from this angle that they can be seen. It was also noted that sensitivity to embodied communication may constitute an individual difference among novice language teachers.

What do teachers notice about students' use of verbal resources?

Chapter 8, like the chapter before it, used the recall, map and interaction data. Again, it acknowledged that the task-in-process is emergent. The language resources negotiated in a task are not entirely predictable from its blueprint. Following usage-based views, data were selected that illustrated semantic and pragmatic meanings that were problematized during the interaction. The following semantic features were the focus of shared attention during the task performances:

- miscomprehension of the teacher's usage
- a new form for an understood meaning
- ambiguous form–meaning mappings
- two forms for one meaning

The tasks provided a context for teachers' observations of student comprehension of their own language usage. In some cases, teachers quickly oriented to the possibility that the student might not immediately comprehend the meaning of certain items (e.g. *crosswalk*). In other cases, they encountered most likely unanticipated miscomprehension (e.g. *walk ... to the end*). In still other cases, the students themselves offered more suitable alternatives to the language used (*street* versus *path*). Collectively, these examples show that students' use of verbal resources can be quite fluid in task-based interaction, and thus teachers must also respond flexibly. The teachers furthermore noticed pragmatic issues arising from the map task content:

- landmark descriptions
- route checking

These examples showed how teachers need to be familiar with the usage events associated with tasks, given the authentic nature of communication that tasks promote. It is worth recalling that aspects of the design (e.g. +/− familiarity, +/− elements, +/− planning time) influenced performance. On the one hand, task design may place demands on teachers in terms of their familiarity with a specific location and the amount of planning time they make use of. On the other hand, additional demands arise in terms of communicating to another person precisely, in real time, how to navigate a route. In Chapter 8, the latter were shown to involve students' spontaneous embodied and verbal responses which were at times unanticipated, or referred to details that the teacher had not considered beforehand.

Again, there was clear support for the close coupling of three processes: attention, interpretation and decision-making during engagement (AIDE). Whereas in Excerpt 7.1 the teacher reported noticing miscomprehension of the word *diagonal* based on his student's facial expression, in Excerpt 8.2 the teacher's noticing involved anticipating a lack of understanding of the word *crosswalk*, combined with the student's partial repetition (*cross-*). These examples highlight noticing of nonverbal versus verbal resources for negotiating meaning, respectively. Regardless of differences in the cues they attended to, however, these teachers both interpreted the evidence for a lack of understanding as important to the task-in-process. They similarly gave thought to how to explain the word in question and intentionally followed up with interactional moves designed to assist comprehension. This indicates that distinct teacher perceptions can give rise to similar actions, when common learning principles are applied in decision-making.

Integrating the Findings

The final research question addressed in this book is: how can the qualitative and quantitative results presented be integrated to form an evidence-based understanding of language teacher noticing? A defining trait of mixed-methods research (MMR) is that quantitative and qualitative results are brought together to form an overall integration of the findings.

As noted before, drawing together quantitative and qualitative strands, with the purpose of understanding their complementarity, is called legitimation (Brown, 2014; Onwuegbuzie & Johnson, 2006). This can then lead to meta-inferences, or inferences at the integration level of MMR (Brown, 2014). Turning the focus now to legitimation, the following strategies are adopted in this section. To begin with, a narrative description of how the quantitative and qualitative strands were interwoven is provided. Then, links between the QUANT and QUAL findings will be displayed (in Table 9.1). This leads to further discussion of connections between the findings. Afterwards, an overall summary and discussion of potential meta-inferences are provided.

Basically, although it was motivated by concerns that tie in directly with language education, the quantitative study reported in Chapter 6 yielded disappointing results. The results for the overall number of comments during the stimulated recalls showed an effect for task complexity, but the findings for noticing instances (a subset of the comments judged to display teacher noticing) were null. Perspective influenced neither comments nor noticing. The small magnitude of such effects must also be considered. Because the confidence intervals for the effect sizes contained zero, it cannot be said that task or perspective influenced quantity of noticing instances, in any clear way.

Table 9.1 Links between the quantitative and qualitative dimensions of the study

QUANT factors			QUAL findings	
Task	Perspective	Score	Noticing of	Excerpt
Station	Field	4	Facial expression (as miscomprehension)	7.1
Shops	Observer	6	Facial expression (as comprehension)	7.2
Station	Field	6	Gaze (as comprehension)	7.3
Shops	Field	6	Gaze (as potential confusion)	7.4
Shops	Observer	6	Nodding	7.5
Museum	Field	6	Lack of nodding	7.6
Campus	Observer	5	Miscomprehension	8.1
Station	Field	6	New form for known meaning	8.2
Campus	Observer	6	Ambiguous construction	8.3
Campus	Observer	6	Synonymous constructions	8.4
Campus	Observer	6	Landmark description	8.5
Museum	Observer	1	Route directions	8.6

Notes: Complex tasks in **bold**. The maximum score was 6.

Instead, language teacher noticing may be susceptible to such a large number of experiential and contextual factors that modelling them in human experiments is impractical. As noted in Chapter 4, teacher noticing is nested within tasks, but also within programs, schools and their communities and the broader social context of education. It would be difficult, at best, to seek to explain how all of these influence instances of noticing, but clearly task design was not a major contributor to the quantity of noticing in this study. That means a different approach to PST noticing is needed, in terms of the thoughts and behaviors surrounding attention, interpretation and decision-making in local contexts of increasing engagement with a variety of students.

Having said that, a closer inspection of the difference scores of certain participants (see the section entitled 'Taking Teacher Noticing to Task' in Chapter 6) indicated areas where the teacher's noticing, qualitatively, appeared to reflect the task designer's intentions. Perhaps studies with other teachers might generate different results. It could be that some participants in this study were too preoccupied with the need to communicate in English to pay much attention to task design features. It also helps to consider that task design is emergent (Samuda, 2015). Imagine the differences between what one notices when viewing a building blueprint versus leading a guided tour of a building. It might be slightly wrong to think of these as cases of more or less noticing. It is instead mainly a qualitative difference. Likewise, PST noticing appears to be shaped more strongly by the immediacy of communication rather than by task specifications, during the live version of a task. Possibly, those teachers who are at ease communicating may find themselves more open to the influence of task design.

As for the field versus observer manipulation, it was noted that this may be a stronger influence when the video depicts large groups of students because it is then that even more noticing may occur. This study used a balanced comparison between a single student in the field view and a single teacher in the observer view. A trend was noted in the direction of more noticing instances in the field condition. Qualitative analyses of data from one participant did show clear differences (see 'Putting Teacher Noticing in Perspective', Chapter 6).

Finally, there was a seeming, but statistically unsupported, interaction between task and perspective, based on the fact that the greatest number of noticing instances occurred during complex tasks viewed from the field perspective (Figure 6.1). This could mean that, along the lines of complex dynamic systems theory (CDST), teacher cognition and noticing are quantitatively different when a teacher leads a complex task while attending closely to student responses. In fact, this possibility seems intuitive and fairly consistent with previous results from studies on teacher responses to simple versus complex tasks (Baralt *et al.*, 2014; Révész & Gurzynski-Weiss, 2016).

Building on the quantitative design, involving as it did tasks offering greater or lesser degrees of challenge, PSTs noticed a variety of things. The quantitative design, and the results for task completion (Chapter 5), provided a useful backdrop for understanding the interactions between participants, and their noticing. These links are displayed in Table 9.1, which shows the tasks and scores alongside each data excerpt.

A few points can be made about this table. The ordering matches the presentation of the 12 excerpts in Chapters 7 and 8. The qualitative analyses drew upon data excerpts taken from both simple (Campus, Station) and complex (Shops, Museum) tasks. The table lists seven simple tasks and five complex tasks. The numbers are the same for perspective: seven excerpts were based on the observer perspective, while five were based on the field perspective. The scores assigned to all these performances tended to be high. In nine of the 12 excerpts, the student's map had been fully completed, with no errors.

To put this in context, in Chapter 5 it was reported that mean scores for the four tasks ranged from 2.56 to 4.56. A significant difference was found across the tasks. Specifically, scores for the Museum task were lower than both the Campus and Station tasks. So, in nearly all cases, these excerpts came from tasks during which performance was above average. It is worth considering whether this success was attributable in part to the teachers' efforts at noticing. What stands out from the qualitative findings is that they paid close attention to a wide array of features that are primary to interaction, whether involving embodied or verbal communication. In the penultimate section of this chapter, these results are further considered in terms of the role they play in teacher education.

To offer a brief overall summary, the following findings emerged from the study reported in this book. As for its quantitative findings, (1) pedagogic task design significantly influenced task outcomes (i.e. successful completion, time on task). However, (2) neither task complexity nor perspectival memory, as operationalized here, influenced PST cognition at the level of noticing. As for its qualitative findings, embedded within the study design, the teachers noticed (3) assorted embodied resources, including facial expression, gaze and nodding, as well as (4) assorted verbal resources, including semantic (i.e. miscomprehended, novel or ambiguous constructions) and pragmatic (i.e. landmark description and route checking) features.

At the level of meta-interpretation, these findings may inform the construct of language teacher noticing. The definition of teacher noticing in Chapter 3 drew upon the literature to put forward AIDE as a model for describing language teacher noticing. Subsequently, in Chapter 4, potential external influences on language teacher noticing were described. These included proximal and distal factors. The main influences considered in the study were those related to task design and recall conditions.

However, the findings can be interpreted as evidence that teachers attended to more than just the inherent features of any given task. Teacher noticing is context dependent and interconnected insofar as PSTs' interpretations and decisions often seemed focused on the students' contributions, which cannot merely be assumed from the design or perspective as they presumably also involve factors such as task motivation (Dörnyei, 2002) and willingness to communicate (MacIntyre et al., 2017).

It may also be that psychological factors complicated the results for perspective. As noted already, perspectival memory can be cognitive, embodied, emotional or evaluative, regardless of whether it is prompted by a field or an observer view (McCarroll & Sutton, 2017). The reconstructive nature of memory does not, to say the least, make its influence on teacher self-report of noticing easy to capture. Moreover, related to this, visualization is complex and changes as PSTs develop (Mäntylä & Kalaja, 2019). Pre-service language teachers' initial experience of AIDE while teaching versus their reconstruction (or visualization) of it at later stages in their development may be a fruitful area for future research.

The qualitative findings additionally inform the construct of teacher noticing. For one thing, the noticing instances revealed that attention is distributed across verbal and nonverbal dimensions of communication. While constantly changing, and open to various cues, the data revealed a close coupling between attention, interpretation and decision-making. Intention also played a role. These processes were reported in ways that are perhaps surprisingly clear and concise. Not only that, but attention was updated constantly during the task-in-process. This quality of noticing, even at the very beginning level, suggests that the participants' understanding of teaching is already highly developed. Teaching is manifested in various ways (social tolerance, opportunity provisioning, enhancement, feedback, direct teaching), which can be regarded as part of human nature, hence the moniker *natural pedagogy* (Atkinson, 2017). The concept of dependence on initial conditions in CDST is relevant here (Larsen-Freeman, 2017). That is, PSTs are already primed to notice, based on their vast experiences of interacting socially in the world, and in classrooms, prior to any teacher education.

Another issue for broader consideration, in connection with construct development and future research, is the inclusion of engagement in the definition of noticing. This project built upon Philp and Duchesne's (2016) work on task engagement to propose that teacher noticing occurs within cognitive, affective, social and behavioral engagement. The qualitative results support this connection and provide useful evidence on how teachers adapt to interactions based on multiple commitments, including a commitment to their interlocutor.

For example, although it is not easy to tease apart these dimensions of engagement, many noticing instances clearly showed evidence of affect or emotion (Dewaele et al., 2018). These were the focus of a separate study based solely on the Museum task data (Jackson & Shirakawa, 2020). Focusing on the original Japanese data, they found that PSTs used a range of emotion words when reporting their noticing, such as *yokatta* ('that was good'), *fuan* ('anxiety') and *anshin* ('relief'). The sources of these emotions were similar to those described here: perceived communication problems or successful interactions with partners. Finally, it was clear that emotions fluctuated, as in the following recall comment from one PST:

> *The city, there was a building, and there were four doors, I knew left side and right side, but I wondered how to say those two in the middle, I really didn't know, I stopped, until then, I wasn't upset but I wasn't really sure and I was like 'hmm'. Then* [my partner] *said 'let's say 1, 2, 3, 4, from the right', to help me and I thought it was great then for the first time, it was only me teaching but my partner was willing to speak, and I was so glad. After that it was so smooth. Yes, thanks to* [my partner]. (Jackson & Shirakawa, 2020: 208)

Such insights into their noticing by PSTs have implications for understanding the complex and dynamic nature of language teacher psychology.

It would be interesting to pursue a meta-interpretation of aspects of individual versus joint attention in teacher noticing, as described earlier in the book. This seems premature, however, considering the limitations of the present study. This study did not measure noticing by the participant in the student role. Future studies should aim to tap into noticing by both teachers and students. One intriguing possibility would be studies that attempt to track students' embodied noticing (Käänta, 2014) in response to teacher AIDE. Other useful data would be those lending insight into the role of intentions. These could perhaps be captured by methods originally developed to understand willingness to communicate, which chart fluctuations in speaker/listener intentions over very brief periods of interaction (MacIntyre *et al.*, 2017). The study of language teacher noticing as a complex and dynamic (Borg, 2015; Feryok, 2010, 2018) phenomenon calls for such methods.

Study Limitations

Before moving on to the implications, it is necessary to fully consider the limitations of the study reported here. Firstly, there were avoidable limitations present in both strands of this mixed-methods study. The sample size was a serious drawback when considering the quantitative results, which were analyzed using non-parametric statistics due to lack of normality. The repeated-measures design can be considered a strength, however. For the sake of future studies, an avoidable issue that affects the qualitative results concerns the recording setup. To capture more detail, particularly nonverbal information, multiple cameras would have been useful.

Secondly, looking at their core assumptions affords insight into caveats inherent to these methods. These are the unavoidable limitations. CA assumes that anything that goes on in an interaction is potentially relevant to the actions performed, yet analysts must be selective when transcribing data. For instance, intonation might be interactionally relevant, but if overlooked during the transcription, its significance in understanding teacher noticing may be missed. Regarding the stimulated recall methodology, one assumption is that individuals are conscious of using attention, reasoning and intentions to guide their actions. Not all of this can be easily recalled by looking at a video-recording, nor should it be assumed that participants reported the cognitions they recalled in full. Thus, it remains possible that inherent methodological limitations may have skewed this study's results.

Implications for Pre-Service Teachers

This section focuses on specific implications of the study for PST education in the Japanese context. In general, these implications concern tasks, interaction and teacher development.

Firstly, regarding tasks in general, the noticing reported by these PSTs suggests that there are indeed challenges and opportunities to be considered when using tasks in the Japanese EFL setting (Butler, 2011). Language usage is not predetermined by tasks and, as noted above, task design can influence both the time it takes to complete a task and its success rate. Teachers new to task-based language teaching (TBLT) should understand that their role is flexible and involves leading students skilfully (Samuda, 2015) while keeping them focused on the task-in-process and its intended outcome. The areas of teacher development mentioned in the following paragraph would seem necessary to becoming a capable task-based teacher. In addition, specifically concerning the direction-giving map tasks, instructions may vary from those used here and so it is important to familiarize teachers with a range of ways to use and modify such tasks (Pica *et al.*, 1993; Samuda & Bygate, 2008; Yule, 1997). The language, while not fixed, does invoke spatial cognition (Denis, 2018) and this could be pointed out to PSTs as an area within which individual differences among learners might be found, as well as an area susceptible to L1 influence during tasks (Cadierno & Robinson, 2009), although it is one in which learners gradually become more linguistically sophisticated.

Secondly, regarding student–teacher interaction, the PSTs noticed many seemingly trivial aspects of interaction that may be taken to indicate learner engagement (Philp & Duchesne, 2016). These included gaze and nodding. In face-to-face classroom settings, it is important to remind new teachers to look for these signals (and not to spend more time than necessary facing the chalkboard or looking at projector screens). This is related to developing teachers' interactional competence (Walsh, 2011) and also to their recognition of students' interactional noticing (Käänta, 2014). The aforementioned concerns on the part of Japanese NNESTs with teaching English in English (Machida, 2019) are also reflected in what these PSTs noticed. Specifically, they were aware of constructions that were likely to be new to their interlocutors and yet they quickly managed to find ways to explain words such as *crosswalk*. Their undergraduate training should help PSTs develop this ability, so that they feel more confident in using English during lessons (Butler, 2004). It would also be valuable for PSTs to consider how teaching is accomplished through embodied interaction (Hall, 2019; Hall & Looney, 2019), which might shift the focus away from anxiety specifically related to language use, including any inaccuracies, which can be handled through self-repair. To this end, videos of their teaching practice should portray teacher–student interaction, rather than showing only the teacher's performance.

Finally, regarding teacher development, this study can help to improve reflective practice (Farrell, 2015). It may do so by building on earlier approaches to advance a form of evidence-based reflection using instances of teacher noticing captured via stimulated recall (Mann & Walsh, 2017). In Chapter 3, a clear distinction was made between the general category of *reflection* and specific *noticing*, whereby noticing is reflection that happens during engagement *with* learners. Teacher noticing can also be distinguished from various subcategories of interactive thought (Anderson, 2019) as it emphasizes temporal continuity across three key processes: attention, interpretation and decision-making. The evidence presented here speaks to the importance of this distinction, because PST noticing revealed the various nuances and complexities of their attempts at communicative teaching practice, which would be difficult, if not impossible, to observe through traditional tools for reflection such as diaries. Thus, these comments could be used to introduce video clubs (van Es & Sherin, 2006, 2008), or class activities in which critical observation of videos of PSTs' teaching demonstrations is intended to support the development of expertise (Yoshizumi, 2018; see also Hüttner, 2019; Yuan *et al.*, 2020). It is important for teachers, beginning with PSTs, to base reflective practice on their actual experiences in the teacher's role, which is crucial to identity formation (Jackson & Shirakawa, 2020; Watanabe, 2017).

More specifically, the qualitative results presented in Chapters 7 and 8 could be used in various ways. For instance, discussion leaders in undergraduate courses or workshops could provide participants with a copy of Table 9.2, along with an explanation of this study. In combination with lectures, readings and videos of lessons that they or other teachers have conducted, this table may help raise awareness and foster discussion of teaching strategies needed to effectively implement task-based instruction.

Table 9.2 Qualitative aspects of teacher noticing and their implications

What the pre-service teachers noticed	Its purpose during task engagement
Facial expressions displaying comprehension and miscomprehension	To confirm understanding and to anticipate questions, in the case of misunderstanding
Gaze as a means of comprehending and displaying comprehension	To confirm whether instructions are understood and foster deeper engagement
Nodding	To determine whether students understand and/or agree
Their miscomprehended usage	To initiate self-repair and improve communication
Constructions that were likely new to students	To facilitate a focus on form, especially if teachers plan ahead to explain new language when the need arises
Constructions ambiguous to students	To identify areas where clarification of task-relevant meanings may be needed
Constructions that can be used synonymously	To illustrate that language use is not predetermined by tasks (introduces language variety)
Landmark description	To foster performance by inviting students to request more detailed information
Route directions	To enhance collaboration toward the goal of task completion

Summary

In this chapter, clear and concise answers were provided to the main research questions, which dealt with the effects of task complexity and recall conditions, the noticing of embodied resources and the noticing of verbal resources. The findings concerning task and recall are merely suggestive, but leaned toward support for the study hypotheses. These hypotheses were that complex tasks and teacher-perspective videos may increase the quantity of PST noticing. The possibility of an interaction between these two factors also exists. The qualitative results, on the other hand, revealed a plethora of influences on noticing besides these factors, including gestures and language (mis)use. These were reported by the PSTs and reflect the complex challenges they face in implementing contemporary language teaching practices, such as TBLT.

One hallmark of MMR is that it seeks to go beyond QUANT or QUAL findings to reach an integrated understanding of the phenomena under investigation, which is greater than the sum of its parts. This was achieved in the present chapter through narrative description, a display combining the QUAL and QUANT results (Table 9.1) and further discussion of the meta-inferences that this integration of findings afforded. Language teacher noticing as a construct in the psychology of language learning and teaching (PLLT) appears to be susceptible to numerous contextual and experiential factors, and may best be regarded as nested within tasks, programs, schools and the wider social context. This is consistent with viewing it as a sociocognitive construct (Jackson & Cho, 2018). CDST seems to be a suitable methodological framework for understanding its complexity, yet the challenge of establishing boundaries remains. Even with the clear boundaries set by this study, it was evident that beyond tasks, videos and communication, affective factors arise from noticing which can also exert a powerful influence on PST development and identity (Jackson & Shirakawa, 2020). Taken together, the results of this research suggest that few, if any, potential influences can be neglected.

Rather than trying to rein these influences in, it may be preferable for the time being to continue descriptive research on language teacher noticing. This study was based on a small sample, after all. Its results cannot be considered generalizable, although they could be used in PST education courses in the present context. Based on the QUAL results, this chapter noted three areas in which the findings of the study could be applied. These were TBLT, classroom interaction and reflective practice. After explaining the tasks used, the comments of the PSTs reported here could be presented and discussed in teacher education courses that focus on any of these areas. This might prompt consideration of unanticipated challenges as well as teaching strategies to overcome these challenges, and it might motivate future PSTs to base reflection on their noticing (i.e. evidence-based reflective practice, Mann & Walsh, 2017). In the final chapter, further potential contributions of the construct of language teacher noticing are considered.

Part 3
Conclusion

10 Future Directions

A Role for Teacher Noticing

Having arrived at the end of this book, one may ask whether language teacher noticing has any future role. In this chapter, I suggest that it does. For this case to be clear, it must be possible to view language teacher noticing as separate from, yet interconnected with, related concepts in language teaching. This interconnection accords with complex dynamic systems theory (CDST), which seeks to highlight the interrelations and dynamics of psychological constructs in order to provide a bird's-eye view of thought and action. To begin with, I briefly review how teacher noticing is positioned with respect to three broader notions: teacher psychology, teacher cognition and teacher reflection. From that starting point, the unique contribution of teacher noticing to pre-service and in-service teacher development and language teaching research can be better understood.

Firstly, language teacher psychology (Mercer & Kostoulas, 2018b: 1) covers a broad range of facets of teachers' mental lives, including 'their characteristics, personalities, needs, motivations and well-being'. The scope of this domain of inquiry is very large and also includes emotion and identity. In general, it places teachers at the center of an expanding circle of contextual factors (Mercer, 2018). This ecological view was used to describe potential influences on pre-service teacher (PST) noticing in Chapter 4. Teacher noticing occurs at the micro level in such analyses. However, meso and macro level influences (Douglas Fir Group, 2016) should also be considered.

Secondly, teacher cognition (Borg, 2015) involves thoughts, or cognitions, arising from or constrained by the following influences: (1) schooling in a general sense, (2) professional coursework, (3) contextual factors and (4) classroom practice. Its relationship to practice is dynamic. As a fundamental element in classroom practice, teacher noticing specifically highlights teachers' interactive thinking (Borg, 2019), or thinking during teaching. Teacher cognition research can help to further narrow down the influences on it. For instance, in the present study the participants' English proficiency, their partners' contributions and task-related factors appeared to be prominent concerns during noticing.

Lastly, practitioner reflection encompasses a wide range of processes that may be situated along a continuum from rapid, spontaneous thinking to slow, careful deliberation (Anderson, 2019). In the English teaching field, reflection is generally thought of as 'conscious, experientially informed thought, at times involving aspects of evaluation, criticality, and problem-solving, and leading to insight, increased awareness, and/or new understanding' (Anderson, 2020: 4). Reflection, and its various uses in second language teacher education (SLTE; Farrell, 2015; Mann & Walsh, 2017), begins with teaching practice. Reflective practice is a process of gathering data about practice and discussing it with others for the purpose of improving teaching, typically over an extended period of time (Farrell, 2015).

As defined in this book, teacher noticing is a facet of the mental lives of all those who identify as teachers, including pre-service English language teachers. It is a form of reflection involving several cognitions: attending to events, interpreting them and deciding how to act on them, while engaged with learners. It thus has the benefit of being grounded in teacher cognition, reflective teaching and recent work on engagement (Baralt *et al.*, 2016; Mercer & Dörnyei, 2020; Philp & Duchesne, 2016). Another benefit is the diverse body of empirical studies in education that have informed it (e.g. Schack *et al.*, 2017; Sherin *et al.*, 2011a; Simpson *et al.*, 2020).

Language Teacher Education

This section presents general implications of language teacher noticing in contexts of PST education. A question-and-answer style of presentation is adopted, which anticipates questions that readers might have at this stage of the book. This discussion will mainly refer to the outcomes of this study.

(1) *Should PSTs be asked to perform and comment on dialogic tasks?* Yes, the rich data from this project indicate that there is much that we can learn about how novice teachers approach teaching, when tasks are used to provide a clear context for their efforts. Moreover, these teachers themselves could benefit by using their comments as the basis for evidence-driven reflection (see Mann & Walsh, 2017). In the case of non-native English speaking teachers (NNESTs), it is advisable to allow teachers-in-training a choice in terms of the language of their reflections, as done here.

(2) *Which tasks are best for promoting noticing and reflection, and how can they be designed to enhance performance?* Tasks that teachers will encounter in teaching materials, which elicit relevant language and are modified to bring to light various conditions that mediate performance and learning (time pressure, elements, familiarity) appear to be suitable choices. Teacher educators should bear in mind these various dimensions of task design, which have been shown to impact language and affective outcomes (Robinson, 2011, 2015). It is also valuable to clearly specify instructions and define the criteria for task completion.

(3) *Which camera arrangements are best for promoting teacher noticing through stimulated recall?* In lieu of a definitive answer, it seems useful to explore this question while considering the purpose of using video. Different angles prompt noticing of different things. Among the many choices are whether to use field or observer perspectives and stationary or moving cameras. Also, with some effort, videos can be prepared that incorporate dual perspectives (see Jackson & Cho, 2018, for a study that employed this option). Additional guidelines and advice can be found in the teaching literature. For instance, Knight (2014) is a practical guide on using video, written for instructional coaches, teachers and principals. Building explicitly on teacher noticing, Sherin and Dyer (2017) offer practical advice on using self-captured video. Also, Calandra and Rich (2015) is an edited collection of research on using digital video for teacher learning. As noted earlier, it seems important not to rely solely on observer perspective videos because these mainly show the teacher rather than student interaction and engagement.

(4) *How can this approach to gathering data on teacher noticing be linked to reflective practice?* This is a very important question. What is suggested here is that teacher educators can and should seek to develop PSTs' capacity to notice. I would argue for 'noticing-based' reflective practice, as a specific form of 'evidence-based' reflective practice. Teacher educators need to be clearer about what is important to classroom performance and teacher development. Mann and Walsh (2017) have paved the way by providing examples from their work with teachers showing the use of stimulated recall as a prompt for reflective commentary, arguing that it can also be used for dialogic reflection, and linking it to other appropriate tools for reflection, such as screen-capture software and self-evaluation frameworks. This helpfully moves stimulated recall away from being solely a methodological tool and toward being a pedagogical tool, in keeping with Swain's (2006b) argument that verbal protocols can be a source of development. Likewise, Mann and Walsh (2017) advocated the use of conversation analysis (CA) to transcribe teaching practice and dialogic reflections among teachers. These written data can be incorporated into assignments, including those that promote language teacher identity (Jackson & Shirakawa, 2020).

(5) *What concepts could be introduced to orient pre-service teachers to the idea of noticing during their teaching?* At a minimum, it might help to consider a more pluralistic, integrative noticing concept. The attentional mechanisms and subjective experiences underpinning noticing occur in teachers, as well as learners, of a second language (L2). This was the focus of Part 1. Based on a sociopragmatic, triadic view of shared attention to linguistic symbols (Tomasello, 2003), this book claims that there are at least four potentially relevant kinds of

noticing in L2 instruction: the teacher's private noticing, the teacher's noticing shared with students, a student's private noticing and a student's noticing shared with the teacher or other students. These categories could be introduced to teacher trainees, and examples of each could be elicited and discussed. These areas would also benefit from additional, classroom-based research, as described below.

Language Teacher Development

Here, I describe the results of my own attempts at reflecting on how an understanding of teacher noticing has altered my experiences of teaching English as a second/foreign language. These are presented as 10 practical suggestions (Table 10.1). Although this advice is intended to be general, it may at times seem more apt in contexts where teachers are working with adult L2 learners. It is based on several shared assumptions within this literature, including that as teachers we should develop a good rapport with students (Dörnyei & Murphey, 2003), support acquisition (Long, 2015), enhance participation (Ortega, 2011), engage in reflective practice (Walsh & Mann, 2015) and, as a valuable component of professional development, conduct focused classroom observations to develop and share our insights (Fanselow, 1988). There are, of course, many other important teacher qualities that SLTE should seek to develop. References to recent work in this area are included below; however, the main purpose of this discussion is merely to pique interest in using noticing to further professional development. The suggestions below are simple and can be woven into lesson plans or informal meetings with teaching peers. They constitute tips based on teacher noticing for busy teachers.

Firstly, teacher–student rapport is an essential ingredient in fostering a positive classroom dynamic (Dörnyei & Murphey, 2003). However,

Table 10.1 Practical suggestions for using language teacher noticing

In order to	Try to
Develop rapport	(1) Ask your students what they want you to notice
	(2) Tell your students what you notice about them
Support acquisition	(3) Predict what you might notice during tasks
	(4) Express feedback in terms of what you noticed
Enhance participation	(5) Avoid prolonged disengagement
	(6) Distribute your attention to all students
Foster reflection	(7) Clear your mind prior to teaching lessons
	(8) Observe your lessons, rather than simply teaching them
Guide observation	(9) Focus on how the teacher 'does noticing' in lessons
	(10) Discuss teacher versus observer perspectives on events

Buchanan and Timmis (2019) observed that some aspects of rapport (e.g. use of names) are more trainable than others (e.g. showing genuine interest in students). Thus, Suggestion 1 aims to develop rapport by eliciting information from students about the particular aspects of their language use that they would like you to notice. Some ways of doing this include adding questions about it to a learner needs survey or, in writing instruction, having students submit assignments with a note requesting specific attention to and feedback on certain areas such as lexis, grammar or organization.

I recently asked a group of first-year undergraduate English majors in Japan to informally jot down their answers to this question, using the prompt, *During pair/group work in English class, I would like my teachers to notice* _____. Edited lightly for clarity, here are some of their responses:

- *students' speaking mistakes*
- *whether students stay on topic*
- *progress at working toward the task's goal*
- *whether everyone participates equally*
- *if other students start speaking in Japanese*
- *whether students can give opinions or not*
- *how we start and finish the conversation*

The main benefit here was to open my mind to actions that my students preferred, without having to guess at this.

Of course, students may not always fully understand (or accept) what they need assistance with, or how instruction can help them. Therefore, teachers should also let students know what they notice (Suggestion 2). Related to classroom rapport, one thing I often notice is how self-imposed seating arrangements in my university classes can restrict students' opportunities to interact with a wider range of interlocutors. By letting students know my concerns prior to group and pair work, they can better understand the purpose of interacting with others during lessons.

A second area in which teacher noticing can enhance language education concerns its potential for supporting second language acquisition (SLA). A great deal has been written in the past two decades about focus on form (e.g. Doughty, 2001; Doughty & Williams, 1998; Kartchava & Ammar, 2014; Long, 2015; Norris & Ortega, 2000; Révész, 2009). It is important to understand that focus on form originated as a description of how instruction can briefly orient learners' attention to form (i.e. linguistic elements that may impede communication, such as pronunciation or morphosyntax) during otherwise meaning-focused lessons (Long, 1991; Long & Robinson, 1998). In practice, teachers implement focus on form when they firstly notice problems with students' production, and secondly deploy recasts, request clarifications or offer explanations in order to address these problems swiftly.

As per Suggestion 3, teachers can try to make predictions about problems they might notice. That is, they can raise their own awareness of the formal aspects of language students are likely to attempt to produce in a given lesson or task. Then, if and when necessary, focus on form will be easier owing to prospective memory, which here involves teachers remembering to carry out more elaborate noticing processes focusing on task-relevant language (Loschky & Bley-Vroman, 1990).

More specifically, based on the notion of proactive focus on form (Doughty & Williams, 1998), it can be useful to think about tasks in terms what you might expect to notice during student performance. Advanced speakers can be helpful informants in this endeavor, if they are willing to perform pedagogic tasks during your preparation time. To exemplify this, I asked a colleague to perform the map gap tasks used in this study with me. To give the directions, this experienced teacher used a combination of verb forms including imperatives and present progressive, as in *turn right ... now you're walking toward the station*, where the latter form describes activity in progress. Hardly any of the PSTs in this study used the present progressive for this function. Nor did they appear to use *going to* to convey intentions, as in *you're going to take the stairs all the way to the top*, which was also used by my colleague. Noticing what you do not hear in language production can be helpful, especially when you convey this observation to students and then ask them to repeat the task, which can allow them to practice underused constructions.

Based on Suggestion 4, and the notion of reactive focus on form (Doughty & Williams, 1998), the other way in which teacher noticing can enhance focus on form regards its execution. For example, while teaching I have found that using the sentence frame *I noticed that you said* _____ serves to orient students' attention to my observations and any subsequent feedback. Thus, Suggestion 4 expands upon the repertoire of discourse moves traditionally employed to implement focus on form (recasts, clarification requests and explanations). It involves framing a repetition of a student utterance such that attention is drawn to it. The declarative nature of this frame supports acquisition when used either to elicit corrections or to highlight valuable contributions. Its advantages are in the former case to cater to a preference for self-repair (Pekarek Doehler & Pochon-Berger, 2015), and in the latter case to orient the discussion toward learning goals. If rising intonation is used, it may further prompt students to repair their quoted utterance (see Doughty & Varela, 1998).

Because L2 learning is as much a matter of participation as it is of acquisition (Ortega, 2011), the third area in which teacher noticing can be valuable is in terms of its importance in managing social interaction in the classroom. The triadic nature of joint attention means that teacher noticing is fundamentally a social process. Teachers should avoid prolonged disengagement (Suggestion 5). Unfortunately, large class sizes and heavy teaching loads often spur disengagement in English as a foreign language (EFL) contexts. It is true that teachers cannot always engage directly with learners. It may even be detrimental if a hovering teacher discourages some students from speaking. During learner–learner interaction, teachers may check in occasionally with students and monitor group performance from afar so as to maintain engagement. Additionally, it can be easy for talkative students to command more than their fair share of the teacher's attention. To ensure that they notice all students, teachers should regroup students, rotate roles and intentionally call on those who are engaged yet seem hesitant to volunteer answers. Sert (2019) described specific frameworks and tools for developing classroom interactional competence (Walsh, 2011), which could be used to promote engagement and to focus on the ways in which teachers distribute attention evenly (Suggestion 6).

Fostering reflection is the fourth area in which noticing can make a direct contribution. Reflective practice (Farrell, 2015), as discussed earlier, is a valuable means of professional development, but questions remain about how it can best be carried out (Walsh & Mann, 2015). Although comprehensive answers to these questions are beyond the scope of this book, teacher noticing is an indispensable data source for reflective practice. Language teacher educators have begun to suggest ways in which the use of video can promote noticing and professional vision (Hüttner, 2019; Mann et al., 2020).

The advice here concentrates on improving the quality of teacher noticing so that it may foster deeper, more personalized reflection. Suggestion 7 concerns clearing one's mind prior to lessons. As a brief anecdote, I worked for several years as a curriculum coordinator in a university intensive language program, where my colleagues and I faced a weekly onslaught of administrative issues. These were important matters, but their relevance to our teaching was tangential and they sometimes resulted in rushed class preparations. While walking to class after a hectic meeting one day, a fellow teacher suggested that we use the brief journey to undertake a 'mood transition'. This idea has stuck with me as a crucial preparatory step before entering the classroom. It can be hard at times not to bring prior thoughts or emotions into the classroom, but there is great benefit to freeing our minds of unrelated distractions before teaching, which means being completely in the moment.

Next, Suggestion 8 is to observe one's lessons, rather than simply teaching them. This assumes that, having cleared their minds, teachers can nurture what Mason (2002: 19) called an 'inner witness'. This internal observer is, helpfully, emotionally distant. From this perspective, teachers can view issues, problems and potential conflicts more objectively. Striving to observe one's teaching in this way can lead to opportunities to use antecedent-focused emotion-regulation strategies (King & Ng, 2018). These are used in anticipation of undesirable outcomes and include modifying classroom situations or tasks while in progress, refocusing attention from negative (but inconsequential) student behaviors to positive ones, and cognitive reappraisal, as when a student's frown is reinterpreted as a sign of concentration rather than one of disapproval.

Classroom observation is the fifth key area that may be informed by the concept of language teacher noticing. Classroom visits by peers or administrators can support dialogue about language teacher professional development. If carefully designed, such sessions enable teachers to see their own teaching differently (Fanselow, 1988). Building on this, based on Suggestion 9, it may be appropriate in certain cases to establish a prior focus on seeing how the teacher does noticing, or carries out interactional sequences that reveal their mental state during classroom discourse. As described by Schegloff (2007: 87), this may be accomplished through verbal (e.g. *oh*, used as a change of state token) or bodily means (e.g. smiling). Teachers convey their surprise, affirmations and denials in a multitude of seeable ways, which may include takes, nodding and frowning, respectively. In addition to verbal indications, how these nonverbal signals of what teachers notice are perceived and understood by others is a ripe area for observation-based discussions.

Equally useful is the opportunity for teachers to compare their noticing of student behavior with that of an independent observer (Suggestion 10). In post-observation conferences (Copland & Donaghue, 2019) the teacher and supervisor/trainer/observer co-construct an interpretation of classroom events that they noticed, based on notes or a video-recording. This could be especially valuable in cases where intercultural communication gives rise to potential misunderstanding. The combined background and experience of the teacher and the observer may ideally lead to a richer interpretation of what is going on in the classroom, as well as, perhaps, suggestions for improving instruction.

Language Teaching Research

This section will briefly note some potential areas for future research. Studies in experimental and classroom settings are needed. Firstly, experimental or laboratory studies can offer insights that are not readily obtainable from classrooms. For instance, stimulated recall methods could be used to examine whether or how teacher noticing changes when the same task is repeated with different groups of students. Eye-tracking (Révész & Gurzynski-Weiss, 2016) could be used to examine the quality and quantity of teacher noticing from field or observer perspectives using split-screen videos (Jackson & Cho, 2018), by measuring gaze toward either side of the screen and attempting to link it to comments on their performance. These types of studies would have pedagogical implications for SLTE. Another intriguing possibility is using stimulated recall to examine both teacher and learner noticing, including private versus shared noticing. A small number of studies have used stimulated recall to investigate both teacher and learner interpretations of classroom interaction (Kim & Han, 2007; Loewen, 2019; Mackey *et al.*, 2007). An integrative view of noticing provides further theoretical justification for such studies, which can be expanded methodologically by adopting multimodal analyses.

In classroom research, more work is needed to address the embodied accomplishment of actions relevant to teaching and learning. Some interesting findings have already emerged from this new area of research, which illustrate that students use embodied noticing to initiate correction (Kääntä, 2014) and that teaching commonly 'involves noticing and deciding when to contribute to ongoing interactions and when to withhold contributions' (Looney, 2019: 219). The insights gained from CA-for-SLA studies could be extended to examine the roles of teachers' use of interactional noticing (Schegloff, 2007) as a public display of teacher cognition, in a wider range of cultural settings. A recent CA study in an English as a second language (ESL) setting by Fagan (2019) presented relevant findings and discussion.

To support these and other studies, wearable cameras should be used to document teaching and noticing (see Russ & Luna, 2013; Sherin *et al.*, 2011b). The field and observer perspectives also warrant additional consideration, to determine their potentially distinct uses (Miller, 2011; see also Libby *et al.*, 2005; McCarroll & Sutton, 2017). Some further specific issues for task-based language education to consider would be how group size influences the capacity to notice among teachers with different levels of expertise. Another question specifically related to TBLT would be how the teacher's noticing shifts across the pre-, during- and post-task phases of a lesson. Classroom studies of corrective feedback could also be theoretically informed by teacher noticing. For instance, Gurzynski-Weiss (2016) addressed the errors noticed by Spanish instructors and probed their decisions to deliver or withhold corrective feedback.

Clearly, there are many horizons to explore in L2 research on teacher noticing.

Reflecting on Noticing as Teacher Psychology

According to psychologists, visual perception makes human beings similar in comparison to other animal species. Nonetheless, all people do not see the world in the same way. Instead, we view it in terms of our goals, beliefs and intentions, how determined and capable we are, how it makes us feel and how closely it resonates with our self-concept. What we see and hear is filtered through professional knowledge, memories of past experiences, the nature of our languages and a subjective understanding of the sociocultural context. Schemata mediate our noticing. It is indeed a complex way of seeing. Our vision also changes over time, which can lead to improvement within domains of professional activity (Goodwin, 1994; Sherin & van Es, 2009; see also Kalaja & Mäntylä, 2018).

This book has sought to establish noticing as a key construct within language teacher psychology. Expert teachers notice, yet inhibit responses to grammatical errors when fluency is the focus. They notice effective student pairings when setting up pair and group work. They notice praiseworthy examples of students' language use to share with the entire class. They also notice features of erroneous production that may benefit from recasts. And they notice student engagement and comprehension while they teach and adjust to it. That is to say, they ground their actions in social tolerance, opportunity provisioning, stimulus enhancement, corrective feedback and direct instruction (Atkinson, 2017). Beyond this, teachers also notice their own teaching capacities and affective responses, which can foster autonomy, identity and well-being.

If there is any role for the instructor in classroom language learning, it involves noticing – at least some part of which is shared between the teacher and students. It remains subjective. This integrative perspective has broad implications. For one thing, it raises the question of whether it is desirable to conduct separate classroom studies of teacher or learner noticing. Doing so has resulted in distinct technical discourses to describe fundamentally similar processes in the psychology of language learning and teaching. A common frame of reference for understanding teacher-learner noticing, and perhaps greater simplicity, may come from models of joint attention (e.g. Tomasello, 2003; see Figure 3.2). Teachers and students are, after all, both human.

Of course, learner and teacher noticing are not exactly the same. There are many obstacles to becoming an expert noticer. Surrounded by values misaligned with the aims of education, language teachers reside within a complex ecology of dynamic influences. They far too often labor within schools and communities that constrain them. With so many issues vying for attention, it seems harder, yet all the more important, to promote reflection based on their noticing. Novice language teachers' limited experience already makes them less selective in what they attend to and reason about (Tsui, 2003). To become expert entails noticing less, albeit more of what matters.

The present volume has revealed how tasks may afford opportunities for pre-service teachers to notice. It has shown how, in their interpretation, embodied and linguistic resources underpin meaning making. Through these momentary reflections, they may realize the extent of their present teaching ability. Teacher development involves building the capacity to notice, and to learn from, significant events during engagement with students. Essential to this process are joint attention and mutual awareness, which are imbued with social meaning. To notice together how we manage interactions and cooperate toward shared goals is fundamental to understanding language teaching, and other forms of dialogue.

Appendices

Appendix A: Map Gap Task Materials (Teacher Versions)

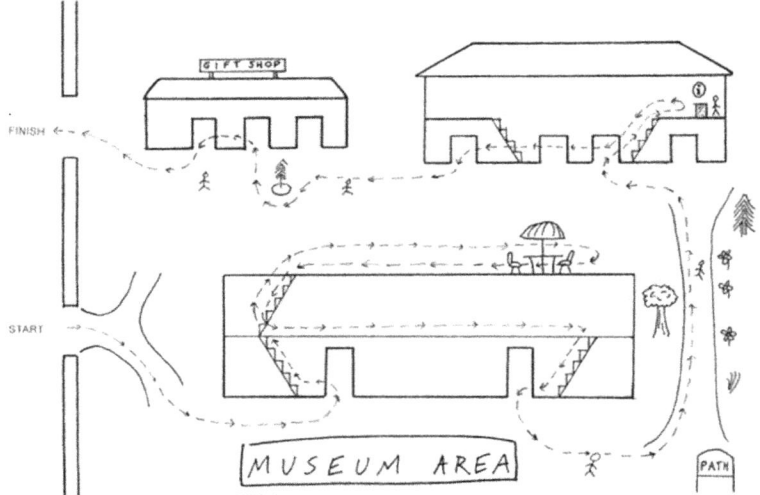

Complex Museum task map

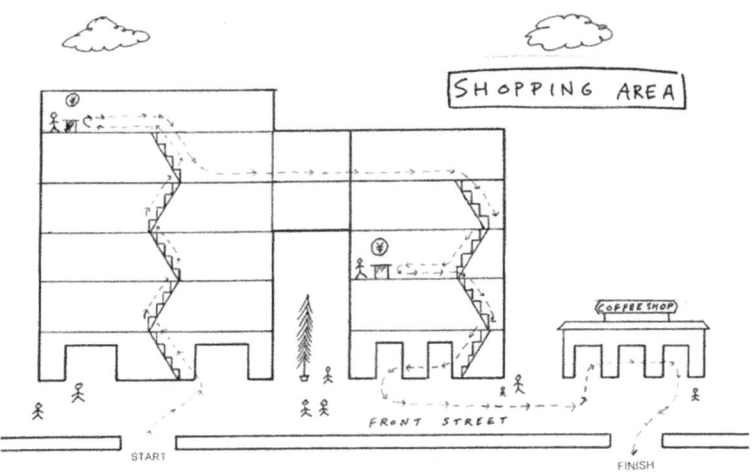

Complex Shops task map

152 Language Teacher Noticing in Tasks

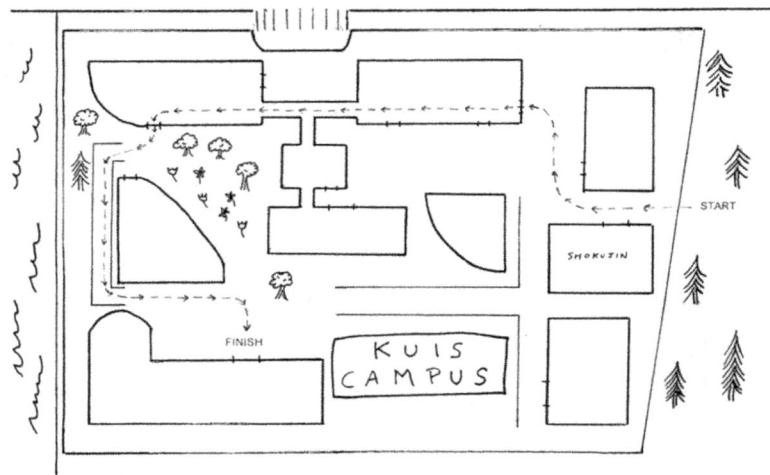

Simple Campus task map

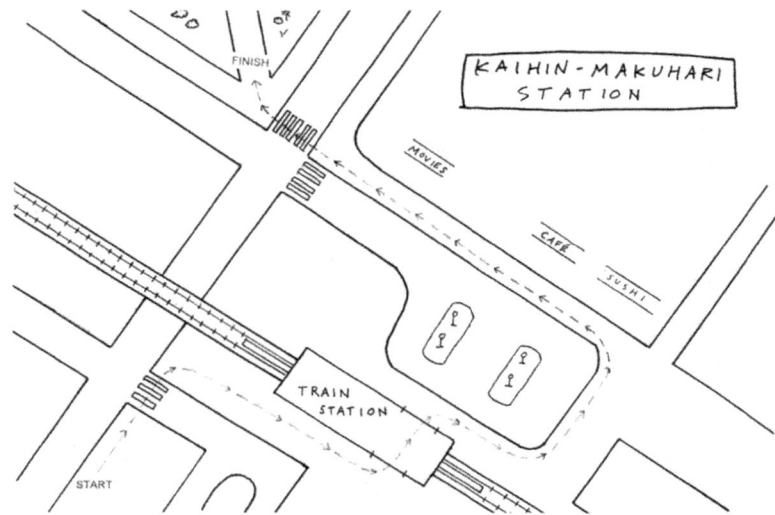

Simple Station task map

Appendix B: Coding Guidelines (Excerpt)

Operational definition of language teacher noticing

Language teacher noticing (henceforth NOTICING) is exhibited in teacher comments that indicate that the teacher had attended to events that occurred during engagement, which is defined as participation in any social, cognitive, emotional or behavioral dimensions of student–teacher interaction while performing the task.

What is NOT noticing? Some things not included in this definition are comments that refer <u>solely</u> to: (a) the teacher's ability (e.g. self-criticisms), or (b) the task materials, or (c) actions described without reference to the student (as if the teacher had been practicing teaching in front of a mirror).

Examples of language teacher NOTICING
<u>Examples 1–5 are NOTICING examples</u>

Example 1: *In the second half, whether or not I sufficiently explained, it was good that my partner did shadowing my direction.*

In Example 1, the teacher commented on the student's verbal behavior (shadowing) during their interaction. Note: the word 'partner' is often used for the person in the student role.

Example 2: *Well, from the view of someone on the stairs, it was right, but from the view of someone looking at this paper, it was left, so I said left a little anxiously.*

In Example 2, the teacher commented on the task materials, what s/he said, and the fact of being anxious, suggesting emotional engagement during interaction. The teacher's consideration of alternate perspectives (or viewpoints) and anxiety (due to communication) imply cognitive and emotional engagement, respectively.

Example 3: *It helped me a lot when my partner told me where s/he was.*

In Example 3, the teacher commented on the fact that his/her partner helpfully engaged during the interaction by reporting where s/he was.

Example 4: *At that moment, I looked at my partner's face and thought he didn't understand the expression 'diagonal', so I was trying to come up with an alternative expression.*

In Example 4, the teacher gleaned from the partner's facial expression that the partner did not understand, which prompted the teacher to reconsider his/her word choice at this stage of the interaction.

Example 5: *Well you know, as I did a couple of times, I felt like I gradually came to understand what way of conveying [things] was easier for the listener.*

Example 5 is a good example because the teacher's comment directly attributes his/her way of conveying information to repeated experiences engaging with this listener/student.

Examples 6–8 are NOT NOTICING examples

Example 6: *When I looked at the map at first, I thought, 'it got more complex than the last one', and I was smiling bitterly.*

In Example 6, it cannot be inferred that the event occurred during engagement with the student. This comment occurred first on the recording and refers to the first time the teacher saw these task materials.

Example 7: *I think I was nervous and fidgeting.*

In Example 7, the teacher commented only on his/her thoughts and behavior without making any connection to engagement with the student.

Example 8: *When it finished, I thought, 'finally it's done', and I was relieved.*

Example 8 comes from the end of a recording when the teacher was finished interacting with the partner. It only concerns the teacher's reaction to finishing, and nothing is said about what the teacher attended to while performing the task.

Appendix C: Transcription Conventions

?	Rising intonation
:	Elongation
[	Overlap
=	Latching
word-	Cut off
°word°	Spoken at quieter volume
WORD	Spoken at louder volume
(1.2)	Pause, measured in tenths of a second
(.)	Pause shorter than 0.2 seconds
(word)	Uncertain hearing
((word))	Transcriber's comment
+	Marks embodied action (described in italics)
L	Left
R	Right
B	Both
H	Hand gesture (LH, RH, BH)
GZ	Gaze

References

Alanen, R. (2013) Noticing and mediation: A sociocultural perspective. In J.M. Bergsleithner, S.N. Frota and J.K. Yoshioka (eds) (2013) *Noticing and Second Language Acquisition: Studies in Honor of Richard Schmidt* (pp. 331–341). Honolulu, HI: National Foreign Language Resource Center.

Allwright, D. (2003) Exploratory practice: Rethinking practitioner research in language teaching. *Language Teaching Research* 7, 113–141.

Allwright, D. and Bailey, K.M. (1991) *Focus on the Language Classroom: An Introduction to Classroom Research for Language Teachers*. Cambridge: Cambridge University Press.

Anderson, J. (2019) In search of reflection-in-action: An exploratory study of the interactive reflection of four experienced teachers. *Teaching and Teacher Education* 86, 1–17.

Anderson, J. (2020) Key concepts in ELT: Reflection. *English Language Teaching Journal* 74, 480–483.

Andon, N. and Eckerth, J. (2009) Chacun à son gout? Task-based L2 pedagogy from the teacher's point of view. *International Journal of Applied Linguistics* 19, 286–310.

Andrews, S. (2007) *Teacher Language Awareness*. Cambridge: Cambridge University Press.

Ankney, K.L. (2016) Studying music teachers' awareness of students' musical thinking through video stimulated recall techniques. *Bulletin of Empirical Music Education Research* 7, 1–14.

Aoki, H. (2011) Some functions of speaker head nods. In J. Streeck, C. Goodwin and C. LeBaron (eds) *Embodied Interaction: Language and Body in the Material World* (pp. 93–105). Cambridge: Cambridge University Press.

Atkinson, D. (2011) Introduction: Cognitivism and second language acquisition. In D. Atkinson (ed.) *Alternative Approaches to Second Language Acquisition* (pp. 1–23). New York: Routledge.

Atkinson, D. (2017) *Homo Pedagogicus*: The evolutionary nature of second language teaching. *Language Teaching* 50, 527–543.

Bailey, K.M. (2012) Reflective pedagogy. In A. Burns and J.C. Richards (eds) *The Cambridge Guide to Pedagogy and Practice in Second Language Teaching* (pp. 23–29). Cambridge: Cambridge University Press.

Baralt, M. (2013) The impact of cognitive complexity on feedback efficacy during online versus face-to-face interactive tasks. *Studies in Second Language Acquisition* 35, 689–725.

Baralt, M., Harmath-de Lemos, S. and Werfelli, S. (2014) Teachers' application of the Cognition Hypothesis when lesson planning: A case study. In M. Baralt, R. Gilabert and P. Robinson (eds) *Task Sequencing and Instructed Second Language Learning* (pp. 179–206). London: Bloomsbury.

Baralt, M., Gurzynski-Weiss, L. and Kim, Y. (2016) Engagement with the language: How examining learners' affective and social engagement explains successful learner-generated attention to form. In M. Sato and S. Ballinger (eds) *Peer Interaction and Second Language Learning: Pedagogical Potential and Research Agenda* (pp. 209–239). Amsterdam: John Benjamins.

Bartels, N. (2005) Applied linguistics and language teacher education: What we know. In N. Bartels (ed.) *Applied Linguistics and Language Teacher Education* (pp. 405–424). Boston, MA: Springer.

Benesch, S. (2017) *Emotions and English Language Teaching: Exploring Teachers' Emotion Labor.* New York: Routledge.

Bergsleithner, J.M., Frota, S.N. and Yoshioka, J.K. (eds) (2013) *Noticing and Second Language Acquisition: Studies in Honor of Richard Schmidt.* Honolulu, HI: National Foreign Language Resource Center.

Borg, S. (2015) *Teacher Cognition and Language Education: Research and Practice.* London: Bloomsbury.

Borg, S. (2019) Language teacher cognition: Perspectives and debates. In X. Gao (ed.) *Second Handbook of English Teaching* (pp. 298–307). Cham: Springer.

Breen, M.P. (1985) The social context for language learning – a neglected situation? *Studies in Second Language Acquisition* 7, 135–158.

Breen, M. (1989) The evaluation cycle for language learning tasks. In R.K. Johnson (ed.) *The Second Language Curriculum* (pp. 187–206). Cambridge: Cambridge University Press.

Brown, J.D. (2004) Research methods for applied linguistics: Scope, characteristics, and standards. In A. Davies and C. Elder (eds) *The Handbook of Applied Linguistics* (pp. 476–500). Oxford: Blackwell.

Brown, J.D. (2014) *Mixed Methods Research for TESOL.* Edinburgh: Edinburgh University Press.

Buchanan, H. and Timmis, I. (2019) Classroom management: Art, craft, or science? In S. Walsh and S. Mann (eds) *The Routledge Handbook of English Language Teacher Education* (pp. 319–334). New York: Routledge.

Burton, J. (2009) Reflective practice. In A. Burns and J.C. Richards (eds) *The Cambridge Guide to Second Language Teacher Education* (pp. 298–307). Cambridge: Cambridge University Press.

Butler, Y.G. (2004) What level of English proficiency do elementary school teachers need to attain to teach EFL? Case studies from Korea, Taiwan, and Japan. *TESOL Quarterly* 38, 245–278.

Butler, Y.G. (2011) The implementation of communicative and task-based language teaching in the Asia-Pacific region. *Annual Review of Applied Linguistics* 31, 36–57.

Bygate, M. (2016) TBLT through the lens of applied linguistics: Engaging with the real world of the classroom. *International Journal of Applied Linguistics* 167, 3–15.

Bygate, M., Skehan, P. and Swain, M. (2001) Introduction. In M. Bygate, P. Skehan and M. Swain (eds) *Researching Pedagogic Tasks: Second Language Learning, Teaching and Testing* (pp. 1–20). Harlow: Pearson Education.

Cadierno, T. and Robinson, P. (2009) Language typology, task complexity and the development of L2 lexicalization patterns for describing motion events. *Annual Review of Cognitive Linguistics* 7, 245–276.

Calandra, B. and Rich, P.J. (eds) (2015) *Digital Video for Teacher Education: Research and Practice.* New York: Routledge.

Carless, D. (2004) Issues in teachers' reinterpretation of a task-based innovation in primary schools. *TESOL Quarterly* 38, 639–662.

Carr, T.H. and Curran, T. (1994) Cognitive factors in learning about structured sequences: Applications to syntax. *Studies in Second Language Acquisition* 16, 205–230.

Carroll, S.E. (1999) Putting 'input' in its proper place. *Second Language Research* 15, 337–388.

Cenoz, J. and Gorter, D. (2015) Towards a holistic approach in the study of multilingual education. In J. Cenoz and D. Gorter (eds) *Multilingual Education: Between Language Learning and Translanguaging* (pp. 1–15). Cambridge: Cambridge University Press.

Chomsky, N. (2000) *New Horizons in the Study of Language and Mind.* Cambridge: Cambridge University Press.

Colestock, A.A. and Sherin, M.G. (2016) What teachers notice when they notice student thinking: Teacher-identified purposes for attending to students' mathematical thinking. In A.D. Robertson, R.E. Scherr and D. Hammer (eds) *Responsive Teaching in Science and Mathematics* (pp. 126–144). New York: Routledge.

Copland, F. and Donaghue, H. (2019) Post observation feedback. In S. Walsh and S. Mann (eds) *The Routledge Handbook of English Language Teacher Education* (pp. 402–416). New York: Routledge.

Coughlan, P. and Duff, P.A. (1994) 'Same task, different activities': Analysis of a second language acquisition task from an activity theory perspective. In J. Lantolf and G. Appel (eds) *Vygotskian Perspectives on Second Language Research* (pp. 173–193). Norwood, NJ: Ablex.

Crandall, J. and Christison, M. (2016) An overview of research in English language teacher education and professional development. In J. Crandall and M. Christison (eds) *Teacher Education and Professional Development in TESOL: Global Perspectives* (pp. 3–34). New York: Routledge.

Creswell, J.W. and Plano Clark, V.L. (2011) *Designing and Conducting Mixed Methods Research* (2nd edn). Thousand Oaks, CA: Sage.

Criswell, B. and Krall, R.M. (2017) Teacher noticing in various grade bands and contexts: Commentary. In E.O. Schack, M.H. Fisher and J.A. Wilhelm (eds) *Teacher Noticing: Bridging and Broadening Perspectives, Contexts, and Frameworks* (pp. 21–30). Cham: Springer.

Crookes, G. (2003) *A Practicum in TESOL: Professional Development through Teaching Practice.* Cambridge: Cambridge University Press.

Day, R.R. (ed.) (1986) *Talking to Learn: Conversation in Second Language Acquisition.* Rowley, MA: Newbury House.

DeKeyser, R. (2003) Implicit and explicit learning. In C.J. Doughty and M.H. Long (eds) *The Handbook of Second Language Acquisition* (pp. 313–348). Malden, MA: Blackwell.

Denis, M. (2018) *Space and Spatial Cognition: A Multidisciplinary Perspective.* New York: Routledge.

Dewaele, J.-M., Gkonou, C. and Mercer, S. (2018) Do ESL/EFL teachers' emotional intelligence, teaching experience and gender affect their classroom practice? In J. de D. Martínez Agudo (ed.) *Emotions in Second Language Teaching: Theory, Research and Teacher Education* (pp. 124–141). New York: Springer.

Dörnyei, Z. (2002) The motivational basis of language learning tasks. In P. Robinson (ed.) *Individual Differences and Instructed Language Learning* (pp. 137–158). Amsterdam: John Benjamins.

Dörnyei, Z. (2017) Conceptualizing L2 learner characteristics in a complex, dynamic world. In L. Ortega and Z. Han (eds) *Complexity Theory and Language Development: In Celebration of Diane Larsen-Freeman* (pp. 79–96). Amsterdam: John Benjamins.

Dörnyei, Z. and Murphey, T. (2003) *Group Dynamics in the Language Classroom.* Cambridge: Cambridge University Press.

Dörnyei, Z. and Ryan, S. (2015) *The Psychology of the Language Learner Revisited.* New York: Routledge.

Doughty, C. (2001) Cognitive underpinnings of focus on form. In P. Robinson (ed.) *Cognition and Second Language Instruction* (pp. 206–257). Cambridge: Cambridge University Press.

Doughty, C.J. (2003) Instructed SLA: Constraints, compensation, and enhancement. In C.J. Doughty and M.H. Long (eds) *The Handbook of Second Language Acquisition* (pp. 256–310). Malden, MA: Blackwell.

Doughty, C. and Varela, E. (1998) Communicative focus on form. In C. Doughty and J. Williams (eds) *Focus on Form in Classroom Second Language Acquisition* (pp. 114–138). Cambridge: Cambridge University Press.

Doughty, C. and Williams, J. (1998) *Focus on Form in Classroom Second Language Acquisition*. Cambridge: Cambridge University Press.

Douglas Fir Group (2016) A transdisciplinary framework for SLA in a multilingual world. *The Modern Language Journal* 100, 19–47.

East, M. (2012) *Task-Based Language Teaching from the Teachers' Perspective*. Amsterdam: John Benjamins.

Eilan, N. (2005) Joint attention, communication, and mind. In N. Eilan, C. Hoerl, T. McCormack and J. Roessler (eds) *Joint Attention: Communication and Other Minds* (pp. 1–33). Oxford: Oxford University Press.

Ellis, N.C. (2005) At the interface: Dynamic interactions of explicit and implicit language knowledge. *Studies in Second Language Acquisition* 27, 305–352.

Ellis, N.C., Römer, U. and O'Donnell, M.B. (2016) *Usage-based Approaches to Language Acquisition and Processing: Cognitive and Corpus Investigations of Construction Grammar*. Malden, MA: Wiley.

Ellis, R. (2018) *Reflections on Task-Based Language Teaching*. Bristol: Multilingual Matters.

Endsley, M.R. (2000) Theoretical underpinnings of situation awareness: A critical review. In M.R. Endsley and D.J. Garland (eds) *Situation Awareness Analysis and Measurement* (pp. 3–32). Mahwah, NJ: Lawrence Erlbaum.

Ericsson, K.A. and Simon, H.A. (1984) *Protocol Analysis: Verbal Reports as Data*. Cambridge, MA: MIT Press.

Eskildsen, S.W. (2008) Constructing another language – usage-based linguistics in second language acquisition. *Applied Linguistics* 30, 335–357.

Eskildsen, S.W. and Cadierno, T. (2015) Advancing usage-based approaches to L2 studies. In T. Cadierno and S.W. Eskildsen (eds) *Usage-Based Perspectives on Second Language Learning* (pp. 1–16). Berlin: de Gruyter.

Eskildsen, S.W. and Wagner, J. (2015) Embodied L2 construction learning. *Language Learning* 65, 268–297.

Evans, V. and Green, M. (2006) *Cognitive Linguistics: An Introduction*. Edinburgh: Edinburgh University Press.

Fagan, D.S. (2019) Teacher embodied responsiveness to student displays of trouble within small-group activities. In J.K. Hall and S.D. Looney (eds) *The Embodied Work of Teaching* (pp. 100–121). Bristol: Multilingual Matters.

Fanselow, J.F. (1988) 'Let's see': Contrasting conversations about teaching. *TESOL Quarterly* 22, 113–130.

Farrell, T.S.C. (2015) *Promoting Teacher Reflection in Second Language Education: A Framework for TESOL Professionals*. New York: Routledge.

Farrell, T.S.C. (2016) The practices of encouraging TESOL teachers to engage in reflective practice: An appraisal of recent research contributions. *Language Teaching Research* 20, 223–247.

Feryok, A. (2010) Language teacher cognitions: Complex dynamic systems? *System* 38, 272–279.

Feryok, A. (2018) Language teacher cognition: An emergent phenomenon in an emergent field. In S. Mercer and A. Kostoulas (eds) *Language Teacher Psychology* (pp. 105–121). Bristol: Multilingual Matters.

Feys, J. (2016) Nonparametric tests for the interaction in two-way factorial designs using R. *The R Journal* 8, 367–378.

Freeman, D. (2016) *Educating Second Language Teachers: The Same Things Done Differently*. Oxford: Oxford University Press.

Freire, P. (2007) *Pedagogy of the Oppressed: 30th Anniversary Edition*. New York: Continuum. (Original work published 1970.)

Fujita-Round, S. and Maher, J.C. (2008) Language education policy in Japan. In S. May and N.H. Hornberger (eds) *Encyclopedia of Language and Education, Vol. 1: Language Policy and Political Issues in Education* (2nd edn) (pp. 393–404). New York: Springer.

Fukuta, J., Tamura, Y. and Kurita, A. (2017) Chūgakkō kyōkasho ni okeru kōtō komyunike-shon o shikō shita katsudō no bunseki – dainigengoshūtoku kenkyū ni okeru tasuku kijun kara no itsudatsu ni shōten o atete [Analysis of oral-communication-oriented activities in junior high school textbooks: Focusing on task criteria proposed by second language research]. *JALT Journal* 39, 165–182.

Gallagher, S. (2011) Interactive coordination in joint attention. In A. Seeman (ed.) *Joint Attention: New Developments in Psychology, Philosophy of Mind, and Social Neuroscience* (pp. 293–305). Cambridge, MA: MIT Press.

Gallo, D.A. and Wheeler, M.E. (2013) Episodic memory. In D. Reisberg (ed.) *The Oxford Handbook of Cognitive Psychology* (pp. 189–205). Oxford: Oxford University Press.

Gass, S.M. (1997) *Input, Interaction, and the Second Language Learner*. Mahwah, NJ: Lawrence Erlbaum.

Gass, S.M. and Mackey, A. (2017) *Stimulated Recall Methodology in Applied Linguistics and L2 Research* (2nd edn). New York: Routledge.

Gass, S.M., Mackey, A. and Ross-Feldman, L. (2005) Task-based interactions in classroom and laboratory settings. *Language Learning* 55, 575–611.

Gass, S.M., Spinner, P. and Behney, J. (eds) (2017) *Salience in Second Language Acquisition*. New York: Routledge.

Gkonou, C. and Mercer, S. (2018) The relational beliefs and practices of highly socio-emotionally competent language teachers. In S. Mercer and A. Kostoulas (eds) *Language Teacher Psychology* (pp. 158–177). Bristol: Multilingual Matters.

Godfroid, A., Housen, A. and Boers, F. (2010) A procedure for testing the Noticing Hypothesis in the context of vocabulary acquisition. In M. Pütz and L. Sicola (eds) *Cognitive Processing in Second Language Acquisition: Inside the Learner's Mind* (pp. 169–197). Amsterdam: John Benjamins.

Goldberg, A.E. (2006) *Constructions at Work: The Nature of Generalization in Language*. Oxford: Oxford University Press.

Goldberg, A.E. (2019) *Explain Me This: Creativity, Competition, and the Partial Productivity of Constructions*. Princeton, NJ: Princeton University Press.

Goodwin, C. (1994) Professional vision. *American Anthropologist* 96, 606–633.

Granena, G., Jackson, D.O. and Yilmaz, Y. (eds) (2016) *Cognitive Individual Differences in Second Language Acquisition and Processing*. Amsterdam: John Benjamins.

Gray, J. and Morton, T. (2018) *Social Interaction and English Language Teacher Identity*. Edinburgh: Edinburgh University Press.

Gregersen, T.S. and MacIntyre, P.D. (eds) (2017) *Innovative Practices in Language Teacher Education: Spanning the Spectrum from Intra- to Inter-personal Professional Development*. Cham: Springer.

Guk, I. and Kellogg, D. (2007) The ZPD and whole class teaching: Teacher-led and student-led interactional mediation of tasks. *Language Teaching Research* 11, 281–299.

Gullberg, M. (2011) Multilingual modality: Communicative difficulties and their solutions in second-language use. In J. Streeck, C. Goodwin and C. LeBaron (eds) *Embodied Interaction: Language and Body in the Material World* (pp. 137–151). Cambridge: Cambridge University Press.

Gurzynski-Weiss, L. (2016) Factors influencing Spanish instructors' in-class feedback decisions. *The Modern Language Journal* 100, 255–275.

Gurzynski-Weiss, L. (2017) L2 instructor individual characteristics. In S. Loewen and M. Sato (eds) *The Routledge Handbook of Instructed Second Language Acquisition* (pp. 114–138). New York: Routledge.

Hall, J.K. (2019) *Essentials of SLA for L2 Teachers: A Transdisciplinary Framework*. New York: Routledge.

Hall, J.K. and Looney, S.D. (2019) Introduction: The embodied work of teaching. In J.K. Hall and S.D. Looney (eds) *The Embodied Work of Teaching* (pp. 1–14). Bristol: Multilingual Matters.

Harley, B. (1993) Instructional strategies and SLA in early French immersion. *Studies in Second Language Acquisition* 15, 245–259.

Hauser, E. (2017) Learning and the immediate use(fulness) of a new vocabulary item. *The Modern Language Journal* 101, 712–728.

Hellermann, J. (2007) The development of practices for action in classroom dyadic interaction: Focus on task openings. *The Modern Language Journal* 91, 83–96.

Hellermann, J. and Cole, E. (2008) Practices for social interaction in the language-learning classroom: Disengagements from dyadic task interaction. *Applied Linguistics* 30, 186–215.

Hodges, C., Moore, S., Lockee, B., Trust, T. and Bond, A. (2020) The difference between emergency remote teaching and online learning. *Educause Review*, 27 March.

Horwitz, E.K. (1996) Even teachers get the blues: Recognizing and alleviating language teachers' feelings of foreign language anxiety. *Foreign Language Annals* 29, 365–372.

Hutchby, I. and Wooffitt, R. (2008) *Conversation Analysis* (2nd edn). Cambridge: Polity Press.

Hüttner, J. (2019) Towards 'professional vision': Video as a resource in teacher learning. In S. Walsh and S. Mann (eds) *The Routledge Handbook of English Language Teacher Education* (pp. 473–487). New York: Routledge.

Ishikawa, T. (2007) The effect of manipulating task complexity along the [+/- here-and-now] dimension on L2 written narrative discourse. In M.P. García Mayo (ed.) *Investigating Tasks in Formal Language Learning* (pp. 136–156). Clevedon: Multilingual Matters.

Jacknick, C.M. and Thornbury, S. (2013) The task at hand: Noticing as a mind–body–world phenomenon. In J.M. Bergsleithner, S.N. Frota and J.K. Yoshioka (eds) *Noticing and Second Language Acquisition: Studies in Honor of Richard Schmidt* (pp. 309–329). Honolulu, HI: National Foreign Language Resource Center.

Jackson, D.O. (2012) Task-based language teacher education in an undergraduate program in Japan. In A. Shehadeh and C.A. Coombe (eds) *Task-Based Language Teaching in Foreign Language Contexts: Research and Implementation* (pp. 267–285). Amsterdam: John Benjamins.

Jackson, D.O. and Burch, A.R. (2017) Complementary theoretical perspectives on task-based classroom realities. *TESOL Quarterly* 51, 493–506.

Jackson, D.O. and Cho, M. (2018) Language teacher noticing: A socio-cognitive window on classroom realities. *Language Teaching Research* 22, 29–46.

Jackson, D.O. and Shirakawa, T. (2020) Identity, noticing, and emotion among pre-service English language teachers. In B. Yazan and K. Lindahl (eds) *Language Teacher Identity in TESOL* (pp. 197–212). New York: Routledge.

Jackson, D.O. and Suethanapornkul, S. (2013) The Cognition Hypothesis: A synthesis and meta-analysis of research on second language task complexity. *Language Learning* 63, 330–367.

Jacobs, V.R. (2017) Complexities in measuring teacher noticing. In E.O. Schack, M.H. Fisher and J.A. Wilhelm (eds) *Teacher Noticing: Bridging and Broadening Perspectives, Contexts, and Frameworks* (pp. 273–279). Cham: Springer.

James, W. (1890) *The Principles of Psychology*. Cambridge, MA: Harvard University Press.

Johnson, R.B., Onwuegbuzie, A.J. and Turner, L.A. (2007) Toward a definition of mixed methods research. *Journal of Mixed Methods Research* 1, 112–133.

Käänta, L. (2014) From noticing to initiating correction: Students' epistemic displays in instructional interaction. *Journal of Pragmatics* 66, 86–105.

Kalaja, P. and Mäntylä, K. (2018) 'The English class of my dreams': Envisioning teaching a foreign language. In S. Mercer and A. Kostoulas (eds) *Language Teacher Psychology* (pp. 34–52). Bristol: Multilingual Matters.

Kartchava, E. and Ammar, A. (2014) The noticeability and effectiveness of corrective feedback in relation to target type. *Language Teaching Research* 18, 428–452.

Kasper, G. and Burch, A.R. (2016) Focus on form in the wild. In R.A. van Compernolle and J. McGregor (eds) *Authenticity, Language and Interaction in Second Language Contexts* (pp. 198–232). Bristol: Multilingual Matters.

Keck, C.M., Iberri-Shea, G., Tracy-Ventura, N. and Wa-Mbaleka, S. (2006) Investigating the empirical link between task-based interaction and acquisition: A meta-analysis. In J.M. Norris and L. Ortega (eds) *Synthesizing Research on Language Learning and Teaching* (pp. 91–131). Amsterdam: John Benjamins.

Kendon, A. (2004) *Gesture: Visible Action as Utterance*. Cambridge: Cambridge University Press.

KGAA (Kanda Gaigo Alumni Association) (2011) Keep changing the curriculum of the ELI [Interview with Francis C. Johnson]. Tokyo: Kanda Gaigo Group.

Kim, J.-H. and Han, Z. (2007) Recasts in communicative EFL classes: Do teacher intent and learner interpretation overlap? In A. Mackey (ed.) *Conversational Interaction in Second Language Acquisition* (pp. 269–297). Oxford: Oxford University Press.

King, J. and Ng, K.-Y.S. (2018) Teacher emotions and the emotional labour of second language teaching. In S. Mercer and A. Kostoulas (eds) *Language Teacher Psychology* (pp. 141–157). Bristol: Multilingual Matters.

Kirby, K.N. and Gerlanc, D. (2013) BootES: An R package for bootstrap confidence intervals on effect sizes. *Behavior Research Methods* 45, 905–927.

Knight, J. (2014) *Focus on Teaching: Using Video for High-Impact Instruction*. Thousand Oaks: Corwin.

Konoeda, K. and Watanabe, Y. (2008) Task-based critical pedagogy in Japanese EFL classrooms: Rationale, principles, examples. In M. Mantero, P. Chamness Miller and J.L. Watzke (eds) *Language Studies, Vol. 1: Language across Disciplinary Boundaries* (pp. 45–72). St Louis, MO: International Society for Language Studies.

Krashen, S.D. (1982) *Principles and Practice in Second Language Acquisition*. Oxford: Pergamon.

Kubanyiova, M. and Feryok, A. (2015) Language teacher cognition in applied linguistics research: Revisiting the territory, redrawing the boundaries, reclaiming the relevance. *The Modern Language Journal* 99, 435–449.

Kumaravadivelu, B. (2006) *Understanding Language Teaching: From Method to Postmethod*. Mahwah, NJ: Lawrence Erlbaum.

Kunitz, S. and Skogmyr Marian, K. (2017) Tracking immanent language learning behavior over time in task-based classroom work. *TESOL Quarterly* 51, 507–535.

LaFlair, G.T., Egbert, J. and Plonsky, L. (2015) A practical guide to bootstrapping descriptive statistics, correlations, t tests, and ANOVAs. In L. Plonsky (ed.) *Advancing Quantitative Methods in Second Language Research* (pp. 66–97). New York: Routledge.

Langacker, R.W. (2008) Cognitive Grammar as a basis for language instruction. In P. Robinson and N.C. Ellis (eds) *Handbook of Cognitive Linguistics and Second Language Acquisition* (pp. 66–88). New York: Routledge.

Lantolf, J. (ed.) (2000) *Sociocultural Theory and Second Language Learning*. Oxford: Oxford University Press.

Lantolf, J.P. (2011) The sociocultural approach to second language acquisition: Sociocultural theory, second language acquisition, and artificial L2 development. In D. Atkinson (ed.) *Alternative Approaches to Second Language Acquisition* (pp. 24–47). New York: Routledge.

Lantolf, J. and Appel, G. (eds) (1994) *Vygotskian Perspectives on Second Language Research*. Norwood, NJ: Ablex.

Lantolf, J.P. and Thorne, S.L. (2007) Sociocultural theory and second language learning. In B. VanPatten and J. Williams (eds) *Theories in Second Language Acquisition: An Introduction* (pp. 201–224). Mahwah, NJ: Lawrence Erlbaum.

Larsen-Freeman, D. (2017) Complexity theory: The lessons continue. In L. Ortega and Z. Han (eds) *Complexity Theory and Language Development: In Celebration of Diane Larsen-Freeman* (pp. 11–50). Amsterdam: John Benjamins.

Lassegard, J.P. (2008) The effects of peer tutoring between domestic and international students: The tutor system at Japanese universities. *Higher Education Research & Development* 27, 357–369.

Lee, J. and Burch, A.R. (2017) Collaborative planning in process: An ethnomethodological perspective. *TESOL Quarterly* 51, 536–575.

Lee, M.Y. and Choy, B.H. (2017) Mathematical teacher noticing: The key to learning from lesson study. In E.O. Schack, M.H. Fisher and J.A. Wilhelm (eds) *Teacher Noticing: Bridging and Broadening Perspectives, Contexts, and Frameworks* (pp. 121–140). Cham: Springer.

Lee, S. and Huang, H. (2008) Visual input enhancement and grammar learning: A meta-analytic review. *Studies in Second Language Acquisition* 30, 307–331.

Lengeling, M.M., Wilson, A.K. and Mora-Pablo, I. (2020) TESOL students' perspectives: Noticing classroom practice. In A. Simpson, F. Pomerantz, D. Kaufman and S. Ellis (eds) *Developing Habits of Noticing in Literacy and Language Classrooms: Research and Practice across Professional Cultures* (pp. 98–115). New York: Routledge.

Leow, R.P. (2015) *Explicit Learning in the L2 Classroom: A Student-Centered Approach.* New York: Routledge.

Leow, R.P. and Hama, M. (2013) Implicit learning in SLA and the issue of internal validity: A response to Leung and Williams's (2011) 'The implicit learning of mappings between forms and contextually derived meanings'. *Studies in Second Language Acquisition* 35, 545–557.

Leow, R.P., Johnson, E. and Záráte-Sandez, G. (2011) Getting a grip on the slippery construct of awareness: Toward a finer-grained methodological perspective. In C. Sanz and R.P. Leow (eds) *Implicit and Explicit Language Learning: Conditions, Processes, and Knowledge in SLA and Bilingualism* (pp. 61–72). Washington, DC: Georgetown University Press.

Leow, R.P., Grey, S., Marijuan, S. and Moorman, C. (2014) Concurrent data elicitation procedures, processes, and the early stages of L2 learning: A critical overview. *Second Language Research* 30, 111–127.

Levinson, S.C. (2003) *Space in Language and Cognition: Explorations in Cognitive Diversity.* Cambridge: Cambridge University Press.

Libby, L.K., Eibach, R.P. and Gilovich, T. (2005) Here's looking at me: The effect of memory perspective on assessments of personal change. *Journal of Personality and Social Psychology* 88, 50–62.

Loewen, S. (2019) Teacher and student perspectives of LREs in a year 1 Spanish class: A stimulated recall study. In R.P. Leow (ed.) *The Routledge Handbook of Second Language Research in Classroom Learning* (pp. 227–240). New York: Routledge.

Long, M.H. (1983a) Linguistic and conversational adjustments to non-native speakers. *Studies in Second Language Acquisition* 5, 177–193.

Long, M.H. (1983b) Native speaker/non-native speaker conversation and the negotiation of comprehensible input. *Applied Linguistics* 4, 126–141.

Long, M. (1991) Focus on form: A design feature in language teaching methodology. In K. de Bot, R.B. Ginsberg and C. Kramsch (eds) *Foreign Language Research in Cross-Cultural Perspective* (pp. 39–52). Amsterdam: John Benjamins.

Long, M.H. (1996) The role of the linguistic environment in second language acquisition. In W.C. Ritchie and T.K. Bhatia (eds) *Handbook of Second Language Acquisition* (pp. 413–468). New York: Academic Press.

Long, M. (2015) *Second Language Acquisition and Task-Based Language Teaching.* Malden, MA: Wiley.

Long, M.H. and Robinson, P. (1998) Focus on form: Theory, research, and practice. In C. Doughty and J. Williams (eds) *Focus on Form in Classroom Second Language Acquisition* (pp. 15–41). Cambridge: Cambridge University Press.

Looney, S.D. (2019) The embodied accomplishment of teaching: Challenges for research and practice. In J.K. Hall and S.D. Looney (eds) *The Embodied Work of Teaching* (pp. 218–226). Bristol: Multilingual Matters.

Loschky, L. and Bley-Vroman, R. (1990) Creating structure-based communication tasks for second language development. *University of Hawai'i Working Papers in ESL* 9, 161–212.

Machida, T. (2019) How do Japanese junior high school teachers react to the teaching English in English policy? *JALT Journal* 41, 5–26.

MacIntyre, P., MacKay, E., Ross, J. and Abel, E. (2017) The emerging need for methods appropriate to study dynamic systems: Individual differences in motivational dynamics. In L. Ortega and Z. Han (eds) *Complexity Theory and Language Development: In Celebration of Diane Larsen-Freeman* (pp. 97–122). Amsterdam: John Benjamins.

Mackey, A. (2012) *Input, Interaction, and Corrective Feedback in L2 Learning*. Oxford: Oxford University Press.

Mackey, A. and Goo, J. (2007) Interaction research in SLA: A meta-analysis and research synthesis. In A. Mackey (ed.) *Conversational Interaction in Second Language Acquisition* (pp. 407–452). Oxford: Oxford University Press.

Mackey, A., Al-Khalil, M., Atanassova, G., Hama, M., Logan-Terry, A. and Nakatsukasa, K. (2007) Teachers' intentions and learners' perceptions about corrective feedback in the L2 classroom. *Innovation in Language Learning and Teaching* 1, 129–152.

Mann, S. and Walsh, S. (2013) RP or 'RIP': A critical perspective on reflective practice. *Applied Linguistics Review* 4, 291–315.

Mann, S. and Walsh, S. (2017) *Reflective Practice in English Language Teaching: Research-Based Principles and Practices*. New York: Routledge.

Mann, S., Crichton, R. and Edmett, A. (2020) Evaluating the role of video in supporting reflection beyond INSET. *System* 90, 1–24.

Mäntylä, K. and Kalaja, P. (2019) 'The class of my dreams' as envisioned by student teachers of English: What is there to teach about the language? In P. Kalaja and S. Melo-Pfeifer (eds) *Visualising Multilingual Lives: More than Words* (pp. 254–274). Bristol: Multilingual Matters.

Markee, N. (2008) Toward a learning behavior tracking methodology for CA-for-SLA. *Applied Linguistics* 29, 404–427.

Mason, J. (2002) *Researching Your Own Practice: The Discipline of Noticing*. New York: Routledge.

Mason, J. (2011) Noticing: Roots and branches. In M.G. Sherin, V.R. Jacobs and R.A. Philipp (eds) *Mathematics Teacher Noticing: Seeing through Teachers' Eyes* (pp. 35–50). New York: Routledge.

Mason, J. (2017) Probing beneath the surface of experience. In E.O. Schack, M.H. Fisher and J.A. Wilhelm (eds) *Teacher Noticing: Bridging and Broadening Perspectives, Contexts, and Frameworks* (pp. 1–17). Cham: Springer.

McCarroll, C. and Sutton, J. (2017) Memory and perspective. In S. Bernecker and K. Michaelian (eds) *The Routledge Handbook of Philosophy of Memory* (pp. 113–126). New York: Routledge.

McIsaac, H.K. and Eich, E. (2002) Vantage point in episodic memory. *Psychonomic Bulletin & Review* 9, 146–150.

Meijer, P.C., Verloop, N. and Beijaard, D. (1999) Exploring language teachers' practical knowledge about teaching reading comprehension. *Teaching and Teacher Education* 15, 59–84.

Mercer, S. (2018) Psychology for language learning: Spare a thought for the teacher. *Language Teaching* 51, 504–525.

Mercer, S. and Dörnyei, Z. (2020) *Engaging Language Learners in Contemporary Classrooms*. Cambridge: Cambridge University Press.
Mercer, S. and Kostoulas, A. (eds) (2018a) *Language Teacher Psychology*. Bristol: Multilingual Matters.
Mercer, S. and Kostoulas, A. (2018b) Introduction to language teacher psychology. In S. Mercer and A. Kostoulas (eds) *Language Teacher Psychology* (pp. 1–17). Bristol: Multilingual Matters.
Mercer, S., Ryan, S. and Williams, M. (2012) *Psychology for Language Learning: Insights from Research, Theory and Practice*. New York: Palgrave.
Mertens, D. (2007) Transformative paradigm: Mixed methods and social justice. *Journal of Mixed Methods Research* 1, 212–225.
MEXT (Ministry of Education, Culture, Sports, Science and Technology) (2010a) *Kōtōgakkō gakushū shidō yōryō eiyakuban* [*The Course of Study for Senior High School, English Version*]. See http://www.mext.go.jp/a_menu/shotou/new-cs/youryou/eiyaku/1298353.htm.
MEXT (Ministry of Education, Culture, Sports, Science and Technology) (2010b) *Chūgakkō gakushū shidō yōryō eiyakuban* [*The Course of Study for Junior High School, English Version*]. See http://www.mext.go.jp/a_menu/shotou/new-cs/youryou/eiyaku/1298356.htm.
MEXT (Ministry of Education, Culture, Sports, Science and Technology) (2017) *Chūgakkō gakushū shidō yōryō* [*The Course of Study for Junior High School*]. See www.mext.go.jp/a_menu/shotou/new-cs/1384661.htm.
Miller, K.F. (2011) Situation awareness in teaching: What educators can learn from video-based research in other fields. In M.G. Sherin, V.R. Jacobs and R.A. Philipp (eds) *Mathematics Teacher Noticing: Seeing through Teachers' Eyes* (pp. 51–65). New York: Routledge.
Mochizuki, N. and Ortega, L. (2008) Balancing communication and grammar in beginning-level foreign language classrooms: A study of guided planning and relativization. *Language Teaching Research* 12, 11–37.
Mondada, L. (2016) Challenges of multimodality: Language and the body in social interaction. *Journal of Sociolinguistics* 20, 336–366.
Morris, S., Roloff Rothman, J. and Owens, J. (eds) (2020) Introduction to the special section: Teaching during a pandemic. *Literacies and Language Education: Research and Practice*. See https://kuis.kandagaigo.ac.jp/eli/publications/?page_id = 510.
Moser, J., Harris, J. and Carle, J. (2011) Improving teacher talk through a task-based approach. *ELT Journal* 66, 81–88.
Murphey, T. (2017) Asking students to teach: Gardening in the jungle. In T.S. Gregersen and P.D. MacIntyre (eds) *Innovative Practices in Language Teacher Education: Spanning the Spectrum from Intra-to Inter-personal Professional Development* (pp. 251–268). Cham: Springer.
Mynard, J., Burke, M., Hooper, D., Kushida, B., Lyon, P., Sampson, R. and Taw, P. (2020) *Dynamics of a Social Language Learning Community: Beliefs, Membership and Identity*. Bristol: Multilingual Matters.
Norris, J. (2011) Task-based teaching and testing. In M.H. Long and C.J. Doughty (eds) *The Handbook of Language Teaching* (pp. 578–594). Cambridge: Blackwell.
Norris, J.M. (2015) Statistical significance testing in second language research: Basic problems and suggestions for reform. *Language Learning* 65, 97–126.
Norris, J.M. and Ortega, L. (2000) Effectiveness of L2 instruction: A research synthesis and quantitative meta-analysis. *Language Learning* 50, 417–528.
Onwuegbuzie, A.J. and Johnson, R.B. (2006) The validity issue in mixed methods research. *Research in the Schools* 13, 48–63.
Ortega, L. (2005) For what and for whom is our research? The ethical as a transformative lens in instructed SLA. *Modern Language Journal* 89, 427–443.

Ortega, L. (2011) SLA after the social turn: Where cognitivism and its alternatives stand. In D. Atkinson (ed.) *Alternative Approaches to Second Language Acquisition* (pp. 167–180). New York: Routledge.

Patton, M.Q. (1997) *Utilization-Focused Evaluation* (3rd edn). Thousand Oaks, CA: Sage.

Pekarek Doehler, S. and Pochon-Berger, E. (2015) The development of L2 interactional competence: Evidence from turn-taking organization, sequence organization, repair organization and preference organization. In T. Cadierno and S.W. Eskildsen (eds) *Usage-Based Perspectives on Second Language Learning* (pp. 233–268). Berlin: de Gruyter.

Philipp, R., Fredenberg, M. and Hawthorne, C. (2017) Examining student thinking through teacher noticing. In E.O. Schack, M.H. Fisher and J.A. Wilhelm (eds) *Teacher Noticing: Bridging and Broadening Perspectives, Contexts, and Frameworks* (pp. 113–120). Cham: Springer.

Philp, J. and Duchesne, S. (2016) Exploring engagement in tasks in the language classroom. *Annual Review of Applied Linguistics* 36, 50–72.

Philp, J., Adams, R. and Iwashita, N. (2014) *Peer Interaction and Second Language Learning*. New York: Routledge.

Pica, T. (1994) Research on negotiation: What does it reveal about second-language learning conditions, processes, and outcomes? *Language Learning* 44, 493–527.

Pica, T., Kanagy, R. and Falodun, J. (1993) Choosing and using communication tasks for second language instruction and research. In S. Crookes and S.M. Gass (eds) *Tasks and Language Learning: Integrating Theory and Practice* (pp. 9–34). Clevedon: Multilingual Matters.

Platt, E. and Brooks, F.B. (2008) Embodiment as self-regulation in L2 task performance. In S.G. McCafferty and G. Stam (eds) *Gesture: Second Language Acquisition and Classroom Research* (pp. 66–87). New York: Routledge.

Plonsky, L. (2015) Statistical power, *p* values, descriptive statistics, and effect sizes: A 'back-to-basics' approach to advancing quantitative methods in L2 research. In L. Plonsky (ed.) *Advancing Quantitative Methods in Second Language Research* (pp. 43–65). New York: Routledge.

Polio, C. and Gass, S. (2017) Preservice instructors' performance on a language learning task: Altering interlocutor task orientation. In L. Gurzynski-Weiss (ed.) *Expanding Individual Difference Research in the Interaction Approach: Investigating Learners, Instructors, and Other Interlocutors* (pp. 281–302). Amsterdam: John Benjamins.

Polio, C., Gass, S. and Chapin, L. (2006) Using stimulated recall to investigate native speaker perceptions in native-nonnative speaker interaction. *Studies in Second Language Acquisition* 28, 237–267.

Prabhu, N.S. (1987) *Second Language Pedagogy*. Oxford: Oxford University Press.

Prabhu, N.S. (1990) There is no best method – why? *TESOL Quarterly* 24, 161–176.

Pukui, M.K. and Elbert, S.H. (1992) *New Pocket Hawaiian Dictionary*. Honolulu, HI: University of Hawai'i Press.

R Core Team (2018) R: A language and environment for statistical computing. Vienna: R Foundation for Statistical Computing. See https://www.R-project.org/.

Rebuschat, P. (ed.) (2015) *Implicit and Explicit Learning of Languages*. Amsterdam: John Benjamins.

Rebuschat, P. and Williams, J. (2012) Implicit and explicit knowledge in second language acquisition. *Applied Psycholinguistics* 33 (4), 829–856.

Révész, A. (2009) Task complexity, focus on form, and second language development. *Studies in Second Language Acquisition* 31, 437–470.

Révész, A. (2012) Coding second language data validly and reliability. In A. Mackey and S.M. Gass (eds) *Research Methods in Second Language Acquisition: A Practical Guide* (pp. 203–221). Malden, MA: Wiley.

Révész, A. and Gurzynski-Weiss, L. (2016) Teachers' perspectives on second language task difficulty: Insights from think-alouds and eye tracking. *Annual Review of Applied Linguistics* 36, 182–204.

Riazi, A.M. (2016) Innovative mixed-methods research: Moving beyond design technicalities to epistemological and methodological realizations. *Applied Linguistics* 37, 33–49.

Riazi, A.M. (2017) *Mixed Methods Research in Language Teaching and Learning*. Sheffield: Equinox.

Ritchhart, R., Church, M. and Morrison, K. (2011) *Making Thinking Visible: How to Promote Engagement, Understanding, and Independence for All Learners*. San Francisco, CA: Jossey-Bass.

Ro, E. (2018) Facilitating an L2 book club: A conversation-analytic study of task management. *The Modern Language Journal* 102, 181–198.

Robinson, P. (2001) Task complexity, task difficulty, and task production: Exploring interactions in a componential framework. *Applied Linguistics* 22, 27–57.

Robinson, P. (2003) Attention and memory during SLA. In C.J. Doughty and M.H. Long (eds) *The Handbook of Second Language Acquisition* (pp. 631–678). Malden, MA: Blackwell.

Robinson, P. (2007) Criteria for classifying and sequencing pedagogic tasks. In M.P. García Mayo (ed.) *Investigating Tasks in Formal Language Learning* (pp. 7–26). Clevedon: Multilingual Matters.

Robinson, P. (ed.) (2011) *Second Language Task Complexity: Researching the Cognition Hypothesis of Language Learning and Performance*. Amsterdam: John Benjamins.

Robinson, P. (2015) The Cognition Hypothesis, second language task demands, and the SSARC model of pedagogic task sequencing. In M. Bygate (ed.) *Domains and Directions in the Development of TBLT* (pp. 87–121). Amsterdam: John Benjamins.

Robinson, P., Mackey, A., Gass, S.M. and Schmidt, R. (2012) Attention and awareness in second language acquisition. In S.M. Gass and A. Mackey (eds) *The Routledge Handbook of Second Language Acquisition* (pp. 247–267). New York: Routledge.

Roehr-Brackin, K. (2018) *Metalinguistic Awareness and Second Language Acquisition*. New York: Routledge.

Russ, R.S. and Luna, M.J. (2013) Inferring teacher epistemological framing from local patterns in teacher noticing. *Journal of Research in Science Teaching* 50, 284–314.

Ryan, J. (2012) Stimulated recall. In R. Barnard and A. Burns (eds) *Researching Language Teacher Cognition and Practice: International Case Studies* (pp. 144–154). Bristol: Multilingual Matters.

Sample, E. and Michel, M. (2014) An exploratory study into trade-off effects of complexity, accuracy, and fluency on young learners' oral task repetition. *TESL Canada Journal* 31, 23–46.

Samuda, V. (2001) Guiding relationships between form and meaning during task performance: The role of the teacher. In M. Bygate, P. Skehan and M. Swain (eds) *Researching Pedagogic Tasks: Second Language Learning, Teaching, and Testing* (pp. 119–140). Harlow: Pearson.

Samuda, V. (2015) Tasks, design and the architecture of pedagogical spaces. In M. Bygate (ed.) *Domains and Directions in the Development of TBLT* (pp. 271–302). Amsterdam: John Benjamins.

Samuda, V. and Bygate, M. (2008) *Tasks in Second Language Learning*. Basingstoke: Palgrave Macmillan.

Samuda, V., Van den Branden, K. and Bygate, M. (eds) (2018) *TBLT as a Researched Pedagogy*. Amsterdam: John Benjamins.

Sano, M., Yamaoka, T., Matsumoto, S., Sato, Y., Aoki, S. and Shimaoka, T. (2006) *Sunshine English Course 3*. Tokyo: Kairyudo.

Sasayama, S. (2016) Is a 'complex' task really complex? Validating the assumption of cognitive task complexity. *The Modern Language Journal* 100, 231–254.

Sasayama, S. and Izumi, S. (2012) Effects of task complexity and pre-task planning on EFL learners' oral production. In A. Shehadeh and C.A. Coombe (eds) *Task-Based Language Teaching in Foreign Language Contexts: Research and Implementation* (pp. 23–42). Amsterdam: John Benjamins.

Sato, C.J. (1986) Conversation and interlanguage development: Rethinking the connection. In R.R. Day (ed.) *Talking to Learn: Conversation in Second Language Acquisition* (pp. 5–22). Rowley, MA: Newbury House.

Schachter, J. (1998) Recent research in language learning studies: Promises and problems. *Language Learning* 48, 557–583.

Schack, E.O., Fisher, M.H. and Wilhelm, J.A. (2017) (eds) *Teacher Noticing: Bridging and Broadening Perspectives, Contexts, and Frameworks*. Cham: Springer.

Schegloff, E.A. (2007) *Sequence Organization in Interaction, Vol. 1: A Primer in Conversation Analysis*. Cambridge: Cambridge University Press.

Schegloff, E.A., Ochs, E. and Thompson, S.A. (1996) Introduction. In E. Ochs, E.A. Schegloff and S.A. Thompson (eds) *Interaction and Grammar* (pp. 1–51). Cambridge: Cambridge University Press.

Schmidt, R.W. (1990) The role of consciousness in second language learning. *Applied Linguistics* 11, 129–158.

Schmidt, R. (1993) Awareness and second language acquisition. *Annual Review of Applied Linguistics* 13, 206–226.

Schmidt, R. (1994) Deconstructing consciousness in search of useful definitions for applied linguistics. *AILA Review* 11, 11–26.

Schmidt, R. (2001) Attention. In P. Robinson (ed.) *Cognition and Second Language Instruction* (pp. 3–32). New York: Cambridge University Press.

Schmidt, R. (2012) Attention, awareness, and individual differences in language learning. In W.M. Chan, K.N. Chin, S. Bhatt and I. Walker (eds) *Perspectives on Individual Characteristics and Foreign Language Education* (pp. 27–50). Boston, MA: De Gruyter.

Schmidt, R.W. and Frota, S.N. (1986) Developing basic conversational ability in a second language: A case study of an adult learner of Portuguese. In R.R. Day (ed.) *Talking to Learn: Conversation in Second Language Acquisition* (pp. 237–326). Rowley, MA: Newbury House.

Schön, D.A. (1983) *The Reflective Practitioner*. Farnham: Ashgate.

Seedhouse, P. (2005) 'Task' as a research construct. *Language Learning* 55, 533–570.

Sert, O. (2019) Classroom interaction and language teacher education. In S. Walsh and S. Mann (eds) *The Routledge Handbook of English Language Teacher Education* (pp. 216–234). New York: Routledge.

Sfard, A. (1998) On two metaphors for learning and the dangers of choosing just one. *Educational Researcher* 27, 4–13.

Sherin, M.G. (2017) Exploring the boundaries of teacher noticing: Commentary. In E.O. Schack, M.H. Fisher and J.A. Wilhelm (eds) *Teacher Noticing: Bridging and Broadening Perspectives, Contexts, and Frameworks* (pp. 401–408). Cham: Springer.

Sherin, M.G. and Dyer, E.B. (2017) Teacher self-captured video: Learning to see. *Phi Delta Kappan* 98, 49–54.

Sherin, M.G. and Russ, R.S. (2015) Teacher noticing via video: The role of interpretive frames. In B. Calandra and P.J. Rich (eds) *Digital Video for Teacher Education: Research and Practice* (pp. 3–20). New York: Routledge.

Sherin, M.G. and van Es, E.A. (2003) A new lens on teaching: Learning to notice. *Mathematics Teaching in the Middle School* 9, 92–95.

Sherin, M.G. and van Es, E.A. (2009) Effects of video club participation on teachers' professional vision. *Journal of Teacher Education* 60, 20–37.

Sherin, M.G., Jacobs, V.R. and Philipp, R.A. (eds) (2011a) *Mathematics Teacher Noticing: Seeing through Teachers' Eyes*. New York: Routledge.

Sherin, M.G., Russ, R.S. and Colestock, A.A. (2011b) Accessing mathematics teachers' in-the-moment noticing. In M.G. Sherin, V.R. Jacobs and R.A. Philipp (eds) *Mathematics Teacher Noticing: Seeing through Teachers' Eyes* (pp. 79–94). New York: Routledge.

Shintani, N. (2015) The incidental grammar acquisition in focus on form and focus on forms instruction for young beginner learners. *TESOL Quarterly* 49, 115–140.

Shintani, N. (2016) *Input-Based Tasks in Foreign Language Instruction for Young Learners*. Amsterdam: Benjamins.

Shirakawa, T. (2018) Categorizing findings on language tutor autonomy (LTA) from interviews. *Relay Journal* 1, 236–246.

Simpson, A., Pomerantz, F., Kaufman, D. and Ellis, S. (2020) *Developing Habits of Noticing in Literacy and Language Classrooms: Research and Practice across Professional Cultures*. New York: Routledge.

Smith, R. and Erdoğan, S. (2008) Teacher-learner autonomy: Programme goals and student-teacher constructs. In T. Lamb and H. Reinders (eds) *Learner and Teacher Autonomy: Concepts, Realities, and Responses* (pp. 83–102). Amsterdam: John Benjamins.

Spivey, M. (2007) *The Continuity of Mind*. Oxford: Oxford University Press.

Stam, G. and McCafferty, S.G. (2008) Gesture studies and second language acquisition: A review. In S.G. McCafferty and G. Stam (eds) *Gesture: Second Language Acquisition and Classroom Research* (pp. 3–24). New York: Routledge.

Storch, N. (2017) Sociocultural theory in the L2 classroom. In S. Loewen and M. Sato (eds) *The Routledge Handbook of Instructed Second Language Acquisition* (pp. 69–83). New York: Routledge.

Streeck, J., Goodwin, C. and LeBaron, C. (2011) Embodied interaction in the material world: An introduction. In J. Streeck, C. Goodwin and C. LeBaron (eds) *Embodied Interaction: Language and Body in the Material World* (pp. 1–26). Cambridge: Cambridge University Press.

Superfine, A.C., Fisher, A., Bragelman, J. and Amador, J.M. (2017) Shifting perspectives on preservice teachers' noticing of children's mathematical thinking. In E.O. Schack, M.H. Fisher and J.A. Wilhelm (eds) *Teacher Noticing: Bridging and Broadening Perspectives, Contexts, and Frameworks* (pp. 409–426). Cham: Springer.

Swain, M. (1995) Three functions of output in second language learning. In G. Cook and B. Seidelhofer (eds) *Principle and Practice in Applied Linguistics: Studies in Honor of H.G. Widdowson* (pp. 125–144). Oxford: Oxford University Press.

Swain, M. (2000) The output hypothesis and beyond: Mediating acquisition through collaborative dialogue. In J.P. Lantolf (ed.) *Sociocultural Theory and Second Language Learning* (pp. 97–114). Oxford: Oxford University Press.

Swain, M. (2006a) Languaging, agency and collaboration in advanced second language proficiency. In H. Byrnes (ed.) *Advanced Language Learning: The Contribution of Halliday and Vygotsky* (pp. 95–108). London: Continuum.

Swain, M. (2006b) Verbal protocols: What does it mean for research to use speaking as a data collection tool? In M. Chalhoub-Deville, C.A. Chapelle and P. Duff (eds) *Inference and Generalizability in Applied Linguistics: Multiple Perspectives* (pp. 97–113). Amsterdam: John Benjamins.

Tomasello, M. (2003) *Constructing a Language: A Usage-Based Theory of Language Acquisition*. Cambridge, MA: Harvard University Press.

Tomasello, M. and Carpenter, M. (2007) Shared intentionality. *Developmental Science* 10, 121–125.

Tomlin, R.S. and Villa, V. (1994) Attention in cognitive science and SLA. *Studies in Second Language Acquisition* 16, 183–203.

Tsui, A.B.M. (2003) *Understanding Expertise in Teaching*. Cambridge: Cambridge University Press.

Tsui, A.B.M. (2009) Teaching expertise: Approaches, perspectives, and characterizations. In A. Burns and J.C. Richards (eds) *The Cambridge Guide to Second Language Teacher Education* (pp. 190–197). Cambridge: Cambridge University Press.

Tyler, A.E. and Ortega, L. (2018) Usage-inspired L2 instruction: An emergent, researched pedagogy. In A.E. Tyler, L. Ortega, M. Uno and H. Park (eds) *Usage-Inspired L2 Instruction: Researched Pedagogy* (pp. 3–26). Amsterdam: John Benjamins.

Van den Branden, K. (2016) The role of teachers in task-based language education. *Annual Review of Applied Linguistics* 36, 164–181.

van Es, E.A. (2011) A framework for learning to notice student thinking. In M.G. Sherin, V.R. Jacobs and R. Philipp (eds) *Mathematics Teacher Noticing: Seeing through Teachers' Eyes* (pp. 134–151). New York: Routledge.

van Es, E.A. and Sherin, M.G. (2002) Learning to notice: Scaffolding new teachers' interpretations of classroom interactions. *Journal of Technology and Teacher Education* 10, 571–596.

van Es, E.A. and Sherin, M.G. (2006) How different video club designs support teachers in 'learning to notice'. *Journal of Computing in Teacher Education* 22, 125–135.

van Es, E.A. and Sherin, M.G. (2008) Mathematics teachers' 'learning to notice' in the context of a video club. *Teaching and Teacher Education* 24, 244–276.

Varonis, E.M. and Gass, S. (1985) Non-native/non-native conversations: A model for negotiation of meaning. *Applied Linguistics* 6, 71–90.

Vygotsky, L.S. (1978) *Mind in Society: The Development of Higher Psychological Processes*. Cambridge, MA: Harvard University Press.

Walsh, S. (2011) *Exploring Classroom Discourse: Language in Action*. New York: Routledge.

Walsh, S. and Mann, S. (2015) Doing reflective practice: A data-led way forward. *ELT Journal* 69, 351–362.

Watanabe, A. (2017) *Reflective Practice as Professional Development: Experiences of Teachers of English in Japan*. Bristol: Multilingual Matters.

Wells, K.J. (2017) Noticing students' conversations and gestures during group problem-solving in mathematics. In E.O. Schack, M.H. Fisher and J.A. Wilhelm (eds) *Teacher Noticing: Bridging and Broadening Perspectives, Contexts, and Frameworks* (pp. 183–204). Cham: Springer.

Widdowson, H. (2003) *Defining Issues in English Language Teaching*. Oxford: Oxford University Press.

Williams, J. (2001) Learner-generated attention to form. *Language Learning* 51, 303–346.

Williams, J.N. (2005) Learning without awareness. *Studies in Second Language Acquisition* 27, 269–304.

Williams, M., Mercer, S. and Ryan, S. (2016) *Exploring Psychology in Language Learning and Teaching*. Oxford: Oxford University Press.

Willis, D. and Willis, J. (2007) *Doing Task-Based Teaching*. Oxford: Oxford University Press.

Willis, J. (1996) *A Framework for Task-Based Learning*. Harlow: Longman.

Woods, D. (1996) *Teacher Cognition in Language Teaching: Beliefs, Decision-Making and Classroom Practice*. Cambridge: Cambridge University Press.

Yamada, M. (2015) *The Role of English Teaching in Modern Japan: Diversity and Multiculturalism through English Language Education in a Globalized Era*. New York: Routledge.

Yamasaki, H. (2016) Teachers and teacher education in Japan. *Bulletin of the Graduate School of Education, Hiroshima University, Part 3: Education and Human Science* 65, 19–28.

Yoshizumi, K. (2018) Investigating student teachers' reflection on microteaching using Japanese Portfolio for Student Teachers of Languages (J-POSTL). *Language Teacher Education* 5, 1–21.

Yuan, R., Mak, P. and Yang, M. (2020) 'We teach, we record, we edit, and we reflect': Engaging pre-service language teachers in video-based reflective practice. *Language Teaching Research* (online), 1–20. doi:10.1177/1362168820906281

Yule, G. (1997) *Referential Communication Tasks*. Mahwah, NJ: Lawrence Erlbaum.

Zheng, X. and Borg, S. (2014) Task-based learning and teaching in China: Secondary school teachers' beliefs and practices. *Language Teaching Research* 18, 205–221.

Index

AIDE mnemonic, 3, 41, 45, 97, 99, 103, 105, 114, 116, 117, 119, 123, 126, 128–129, 132–134
    attention, 25, 41–42, *see also* joint attention
    interpretation, 39, 42–43
    decision-making, 39, 43
    engagement, 5, 43–44
attention, *see* AIDE mnemonic
autonomy, 53, 62, 150
awareness, 13–16, 24–25, 32, 66
    mutual awareness, 42, 150
    situation awareness, 25, 42, 60
    teacher language awareness, 23

beliefs, 30, 43, 58, 149
Brazilian Portuguese, 13

Chinese, 95
classroom-based research, 65, 148–149
classroom interactional competence, 21, 136, 147
cognition hypothesis, 57–58, 80, 89, 127
cognitive-interactionist approach, 17–19
complex dynamic systems theory (CDST), 49–50, 62, 141
consciousness, 13, 25, 32
constructions, 108–111, 113, 130, 137, 146
    lexical, 88, 115, 119, 124, 136
    motion verb, 58, 117, 123–124
    you can see + noun phrase, 100, 103, 109, 114, 118
context of the study, 50–55
continua for observing teacher noticing, 40
conversation analysis-for-SLA (CA-for-SLA), 20–21, 96, 149
cultural understanding, 51, 52, 56, 109, 111, 119, 120, 148

data triangulation, 9, 70
decision-making, *see* AIDE mnemonic
direction-giving map gap tasks, 55, 58, 73, 120

ecological approach, 44, 50–51, 141, *see also* multi-level framework
effect sizes, 74–75, 85–87, 130
embodied noticing, 94, 100, 106, 134, 149
embodied resources, 93–97, 106, 121, 127, 132, 137
    dancing, 95–96
    drawing, 101–102, 104
    facial expressions, 97–100
    gaze, 100–103
    gesture, 103, 115–116, 121, 128
    nodding, 94, 99–100, 103–105
    tapping, 99–100, 105
emotions, 35, 43, 59, 80, 96, 133–134, 147, 153
engagement, *see* AIDE mnemonic
English as a foreign language (EFL) context, 33, 57, 144, 146–147
epistemology, 8–9, 64
explicit/implicit learning, 14, 17, 25

focus on form, 5, 12, 21, 26, 32, 109–110, 137, 145–146
form-meaning mappings, *see* constructions

gesture, *see* embodied resources

Hawaiian, 15–16
hypotheses tested in the study, 80–81, 86, 127

identity, 67, 136, 138, 141, 143, 150
implications for language teacher education, 135–137, 142–144

intention, 13–14, 17, 34, 36, 41–42, 50, 63, 96, 101, 106, 116, 129, 133–135, 146–147, 149
interactional competence, 21
interactional noticing, 21, 136, 149
interactive thought, 3, 33–34, 61, 136, 141
interpretation, *see* AIDE mnemonic
interpretive frames, 31, 42–43
intersubjectivity, 42

Japan, 4, 7–8, 22, 50–57, 62, 76, 103, 120, 135–136, 145
Japanese, 58, 70–72, 81–82, 121, 134, 145
joint attention, 41–42, 50, 94, 116, 120, 134, 146, 150

L1 influence, 16, 21, 22, 43, 67, 79, 135
landmark descriptions, 108, 121–123, 130, 137
language teacher noticing, 3, 29, 34, 40–44
  coding of, 81–82
  construct development, 28–63, 65, 132
  descriptive statistics, 82–83
  individual differences in, 61, 92
  methods of investigating, 66–67
  operational definition of, 153
  versus L2 learner noticing, 26, 41, 150
learning as acquisition/participation, 5, 111, 146
limitations of study, 134–135
listening, 22, 54, 95, 99, 105, 112, 116, 118

mathematics teacher education, 3, 7, 9, 11, 35–40, 51, 128
mediation, 19–20, 80, 149
memory, 34–35, 78–79, 110; *see also* perspectival memory
  as reconstructive, 79–80
  episodic, 79
  long-term, 16
  prospective, 146
  working, 14, 49
Ministry of Education, Culture, Sports, Science and Technology (MEXT), 52, 55, 57
mixed-methods research (MMR), 9, 13, 64, 68, 76, 87, 130
  innovative MMR, 64, 76
  legitimation, 67, 76, 130

study design, 67–68, 76
morphosyntax, 18, 20, 145
motivation, 14, 24, 53, 133
multi-level framework, 50–51, 63, *see also* ecological approach
multimodal conversation analysis, 42, 93, 97, 105, 127, 149

natural pedagogy, 35, 133, 150
negotiation of meaning, 17–18, 110
non-native English speaking teachers (NNESTs), 76, 113, 136, 142
non-parametric analyses, 73, 85
nonverbal communication, 20, 64, 88, 93, 96, 99, 100, 104, 105–107, 121, 128–129, 133–134, 148, *see also* embodied resources
noticing hypothesis, 7, 13–17, 65

observation, 6, 30, 33, 38, 56, 66, 136, 144, 148

participants, 69–70
  eligibility for study, 55
  familiarity, 106
participation, *see* engagement under AIDE mnemonic
perspectival memory, 59–61, 87, 90–91, 107, 126, 132–133
  field/observer perspectives, 60–61, 80–81, 84–86, 89–91, 127, 128, 130–132
planning time, 58, 80, 89, 116, 127, 129
pluralism, 9, 64–65, 68, 76–77, 143
practicum, 54, 65
pragmatic knowledge, 22, 108–111, 119–120, 124–125, 129
professional vision, 26, 36–39, 147
proficiency, 19, 55–56, 66–67, 141
pronunciation, 6, 23, 145
psychology of language teaching and learning (PLLT), 29, 44, 49, 62, 126, 137, 150

R software, 84–85
rapport, 5, 144–145
reading, 23, 36, 54, 60
recall comments, 82–92, 97, 127, 134
reflection-in-action, 32–35
reflective practice, 4, 6, 32–35, 45, 54, 62, 80, 136, 138, 142–143, 147

reliability, 72–75
  of task scoring, 73
  of recall coding, 82
repair, see verbal resources
repeated-measures design, 67, 79, 134
repertoires, 59, 99, 113, 116, 146
research questions, 9, 68, 78, 108, 126–134
route directions, 90, 105, 108, 119–121, 130, 132, 137

sampling procedures, see eligibility under participants
school/community description, 52–53
second language acquisition (SLA), 5, 11, 49, 65, 145
second language teacher education (SLTE), 29, 45, 54–55, 60, 62, 76, 91–92, 142
self-concept, 149
semantic knowledge, 18, 108–111, 113–114, 124, 128, 132
sociocultural theory (SCT), 17–20, 80, 91, 143
Spanish, 149
spatial cognition, 120–121, 135
  mental models, 90
spatial frames of reference, 101, 103
speaking, 22, 54, 145, 147
stimulated recall methodology, 7, 33, 59–60, 66, 68, 70, 143, 148
  procedures, 71–72, 81–82,
  reactivity, 79–80
  veridicality, 79–80
subjectivity, 11, 13–14, 16, 20, 24, 25, 78, 143, 149–150
suggestions for teachers, 144
Swahili, 94

task-based language teaching (TBLT), 4, 18, 28–30, 55, 108–109, 111, 135, 149
  in Japan, 55–57
  re-tasking/de-tasking, 36
  target tasks, 119
  task completion, 73–74, 94, 142
  task complexity, 4, 9, 58–59, 68, 78, 81, 84, 87, 126–127, 130, 132, see also cognition hypothesis
  task features, 57–59, see also direction-giving map gap tasks
  task-in-process/task-as-workplan, 81, 88, 107, 124–125, 128–129, 131, 133, 135
  task-relevant language, 58, 137
teacher cognition, 29–31, 34, 44, 50, 60, 62, 92, 141
teacher education program, 50, 54–55
teachers, xi, 4, 5, 13, 19, 21–24, 26, 28, 54, 56–57, 61, 65, 93, 107, 113, 135, 144, 150
  expert, 37, 61, 65, 150
  in-service, 7, 28, 30, 56
  novice, 5, 37, 61, 142
  pre-service, 3, 47, 54, 135, 137, 143
time on task, 74–75, 91, 132
transcriptions, 68–69, 70, 72, 81–82, 96–97, 113, 135, 155
transdisciplinarity, 8, 12, 28
translanguaging, 22
triangulation see data triangulation
tutoring, 53, 69

United States of America, 36
usage-based learning, 108–111
  associative learning, 109–110
  cognitive semantics, 109
  usage event, 108, 111, 119–120, 123–124, 129

validity, 60, 66, 72–76, 89
  of mixed-methods study, see legitimation under mixed-methods research
  of stimulated recall interviews, 71–72, 79, 81–82
  of tasks used, 73–75
verbal resources, 9, 93, 94, 97, 108, 127–129, 132, see also constructions
  change of state token, 119, 123, 148
  circumlocution, 116
  comprehension check, 103–104
  continuer, 103, 112
  explanation, 102, 112–114, 116–117
  intonation, 119, 123, 135
  pause/filler, 99, 102, 115–116
  repair, 20, 65, 94, 98–99, 102, 113, 115–117, 121–123, 136–137, 146
  repetition, 98, 101–102, 104, 115–116, 121, 123, 129, 146
  segmentation, 98, 115

verbalization, 19, 65, 79–80
video, 33, 59–60, 70, 91, 135
    clubs, 37–38, 66
    split-screen videos, 148
    wearable cameras, 39, 64, 66, 149
visual narratives, 60–62

well-being, 5, 8, 141, 150
willingness to communicate, 69, 133–134
writing, 23, 54, 145

zone of proximal development (ZPD), 19–20

For Product Safety Concerns and Information please contact our EU Authorised Representative:

Easy Access System Europe

Mustamäe tee 50

10621 Tallinn

Estonia

gpsr.requests@easproject.com

www.ingramcontent.com/pod-product-compliance
Lightning Source LLC
Chambersburg PA
CBHW070614300426
44113CB00010B/1522